JEFF APTER

GWEN STEFANI
& NO DOUBT

A SIMPLE KIND OF LIFE

OMNIBUS PRESS

London/New York/Paris/Sydney/Copenhagen/Berlin/Madrid/Tokyo

In memory of Jack Apter, 1928–2006

Copyright © 2008 Omnibus Press
(A Division of Music Sales Limited)

Cover designed by the Design Corporation

ISBN 13: 978.0.8256.3603.5
Order No: OP52525

Exclusive Distributors
Music Sales Limited,
14/15 Berners Street,
London, W1T 3LJ.

Music Sales Corporation,
257 Park Avenue South,
New York, NY 10010, USA.

Macmillan Distribution Services,
53 Park West Drive,
Derrimut, Vic 3030,
Australia.

Every effort has been made to trace the copyright holders of the photographs in this book but one or two were unreachable. We would be grateful if the photographers concerned would contact us.

Typeset by Phoenix Photosetting, Chatham, Kent
Printed in the United States of America by Quebecor World

A catalog record for this book is available from the British Library.

Visit Omnibus Press on the web at www.omnibuspress.com

Contents

Prologue

No one understood New York City better than the blue-eyed king of the crooners, Frank Sinatra. When Cranky Frank told the world "if you can make it there, you can make it anywhere", he wasn't just riffing on a choice rhyming couplet.

In a million different ways, New York really is the centre of the universe, and no more so than in the feverish world of rock'n'roll. Although, truth be told, if a band can make it in New York City, well, they've probably *already* made it everywhere else. It's the Everest of entertainment. If you were planning on proving just how high you'd climbed, there's no better stage than Madison Square Garden, or a bigger occasion than the Grammy Awards, the annual backslapping celebration of pop music success and excess. Backstage, however, Madison Square Garden on Grammy night in 2003 wasn't that different from any other cavernous entertainment bunker. A vision in concrete, with rabbit-warren corridors leading off to mysterious corners, it could, for a moment, make you forget about the 20,000 anxious, eager fans awaiting your presence in the darkness.

Not that No Doubt seemed to mind. Sixteen years down the line, this Orange County, California, gang of four were finally, irrefutably, comfortable in their own skins. They didn't even seem to be overly concerned that outside, during rehearsals on the main stage, R&B princess Ashanti was having technical difficulties involving a group of performing children and some kind of hydraulic mechanism, which meant that No Doubt's rehearsal time had been delayed. It had taken them a long time to get here; so they were soaking up the moment.

Even though life was sweet right now, five albums and 20-odd million record sales into their long, weird musical trip, the majority of those 16 years had been hard going. For longer than they would care to recall, No Doubt had been little more than darlings of the tight-knit and undeniably parochial So-Cal ska scene. Not only had they been famously rejected by taste-making Los Angeles radio station KROQ, they had also been told that they lacked focus by one of their early A&R guys at Interscope Records, a man paid to be a true believer in this band-cum-gang. And it'd be wrong to say that Interscope, the label founded by major industry player Jimmy Iovine, had always been No Doubt's biggest champions. There was even a stage in the early Nineties when the band pooled their cash to release their second LP, *Beacon Street Collection*, out of pure frustration with the never-ending sessions for what would turn out to be their career-making LP, *Tragic Kingdom*. They were forced to sell *Beacon Street* via mail order and at gigs.

Yet for No Doubt, through adversity, came success – ultimately on a scale once totally unfathomable to the ska-pop hopefuls from Anaheim. Gwen Stefani's brother Eric, the co-founder, songwriter, and chief motivator of the band, walked away from No Doubt in late 1994, opting for a career as an animator for *The Simpsons*. Seven years earlier, the band had suffered an even more painful loss when their original singer, John Spence, committed suicide. Around the time of Eric's departure, the seven-year romance between Gwen Stefani and No Doubt bassist Tony Kanal also fell apart. Within months back in 1994 No Doubt had taken not one, but two hits to the head, the kind of internal turmoil that would kill most under-achieving bands stone dead. Yet No Doubt was no under-achieving band. Kanal and Gwen Stefani found a way to play together on-, but not off-stage, without killing each other. Gwen – in her unexpected role as band lyricist – discovered her split with Kanal gave her plenty of juicy subject matter for songwriting.

And so No Doubt as we know it was born.

'Don't Speak', which quoted directly from intimate exchanges between Kanal and Gwen, became an anthem for millions of broken-hearted teens in 1996, while the video became an MTV staple. Somewhere in the midst of all this activity, Gwen, a self-confessed "nerd" and "geek", transformed herself into what one critic would call "Doris Day in a tank top and bondage pants", a pin-up for teens not quite prepared to embrace the raw junkie-chic of Hole shouter (and recent rock'n'roll widow), Courtney Love. The cult of the Gwenabees began. A star was unmistakably born.

And just 18 months after its 1995 release, *Tragic Kingdom*, the band's third album, redefined the term "ubiquitous". As "sleepers" go, Rip van Winkle had nothing on *Tragic Kingdom*. Within a couple of years it would become that rarest of beasts: a Diamond album, which meant that it had shifted more than 10 million copies in the US. It briefly propelled this remarkably self-effacing Anaheim crew into the lofty company of such mega-selling legends as Pink Floyd and The Eagles, whose *Dark Side of the Moon* and *Hotel California*, respectively, had also gone Diamond.

Meanwhile, backstage at the Garden, several years and several million albums later, the members of No Doubt were engrossed in their own worlds. Drummer Adrian Young, the first No Doubt parent – and one of the few golf junkies to sport both a Mohawk and a single-figure handicap – was absorbed in his iBook, checking out images of his recently born son, Mason. (Keeping it very much in the family, Young's wife, Nina, is No Doubt's former production co-ordinator.) If there was anyone in No Doubt who'd stayed relatively true to his punkish roots, it would be Young, a frenetic flurry of hands, legs and arms behind his kit, who'd strip down to his boxers – or less – to perform.

Guitarist Tom Dumont was nearby, with a knit cap pulled down low over his eyes and sandy hair. An adopted middle child, Dumont didn't really share the same musical bent as his bandmates growing up. Rather than the interracial ska of such revered UK acts as Madness and Specials AKA, or the Eighties new wave peddled by LA station KROQ, Dumont fancied the brawny, brainy prog rock of Canadians Rush, and the cartoon riffs of Kiss. Dumont loved Kiss so much, in fact, that he bought his first electric guitar, a black Les Paul Gibson, primarily because it was the chosen axe of Kiss guitarist Ace Frehley. While No Doubt never claimed to be "muso's musos", Dumont was as close as the band would come to having a "serious" player amongst their numbers.

Seated on a sofa was bassist Tony Kanal, his eyes hidden by completely unnecessary dark glasses. The son of Indians, London-born and a Californian since the age of 11, Kanal, like the rest of the band, knew his place in No Doubt. Not only did he keep down a tight bottom end on stage and in the studio, Kanal was also the most business-minded of the group. He lived and breathed No Doubt, and spent much of his time planning the band's next move, alongside their official management and crew. Recently, it had been Kanal's idea to investigate dancehall, a juicy variant of reggae that is the flavour of Jamaica. That led to No Doubt's hugely successful *Rock Steady* album, a record that proved the band could bounce back from the comparatively meagre sales of 2000's *Return Of Saturn* LP. (Admittedly, it's a tough call for anyone to follow up on a Diamond album; just ask Alanis Morissette.) *Rock Steady* was also the record that led No Doubt to the 2003 Grammys, where the hit single 'Hey Baby' had been nominated for Best Pop Performance By A Duo Or Group With Vocals.

Kanal was doing his best not to fall asleep when Patti and Dennis Stefani, Gwen's parents, walked into the Madison Square backstage bunker. At the sight of her buff, near-perfectly toned daughter, dressed down in a cashmere top and combat trousers, Patti Stefani couldn't help but observe: "You look very Californian".

As decidedly un-rock'n'roll as it seems, the influence of the clean-living, folk-music-loving, very upper-case-c Catholic Stefanis had helped define No Doubt as much as anyone, or anything, else. They favoured a strict-but-fair style of child rearing, which meant that their daughter now presented one of the more wholesome images in modern music. She might flash a little celebrity skin – anyone who's seen a No Doubt video or show can attest to that – but Gwen Stefani had her limits. Unlike the anything-goes attitude of the Britneys, J Los, and Courtney Loves of the world, Stefani wasn't tabloid fodder. Her Cinderella-worthy 2002 wedding to Bush singer Gavin Rossdale –all warm smiles and designer labels, more *Vogue* than *US Weekly* – was as close as Gwen would come to doing anything faintly sensational. Like any So-Cal princess, peppered her "dudes" and "likes" with the occasional curse word, but she did so reluctantly. Her mother did not approve.

Case in point: the *Tragic Kingdom* single 'Just A Girl', in which Stefani screamed the sarcastic kiss-off, "Fuck you / I'm just a girl". During a show, as Patti Stefani looked on in horror, her much-loved, properly raised daughter used *that* word in front of thousands. Angry mother refused to speak to devastated daughter for a week. Gwen became a little more cautious with this type of thing: She might have been in her thirties, and a woman from the top of her platinum blonde bob to the tips of her designer-clad toes, but she still respects her parents deeply. So while the boys in the band weren't teetotallers by any stretch, and the Anaheim four certainly knew how to turn on a party both on-stage and off, the only drug you'd be likely to find here is the caffeine in Gwen's preferred blend of tea, Celestial Seasonings Bengal Spice. You'd struggle to even score a cigarette from the No Doubt crew. Not surprisingly, the best stories concerning No Doubt typically involve the harder-living bands in whose circles they moved, like Long Beach fuck-ups Sublime and ska wild boys The Untouchables.

Many bands talk themselves up as happy families, but No Doubt actually seem to live it out. In fact, there were just a few people missing from this cheery extended family tableau backstage at the Garden. Gwen's brother Eric wasn't there. Nor was his fellow No Doubt founding member John Spence, whose over-used response to virtually every question gave the band its name – "no doubt" he'd say, and No Doubt they became.

When Spence killed himself in 1987, just as it seemed like the band was beginning to outgrow its So-Cal roots, Gwen Stefani, who always considered herself to be her brother Eric's follower and "puppet", who had no life dreams outside of marriage and children, and mastering all the songs in *The Sound Of Music*, was suddenly a lead singer. And now, several years later, a solid-gold star.

★　★　★

Finally, Ashanti and the kids got it together and No Doubt bounced through a typically good-natured rehearsal of 'Hey Baby'. Later, the band would win the Grammy, their first after many years of nominations and crossed fingers. But while most of the high-profile Grammy guests would obligingly troop off to the annual after-party bash hosted by music biz legend Clive Davis, No Doubt, very typically, disappeared to the best party in town, at the Bryant Park Grill. Locked in a girlish embrace with R&B queen Mary J Blige, Stefani, resplendent in a Vivienne Westwood-designed polka-dot number, posed sweetly for the camera. Hers was the smile of a lucky woman, the "who'd-have-thought it" grin of an accidental star. As she looked around and took in the million-dollar glow of her A-list peers, this woman with a propensity for chubbiness, who once played the piccolo in the school band, realised something significant: She was now undeniably, irrefutably famous. And, finally, after a lifetime of deep personal insecurities, uncertainties and dramas, that felt just fine.

CHAPTER ONE

Ska'd For Life

"The guitar player was playing straight, and [Lester] "Ska" Sterling, the alto player, he tell the guitar: 'Just play ska-ska-ska-ska guitar'. Everybody laughed, and named the music ska."

–Lloyd Brevett of The Skatalites

While talking up their 2001 album, *Rock Steady*, the members of No Doubt, somewhat disingenuously, expressed their newfound love for Jamaican sounds of dancehall and rock steady. They spoke about the forms with such a deeply felt reverence that it seemed as if some lucky musical anthropologist had just unearthed the styles. They should have known better, especially for a band that, during the first, relatively fruitless phase of its evolution, would gladly hitch its star to the ska-punk bandwagon. Truth of the matter is, when The Grateful Dead lamented "what a long, strange trip it's been", they might well have been describing ska and its wayward journey from the resorts and dancehalls of post-war Jamaica, via the pork-pie-hat-wearing rude boys of 2-Tone England, to the green and manicured lawns of Orange County, California – and, eventually, to the ubiquitous boom box positioned backstage at the many after-show parties held by No Doubt and its crew in the late Nineties. What No Doubt didn't realise was that it took a good 40 or so years for ska to complete that relatively short jump from the Caribbean to the OC.

Long before the CD age – and well before US Vice President Al Gore, apparently, invented the Internet – the humble wireless was king. And one of the fortunate end results of WWII was the proliferation of radios that flooded Jamaica; suddenly locals could tune into the juicy, raunchy R&B that was pumping out of such US cities as New Orleans. Fats 'Blueberry Hill' Domino was an early favourite of the Caribbean music lovers who would eventually breathe life into ska. And Jamaica was a country never short of savvy entrepreneurs, willing to squeeze a buck out of virtually anything, so it didn't take long for a few locals to take a ride on this musical bandwagon. They could see that music lovers were hot for R&B, but how could they get it to a mass audience (and collect a few bucks along the way)? So such players as Duke Reid, Clement "Coxsone" Dodd – both of whom would eventually establish their own record labels and recording studios – and Prince Buster were among the first promoters to establish sound systems. These were basically portable discotheques that were set up at dances and pretty much anywhere else that young people gathered to cut loose.

The promoters of these wild parties would ship in the latest R&B platters from Miami and New Orleans, as there were no record labels, yet, in Jamaica. (In fact, the so-called mento scene, known as the "grandpappy of reggae" amongst musicologists, was the only music industry in existence there at the time.) The 78RPM platters themselves became such hot properties that the sound system operators would scratch the label off each record, masking its identity and thereby establishing a monopoly of the tunes most favoured by locals. And, inevitably, if you were the guy playing the best music, the people came to listen and dance. The legend and legacy of these sound systems was such that several decades later they'd be celebrated in song – called simply 'Sound System' – by Operation Ivy, just like No Doubt, were Californians. (Operation Ivy, deeply in love with the anything-goes spirit of The Clash, would eventually morph into the hugely successful and no less derivative band Rancid.)

Like most musical trends of the past half century, R&B – especially the New Orleans variety – fell out of favour Stateside, as the earthy rock'n'roll swagger of Elvis Presley, Jerry Lee Lewis and their many slicked-back, hip-swivelling imitators became the latest sensation. But Jamaicans still loved what was to them a relatively new music, so shrewd local artists took advantage of the few recording studios that were gradually being established, such as Duke Reid's Treasure Isle studio, and began recording their own variation of R&B. With its accentuated guitar and piano rhythms on the upbeats, this style was only one skanking step away from evolving into what would become known universally as ska.

There's more than one interpretation of how ska's heavy beat evolved.

Pointy-headed musicologists with a purist bent blame the sometimes-unsteady radio signals that were beamed into Jamaica; they figure that ska's woozy rhythms were the end result of a misreading by local musicians of the sounds emerging from America. The more generous think it was simply the homegrown musicians' own funky spin on American R&B. Lloyd Knibb, drummer for the immortal Skatalites, has said that ska was a "new beat" concocted in the studio, on the request of Clement Dodd, to cater to the proliferation of sound systems springing up all over Jamaica. Others saw it as the next natural step from the aforementioned mento, a style with deep African and European roots, which had been first recorded by Caribbean jazz artists in the Twenties and had gone through a golden age in the Fifties. And it's true that many mento songs would be remade in the dancehall style fancied by many of ska's biggest names, so that's as reasonable as any other explanation of ska's origins.

The roots of the term ska were almost as intriguing as the form's long and winding evolution (conveniently broken down into the so-called "three waves" of ska: its Jamaican birth, its 2-Tone resurrection in the UK, and its ska-punk, American-led makeover in the 1980s). One theory has it that the phrase came from Cluet Johnson, bassist for the Blues Blasters, "Coxsone" Dodd's house band. The gregarious Johnson had a habit of greeting his many friends as "skavoovees", which was most likely his own take on American hipster slang, although he later explained that it was simply his way of asking "do you understand?" But legendary Jamaican guitarist Ernest Ranglin – who, way back in 1958, would play on the first release on Chris Blackwell's Island label, and who later teamed with Jamaican singer Millie Small for the smash single 'My Boy Lollipop', ska's first legitimate global hit – held another view. He insisted that the term referred to the curious "skat, skat, skat" scratching sound that he and other axe-men produced while playing. Skatalite Lloyd Brevett agreed that it did emerge from a studio session, when asked many years later. "The guitar player was playing straight, and [Lester] "Ska" Sterling, the alto player, he tell the guitar: 'Just play ska-ska-ska-ska guitar'. Everybody laughed, and named the music ska." (This might also explain how Sterling got his nickname.) Some even believe that the term ska is simply a shortened form of the phrase "speed calypso", which is a pretty fair summation of the music itself. Whatever the true explanation, the word seemed a natural fit, and the sound now had a name.

★　★　★

Every movement needs its heroes: punk has its Sex Pistols, folk-rock has its Byrds, Britpop its Beatles and rockabilly its Sun Studio all-stars. And the

3

band at the centre of ska's Jamaican birth – its first genuine superstars – was The Skatalites. Even though it lasted for little more than a year, at least in its original form, The Skatalites' impact on ska, ska-punk and its many and varied offspring was indelible. "More than a band," wrote *The All Music Guide's* Jo-Ann Greene, "The Skatalites were and are an institution, an aggregation of top-notch musicians who didn't merely define the sound of Jamaica, they *were* the sound of Jamaica across the Fifties and Sixties." *Rolling Stone* agreed. "In the early Sixties," they declared, "The Skatalites were [ska's] masters, incredibly assured instrumentalists who, over an endless, pumping beat, wailed wildly melodic jazz riffs."

As was the trend among many other foundation ska acts, The Skatalites remade popular American (and British) songs of the time, everything from sugary doo-wop ballads to cool jazz and slinky R&B. But they did it with such élan, such seemingly effortless grace, that they stood above the pack. It also helped that the group's many members would play on virtually every notable ska recording to come out of the Caribbean during its heyday in the Fifties and Sixties: As monopolies go, theirs was virtually unbeatable.

Like so many great bands, such as The Easybeats and AC/DC, whose roots can be traced to the rough and tumble of Sydney's Villawood Migrant Hostel, The Skatalites had pretty damned humble beginnings. Four of its nine original members – trumpeter Johnny "Dizzy" Moore, Cuban-born tenor saxophonist Tommy McCook, alto saxophonist Lester Sterling and trombonist Don Drummond – met at the Alpha Cottage School, an educational institution for wayward Kingston kids that was run by the Catholic diocese. Fortunately for the future Skatalites, the school ran a high-quality music program, and they all would eventually get gigs playing on Jamaica's resort and hotel circuit, faithfully pumping out jazz and R&B favourites for rum-swilling tourists.

Given that Jamaica's music scene was so small, it was inevitable that by the time The Skatalites officially formed in 1964, many of the members had already played in bands together. Drummond and Skatalite drummer Lloyd Knibb, for example, had worked together in Eric Dean's Band; when Knibb split to join a band called the Sheiks, he became part of a band that already included pianist Donat Roy "Jackie" Mittoo and trumpeter Moore, whom he'd meet again in The Skatalites. And so the dance continued.

Between 1959, when Duke Reid released the first vinyl single on his Treasure Isle label, and 1962, when Jamaica finally gained its independence, most of the men who would become Skatalites found regular recording work at Reid's Treasure Isle studio, cutting a mix of R&B, boogie and ballad standards, best heard on The Heartbeat label's *Ska After Ska After Ska* collection (or the Dutch release *Jamaica Gold*). In 1962, Clement Dodd opened his legendary Studio One, and most of The Skatalites found work there as well. The first recording made in the studio was entitled *Jazz Jamaica From The Workshop*, which featured the musical stylings of guitarist Ernest Ranglin, as well as tenor sax man Roland Alphonso, Drummond and McCook. When The Skatalites began to record in 1964, they were effectively Clement Dodd's house band.

Although there is no question that McCook christened the band, for many years after there was ongoing debate as to just who brought the ensemble together: Ranglin (who was not a Skatalite, although he did record with them) gives Moore the credit, while Knibbs believed that it was his work. When they made their public debut on June 27, 1964, at the Hi-Hat Club in Rae Town, The Skatalites hired several vocalists, including calypso star Joseph "Lord Tanamo" Gordon, plus Jackie Opel, Doreen Schaeffer and Tony DaCosta. Soon after, they'd established residencies at the Bournemouth Beach Club in Eastern Kingston (where they played two sets a night three times a week) and the Orange Bowl on Kingston's Orange Street. And with that, the style that would forever be known as ska was introduced to a music-hungry Jamaican public.

Their repertoire was all over the shop: they played "ska'd up" versions of such Beatles songs as 'I Should Have Known Better' and 'This Boy' as well as reworking popular movie themes and surf instrumentals. In the process they accidentally established the tendency of most ska bands to flesh out their set with unexpected covers. (No Doubt's early shows featured numerous songs from Madness, The Specials and The Selecter, as well as their own spins on such ska cuts as 'Mr Big Stuff' by Jene McKnight, plus a makeover of Blondie's 'One Way (Or Another)' and the Bad Brains' 'Sailin' On'.) And again, just like No Doubt many years down the line, The Skatalites were unbelievably hard workers: in between their own residencies, and frequent touring in support of most of the acts on Dodd's Studio One label, they spent almost all their waking hours in the studio – when they weren't hanging out at a rural encampment where Rastafarians liked to gather, soaking up the sounds that would rub off on ska and eventually become known as reggae. (Members of The Skatalites would go on to record with Bob Marley and Toots Hibbert.) And not only did they record session after Studio One session for Dodd – with whom Jackie Mittoo had a standing deal to deliver five 'new rhythms' per week – and Reid, but they also recorded for label owners Prince Buster and brothers Duke and Justin Yap. It's not known exactly how many recordings The Skatalites made; most players went uncredited on the singles that they helped create, and the platter would typically contain little more than the vocalist's name, the title of the track, its composer and the parent label. The name Skatalites simply didn't mean that much to the record-buying public. In fact, their seminal ska instrumental, 'The Guns of Navarone' – later covered by The Specials – was released under Roland Alphonso's name, not the band's. But there was no doubt that these esteemed session men helped sprinkle fairy dust all over recordings from Prince Buster ('Al Capone'), Stranger Cole, Eric 'Monty' Morris, Jackie Opel, Doreen Schaeffer and many other silky-smooth crooners.

Well-meaning ska-chivists have attempted to redress this oversight: The West Side label's *Skaravan – Top Sounds From The Top Deck* series, for one, has uncovered eight discs' worth of Skatalites recordings, and these only include tracks cut for the Yap brothers. (*Foundation Ska* compiles many of their Studio One recordings.) But The Skatalites' signature sound – jazz-inflected brass, a genuine sense of swing, and that trademark skanking beat, as steady as a metronome – is hard to miss; it's the key to such genre-defining early tracks as 'Phoenix City', 'Corner Stone', 'Silver City' and many, many others.

And yet, oddly, despite the band's fast-growing reputation, The Skatalites were overlooked when it was agreed that this new thing called ska should be showcased at the 1964 New York World's Fair. Instead, the honour went to an outfit called Byron Lee & the Dragonaires, while Prince Buster, Eric 'Monty' Morris and future reggae hero Peter Tosh were there to help them out. (Buster would soon play a crucial role in exporting ska to the UK, where it would languish for some time before being embraced by genre-jumpers The Beat, Bad Manners and such big favourites of Eric and Gwen Stefani as The Selecter, The Specials and Madness.)

The Skatalites, however, had no time for grumbling about this oversight; they were about to implode. While the rest of the band were cutting loose at a New Year's Eve show at the La Parisienne Club in Harbour View, trombonist Drummond, who had a history of mental illness and had been institutionalised while still playing with the band – Dodd had nicknamed him 'Cosmic Don' for good reason – was stabbing his common-law wife, band vocalist Marguerita, to death in a fit of rage. Swiftly arrested, Drummond was committed to Bellevue Sanatorium, where he died of leukaemia in 1969. "From youth, Don is a slightly damaged guy," Lloyd Knibb would tell the *Los Angeles Times'* Mike Boehm almost 30 years on, during another revival of interest in the music of The Skatalites. "I don't know what caused it, really. He was a nice quiet guy, don't make no trouble."

It didn't come as a huge surprise that this bloody tragedy effectively derailed The Skatalites, who never completely recovered from the shock, and split in July 1965. They resurfaced frequently over the following three decades, when they discovered that a renewed interest in ska, especially on the US West Coast, offered some lucrative live work. A reformed band, including foundation members Alphonso, Sterling and Knibbs, would also cut several new albums in the 1980s. However, even though they were obviously chuffed at the renewal of interest in their music, and the reverential attitude of the new bands who had researched their ska history, these founding fathers weren't totally sure that the music of such bands as Boston's Mighty Mighty Bosstones and Orange County kids Sublime and No Doubt – all by that time making waves at radio and MTV – should be called ska. "Yeah, yeah, yeah. [They're] all right," Knibb shrugged, when asked by the *Los Angeles Times'* Boehm. "They're trying their best. They call it ska, but it's not ska, really. They're playing like the English guys. We play the true ska."

Although the tragic, bloody demise of The Skatalites signalled the last gasp of ska's first wave, many of the band's members, including pianist Jackie Mittoo (who would find a new home playing ska and reggae in Toronto, where he moved in 1968), would deliver solo records. Lloyd Brevett and Tommy McCook did likewise. Alphonso, Moore, Mittoo and Brevett, meanwhile, would go on to form the Soul Brothers (later the Soul Vendors), while McCook also formed a band called the Supersonics. And it wasn't as if The Skatalites worked in isolation; there were numerous other Jamaican acts playing 'the ska' during its heyday, including Justin Hinds and the Dominoes, and vocal harmonisers with such then fashionable tags as the Techniques, the Sensations, the Uniques, and so on. Ska was also an adaptable musical form; during the mid '60s, as American soul turned slower and funkier, ska varied its rhythms accordingly, which led to the birth of rocksteady, with its emphasis on silky vocals and slower tempos. (*Rock Steady*, of course, also just happens to be the name of No Doubt's fifth studio album, so its legacy is abundantly clear.) The leading purveyors of this variation on ska included the Melodians, who hit big with the original version of 'Rivers Of Babylon', a far more mellow and soulful version of the song than Boney M's discofied confection of 1978. There was also The Ethiopians, led by singer/songwriter Leonard Dillon, a Christian with strong Rastafarian connections, whose 'Train To Skaville' even scraped into the lower reaches of the UK Top 40 in 1967. Another member of the rocksteady crew was one Desmond Dekker, who would soon play a key role in helping ska jump the Atlantic to the UK.

Dekker shared more than a love of ska's skanking beat with The Skatalites: he'd also done hard time in the Alpha Cottage School for Boys.

He was born Desmond Adolphus Dacres in Kingston on July 16, 1941; his mother died when he was an infant, so, along with his father, he spent the early part of his life in Seaforth, St Thomas, where he sang in church. The list of artists Dekker emulated was impressive: he cited such legends as Nat King Cole, Sam Cooke, Louis Armstrong, Jackie Wilson and Mahalia Jackson as early influences. He was apprenticed to a tailor before he returned to Kingston, where he found work as a welder, singing in the factory while his workmates shouted encouragement.

This was all the motivation he needed to try and score work with a record label. But although he auditioned for both Coxsone Dodd and Duke Reid, neither was terribly impressed, so Dekker tried out at Leslie Kong's Beverly Record label, where he found a champion in Derrick Morgan, then the label's brightest star. Two years passed before he made his recording debut with 'Honour Your Mother and Father', a song handpicked by Kong. It became a number one hit in Jamaica, while such follow-ups as 'Sinners Come Home' and 'Labour For Learning' also did big business locally. And in the process, Desmond Dacres was reborn as the far cooler Desmond Dekker. His next hit, the buoyant 'King of Ska', recorded with the Cherrypies (aka the Maytals), also earned him a tag that stayed with him until his death in 2006: to many, the movie-star handsome Dekker truly was the 'King of Ska'.

Flushed with success, Dekker set about recruiting the Four Aces, his own version of Presley's Jordanaires, a group that featured the voices of brothers Carl, Patrick, Clive and Barry Howard. Together they cut more hits, including the singles 'Get Up Edina', 'Mount Zion' and 'This Woman'. Until this point, however, Dekker was an artist swimming in the mainstream, singing polite, inoffensive tunes for the masses. But in 1967 he appeared on Derrick Morgan's *Tougher Than Tough*, a celebration of the local rude boy culture. His song '007 (Shanty Town)' was inspired by the 'rudie' mayhem that Dekker had witnessed on the mean streets of Jamaica. Dekker was swiftly embraced as a rude boy icon. The English mod scene also went ape for Dekker, and the song reached the UK Top 20. When he toured the UK, a gaggle of mods followed his every move.

Dekker stuck with the rude boy template for such subsequent hits as 'Rudie Got Soul' and 'Rude Boy Train', while he tapped into more humanist themes with the songs 'Wise Man', 'Unity' and 'Sabotage'. Many of these tracks turned up on his debut LP, *007 (Shanty Town),* along with 'Pretty Africa', one of the earliest songs to broach the theme of repatriation. It would quickly become a staple of his live set.

But all this was a prelude to Dekker's biggest hit, 'The Israelites', which would surface in 1969. Co-written by Dekker and Leslie Kong, the song topped both the UK and US singles charts, and did likewise in Dekker's home of Jamaica, as well as South Africa, Canada, Sweden, West Germany and elsewhere. Given that the charts in the UK were awash at the time with the lily-white, sugary-sweet pop of Lulu, Mary Hopkins, Cilla Black, the Hollies and others, it was a monumental accomplishment on the part of Dekker and Kong. And along with Millie Small's 'My Boy Lollipop', 'The Israelites' would be widely regarded as one of the first tracks with a strong ska / reggae flavour – not to mention its weighty social comment – to be embraced by a mainstream, global audience. (The track was so popular, in fact, that when it was reissued in 1975, it scaled the UK Top 10 all over again; it was later used in an ad for Maxell and was covered with due reverence by ska-pop chart-busters Madness.) Despite the song's heavy historical references – the Israelites were a group of Hebrews, members of the Twelve Tribes of Israel, mentioned in the Hebrew Bible – the lyric came to Dekker in the most innocuous way. "I was walking in the park, eating corn," he explained. "I heard a couple arguing about money. She was saying she needed money and he was saying the work he was doing was not giving him enough. I relate to those things and began to sing a little song – 'You get up in the morning and you slaving for bread.' By the time I got home it was complete."

Now a star, Dekker relocated to the UK, where he became a friend to the even-more famous, including Beatle Paul McCartney, who name checked him in the cod-reggae cut 'Ob-La-Di, Ob-La-Da', on the White Album. Curiously, this was a track that would be used by No Doubt as a set closer pretty much whenever they played in the late 1990s. Whether they knew that the song's 'Desmond' was the same man who helped import ska and in the process helped kickstart the 2-Tone revival, however, remains unclear.

Although Dekker couldn't replicate 'Israelites'' success in the US, he did deliver the occasional standout single, such as a sterling cover of Jimmy Cliff's 'You Can Get It If You Really Want', which was recorded on the insistence of Kong. His instincts were good, because the song reached number two in the UK during September 1970, rubbing shoulders in the charts with everyone from Smokey Robinson & the Miracles ('Tears Of A Clown'), to a resurgent Elvis Presley ('The Wonder Of You') and such one-hit wonders as Freda 'Band Of Gold' Payne. It was Dekker's final chart appearance; when Kong died of a heart attack in 1971, the hits dried up for the King of Ska.

Dekker continued to play live and his career was revived with the emergence of the 'second wave' of ska, the era of 2-Tone and such mixed-race

UK acts as The Specials, The Selecter and the Beat (all of whom would leave a sizeable impression on No Doubt in the years before they morphed into a slick, successful mainstream pop act). A few years before Dekker declared bankruptcy in 1984, he signed with Stiff Records, a label strongly connected with the 2-Tone / rude boy movement, and it was there that he cut the album *Black & Dekker* with the help of The Rumour, Graham Parker's backing band. This was released in 1980, which turned out to be a banner year for the so-called 'second wave' of ska.

★ ★ ★

While it may have been the flood of radios into Jamaica that gave life to the first wave of ska, it was the export of flesh-and-blood Jamaicans that started ska's rebirth. With the onset of a post-war labour shortage in the UK, and with no restrictions, at the time, on the amount of immigrants pouring into the United Kingdom from Jamaica – which was part of the Commonwealth – the West Indian population exploded in England after WWII. Although there had always been some West Indians residing there – at the turn of the 19th century their numbers totalled roughly 8,600 – by 1951 this figure had almost doubled to 15,300, and by 1961 the Caribbean population topped a whopping 170,000. Within a year, however, a quota system was introduced under which vouchers would be issued to prospective immigrants, with no more than a quarter of those vouchers going to any one country. This system was introduced to slow down the immigrant explosion. These changes were, in part, brought on by race riots that had occurred in such melting-pots as Nottingham and Notting Hill during 1958, where nightly clashes between whites and West Indians resulted in some of the worst racially-inspired violence to ever happen in the UK.

Of course, the West Indians relocating to the UK also brought their music with them: ska, reggae, rocksteady. And it was only a short while until the aforementioned Millie Small was all over the English radio and charts with her sticky-sweet 'My Boy Lollipop', which reached critical mass in April 1964. And between then and 1969, when Dekker's 'The Israelites' spread the good word of ska all the way to the number one spot, there was some commercial interest in the form, with hits from Dave and Ansil Collins (their 'Double Barrel' was the recording debut of studio ace Sly Dunbar, later to record with No Doubt), Ken 'Mr Rocksteady' Boothe (who, bizarrely, cut a version of Sandie Shaw's snow-white 'Puppet On A String' in 1967) and John Holt. Meanwhile, Duke Reid's Trojan Records – its name swiped from the logo that was emblazoned on the side of the Leyland trucks that lugged sound systems from one side of Jamaica to another, that read 'Duke Reid: The Trojan King of Sounds' – was formed in 1968. The label's first UK hit was Jimmy Cliff's peerless 'Wonderful World Beautiful People', which made the Top 10 in November 1969. It was the first in a string of almost 30 UK charting singles for the label, whose releases included choice ska-flavoured cuts from the Heptones, Lee Perry, the Maytals and The Skatalites' many members gone solo, including Roland Alphonso and Tommy McCook.

Yet it still took many years and more than one musical revolution – both disco and punk came, flickered briefly and then faded almost as quickly – before the idea of 2-Tone came to one Jerry Dammers, and returned ska to the mainstream. Dammers, the future Specials leader, 2-Tone figurehead and No Doubt icon, was an immigrant himself; he was born Gerald Dankin, in India on May 22, 1954. His father, a clergyman, had relocated the family to the industrial centre of Coventry, 80 miles out of London, when Dammers was two. The teenage Dammers enrolled as an art student at Lanchester Polytechnic and soaked up the local music scene. Being 1977, it was the year that punk broke, with the Sex Pistols having barnstormed the UK charts in January with 'Anarchy In The UK', followed swiftly by their anti-anthem, 'God Save The Queen', the perfect poison pen letter for the royal jubilee. Their peers and friendly rivals The Clash had delivered their self-titled debut in spring, having stitched up a useful $200,000 advance from the UK branch of CBS Records a few months earlier. Stiff Records, meanwhile, were banking on the Damned, whose debut LP, *Damned, Damned, Damned*, was produced by Nick Lowe. Scruffy punks the Stranglers were also having their days in the sun, with their joyously sleazy single 'Peaches' rubbing shoulders with the Brotherhood of Man and Olivia Newton-John in the UK charts during the northern summer of 1977. Even American misfit Jonathan Richman was cashing in on the seismic shift in the charts; out front of the Modern Lovers, his punk-pop chant 'Roadrunner' reached the UK Top 20 in August 1977. If there was ever a time to start a band – and a label, in Dammers' case – it had to be right now.

Like future Pogue Shane McGowan, Elvis Costello, and so many others, Dammers was inspired by the anything-goes attitude of punk, and along with black guitarist Lynval Gooding and bassist Horace Panter, he formed his first band, The Automatics (aka The Coventry Automatics). Dammers could see that punk acts such as The Clash were very open to the multi-racial sounds of reggae – reggae's outlaws Bob Marley and Peter Tosh were lionised by punks almost as fervently as their own Johnny Rotten or the doomed Sid Vicious – and he was leading a multi-racial outfit, so he tried to mix punk's warp-speed riffing with what bandmate Panter referred to as 'heavy reggae'. The experiment failed, so Dammers, Golding and Panter (now reborn as one Sir Horace Gentleman) chose to play ska instead – albeit ska infused with the maverick spirit and cartoonish nicknames of punk, and more than a hint of melody. With the addition of guitarist Roddy Byers (aka Roddy Radiation) and two singers, Jamaican-born Neville Staples, a man with a seemingly bottomless baritone, and Coventry local Terry Hall, The Specials (aka the Special AKA) line-up was complete. And in the process, the second wave of ska – the '2-Tone' era – had begun.

Just like ska innovators The Skatalites before them, neither The Specials, nor the commercial resurgence of ska in the UK, was destined for an especially long life. Although Dammers' 2-Tone label would stumble along for seven years, releasing 29 singles and seven albums, the peak of the ska explosion could be plotted by the Special's first single, 'Gangsters', which surfaced in August 1979, and the band's appearance in the 1981 feature film, *Dance Craze*, alongside Bad Manners, the Beat, The Selecter and the Bodysnatchers, a helter-skelter snapshot of a time when ska officially went mainstream. From then on in, with the notable exception of Madness, ska offered gradually diminishing returns for the many bands that'd climbed aboard the bandwagon. Nonetheless, during its heyday, few styles of music have made the trip from the fringes to the spotlight so swiftly, nor have they left behind so many eminently hummable tunes – or such a readily identifiable look. And Madness have managed to resurrect their career many times over the past few decades, proving that there are enough true believers out there to still make it viable. (No Doubt even tapped them as a support act for some 1998 shows in Hawaii.) 'Updated' line-ups of the Beat and The Selecter also hit the reformation trail during the 'third wave' of ska.

Ska's 'rude boys' (and the occasional rude girl) were hard to miss: they were decked out in sharp three-button 'tonic' suits, usually matched with 'stingy brim' or pork pie hats, or wore pegged and bleached Levi's with 10-hole Doc Martens or loafers, and Ben Sherman or Fred Perry polo necks. Crombie overcoats, Harrington jackets and/or nylon flight jackets, usually littered with badges and pins declaring allegiance to various bands and scooter clubs, typically rounded off the ensemble. Ska was the complete lifestyle package, a fact not lost on the many Americans – including No Doubt co-founders Eric Stefani and John Spence – who, a few years later, 'discovered' such bands as The Selecter, Madness and The Specials. Jerry Dammers, especially, was a role model for the members of the original line-up of No Doubt. As one band insider would tell me, "Eric Stefani was very influenced by Jerry Dammers." Dammers' impact on Jerry McMahon, No Doubt's first guitarist, was even stronger. According to the same source, "He actually wanted to be Jerry Dammers." At least as much as a polite, middle-class kid from comfortable Orange County could, of course. McMahon and John Spence were the true ska 'purists' amongst No Doubt Mark I. Doug Fatone, who'd co-manage the band for a time, recalled seeing them both at numerous scooter rallies and ska gigs. "Yeah, John and Jerry were around a lot," he said.

And in the late Seventies, it was Dammers and The Selecter who were taking the lead. Having been hand-picked by The Clash as openers on their 'On Parole' British jaunt of June and July 1978 – Joe Strummer was a particularly dedicated fan – it seemed a natural next step that the band would sign with Clash manager Bernard Rhodes, whom Dammers had approached regarding management. And even though the band did as Rhodes suggested, spending six months rehearsing at his rat-infested dump on the Chalk Farm Road on London, and then doing hard yards playing to nobody in France, the independently minded Dammers soon had other ideas. Inspired by the success of such maverick American labels as Motown and Stax, he figured that The Specials should establish their own label, to be named 2-Tone as a nod towards the inclusive, multi-racial style of music that they'd almost mastered. It didn't seem to concern Dammers that he had to borrow money from friends and family to record 'Gangsters', their debut single. (Ska star Prince Buster, in his own way, also helped out, because the song's brakes-screech was 'sampled' from his 1964 track 'Al Capone', while some of Buster's lyrics were reworked for 'Gangsters'.) In fact, the recording was made on such a shoestring budget that no money was left in the kitty for a B-side, so Golding got in touch with a guitarist friend of his, Noel Davies, whom he recalled had home-recorded an instrumental track some time earlier. With the addition of an over-dubbed ska rhythm guitar track, it became known as 'The Selecter', providing both a B-side for 'Gangsters' and a name for another act about to become 2-Tone recording stars – which just so happened to include Davies among its members. It went to show just how incestuous the 2-Tone world would become.

Every bit the independent man, Dammers even designed the 2-Tone logo, with some help from Panter. Based on the cover image of an old Peter Tosh LP, it featured the dapper figure that would forever be known as Walt Jabsco, who made his first appearance in the artwork for 'Gangsters' and then appeared on every subsequent 2-Tone release. No Doubt's Eric Stefani, a budding artist himself, was one of many southern Californian ska fanciers who would emulate Dammers' artwork – almost to the point of shameless imitation – when creating a logo for his own band, and for the So-Cal-based radio show, The Ska Parade.

'Gangsters' emerged amidst a northern summer that mixed the usual pop fluff – pop's own Peter Pan, Cliff Richard, grumbling how 'We Don't Talk Anymore', Abba's disco-style 'Voulez Vous', ELO's ridiculous 'The Diary Of Horace Wimp' – with much more interesting and innovative fare from The Police (the white-man's reggae of 'Can't Stand Losing You'), Ian Dury & the Blockheads' 'Reasons To Be Cheerful, Part 3' and the Gary Numan-led Tubeway Army, whose chilly electro-pop anthem 'Are Friends Electric' was virtually inescapable. As was the Boomtown Rats' signature song, 'I Don't Like Mondays', which was perched atop the UK singles chart when 'Gangsters' began its unexpected yet unstoppable climb.

'Gangsters' namechecked Bernie Rhodes, and documented, in very specific detail, the hardships that The Specials experienced while touring France (Rhodes ditched them at the Dover ferry; their visa-less drummer was turned around at Calais; they had an 'incident' with the French constabulary which led to the 'confiscation' of their instruments). The single quickly picked up both radio airplay and a collective thumbs-up from the press. Dammers approached the Rough Trade label, who agreed to press 5,000 copies of the single. But when Dammers and the band turned up for a gig at London's Moonlight Club, they knew that they'd underestimated their commercial worth: amidst the full house of diehard fans, new converts and music biz execs was Mick Jagger, keen to sign the band to his own Rolling Stone records. Although impressed, The Specials passed; instead they stitched up a deal with Chrysalis Records, who signed the band to a five-album deal and the promise to release 10 2-Tone singles per year. Clearly on a 2-Tone roll, The Specials' 'Gangsters' peaked at No 6 in the UK chart in September 1979; the label signed Madness and The Selecter; and Dammers hired another of his admirers, Elvis Costello, to produce The Specials' debut album. It was very clearly the best of 2-Tone times. (In another curious No Doubt-related twist, Costello would later produce a single for the Anaheim-based ska-pop stars.)

If Jerry Dammers was a major role model for No Doubt's Eric Stefani and Jerry McMahon, then The Selecter's Pauline Black would truly mean the world to Gwen Stefani, once she had outgrown her obsessions with *The Sound Of Music* and Madonna, that is. According to one No Doubt insider, who preferred not to be named for this book, he spotted an autographed copy of No Doubt's breakthrough album, *Tragic Kingdom*, while interviewing Black at her home in England. The album came with an inscription from Stefani that read: 'Thanks for being such a hero to me.' Stefani meant what she wrote, too; one of the first songs she chose to perform in public, while still at Anaheim's Loara High School, was none other than The Selecter's 'On My Radio'.

Like The Specials, The Selecter – which comprised Black, guitarists Noel Davies and Compton Amanor, bassist Charley Anderson, drummer Charley 'H' Bembridge, back-up vocalist Arthur 'Gaps' Hendrickson and Desmond Brown on keys – emerged from the less-than-sexy hotspot of Coventry, better known for having once been the centre of Britain's car industry than its music. And again like their mentors, The Selecter was a multi-racial band, the physical (and musical) manifestation of 2-Tone's 'black and white' mission statement. The bulk of the band, excluding Black and Brown, had been united in a roots-reggae outfit called Hard Top 22, while Black and Brown had worked together in another local reggae-fusion combo, so when they came together as The Selecter, the fit was natural.

If Dammers' independent spirit was the force behind The Specials, then Black was The Selecter's not-so-secret weapon. The self-assured vocalist gave their irresistible debut single, 'On My Radio', just the right blend of understated sexiness and forthright assertiveness. Released in November 1979, the single raced into the UK Top 10 – a delicious irony, given that its lyric lambasted the crap that Black heard on the radio at the time – just as The Specials' next release, the equally hummable 'A Message To You Rudy', also began its climb towards the top of the UK charts. It seemed as though 2-Tone could do no wrong.

While 'Gangsters' may have been a near-perfect introduction to The Specials, their cover of 'A Message To You Rudy' was probably their finest few minutes. Combining a cautionary lyric about the limited possibilities of life as a rude boy with a deliciously sleepy solo from legendary ska trombonist Rico Rodriguez   who had recorded with The Skatalites and Prince Buster, and had actually played on the 1967 Dandy Livingston original of 'Rudy' – the single was a runaway success. And their Elvis Costello-produced LP, simply titled *Specials*, was welcomed like some homecoming hero. Even though 2-Tone would prove to be a very English success story – songs about "rudies" and "night boats to Cairo" proved a hard sell Stateside – the album received gushing praise from *Rolling Stone*, a magazine more comfortable with the Trans-Atlantic sounds of such UK rock monsters as Led Zeppelin and the Who. "*The Specials* is about as good as the British variant [of ska] gets," they wrote of the band's debut long-player.

Dammers and co celebrated their good fortune with the 40-date 2-Tone UK tour, with The Specials headlining and The Selecter and then-2-Tone labelmates Madness also on the bill. Despite some unwelcome appearances from racist collective the United National Front and the BNP, both of which actually attempted recruiting drives at some gigs, the tour was a huge, full-house success. At its end, The Specials reminded everyone of their right-mindedness by appearing at the UNICEF Concerts for Kampuchea, sharing the stage with such million-dollar stars as Paul McCartney, The Clash, Queen and their album producer, Elvis Costello.

The 2-Tone label's ear for talent was remarkable: soon after signing The Selecter, Dammers spotted Birmingham ska-pop outfit The Beat, who kept the label in the charts with their upbeat take on Smokey Robinson's 'Tears Of A Clown' (followed by some of ska-pop's best tunes, including 'Mirror In The Bathroom', 'Hands Off She's Mine' and 'Can't Get Used To Losing You'). And 2-Tone also released the debut single of self-proclaimed London "nutty boys", Madness, whose cover of Prince Buster's 'The Prince' went Top 20 in late 1979. (Soon after, Madness defected to Stiff Records, the home of Elvis Costello, Ian Dury, Nick Lowe, The Damned and others, and found even bigger success with the party track 'One Step Beyond', which came complete with its own "nutty" dance steps, a sort of rude boy variation on John Cleese's silly walk.)

Just like The Selecter, Madness was another ska-pop band that'd leave a strong impression on the future members of No Doubt. Eric Stefani's first introduction to ska–pop was an import single of their 1980 hit, 'Baggy Trousers'. In fact, the entire existence of No Doubt could probably be traced to the moment when Eric Stefani weaned his sister off Madonna and *The Sound Of Music* and pointed her in the direction of Madness' hugely accessible ska-pop rhythms. "I would never have been into. . . Madness if it wasn't for him," she would admit in a 1995 interview. "He was my main influence. When I got into the band, I learned everything from my brother."

As easy transitions go, Madness would be the perfect band for a pop fan such as Gwen Stefani to digest. Most ska purists, who felt they lacked the political edge and social agenda of The Specials, considered the group light-weight. Howard Paar, an expat Brit who, during the early 1980s, ran Los Angeles' first genuine ska venue, the ON Klub, agreed with this. 'The Specials,' he said, 'meant a lot to me, in the way that The Clash did. [But Madness] always seemed a bit jokey to me.' In the same way that Madness were considered fringe dwellers by 2-Tone devotees, No Doubt were always on the fringes of the so-called 'third wave' of ska, the movement that helped shift them into the spotlight. Such peers as The Untouchables and The Skeletones – bands who would share early bills with No Doubt – would pursue a more 2-Tone / Skatalites influenced path, and, of course, come nowhere near the monumental sales and huge success of No Doubt. Such is the lot of the musical purist – relegated to the outskirts of the mainstream, where the kudos are nice, but the financial rewards are notice-ably smaller.

★ ★ ★

Of all the 2-Tone-era bands, only Madness would continue to generate hits on a steady basis, or maintain any real career momentum, and that was mainly because they inched closer and closer to the mainstream, despite maintaining the trappings (mainly sartorial) of ska. They were also dab-hands at producing amusing videos which emphasized their image as 'nutty boys', out to have fun. 'Grey Day', 'Cardiac Arrest', 'Driving In My Car', 'House of Fun' and 1982's 'Our House' – the only Madness single to suc-cessfully leap the pond and reach the US Top 20, in July 1983 – all did seri-ous business at or near the top of the UK singles chart. History wasn't so kind to most of their peers. Despite a hit with the single 'Three Minute Hero', and a US release for *Too Much Pressure* on Chrysalis Records, Gwen Stefani's hero, Pauline Black of The Selecter, found it hard to move forward. After leaving 2-Tone (along with the Beat), the group eventually folded, at least in their original form, after 1981's *Celebrate The Bullet* LP. For a time, Pauline Black left music altogether, resurfacing on the UK kids' show *Hold Tight*.

The Specials managed to hang on a little longer. They strung together a handy sequence of hits – February 1980's 'Too Much Too Young', a live five-tracker, followed by 'Rat Race' and the muzak-y 'Stereotype', in June and October of the same year. But during an attempt to tap into the US market, which included some opening slots with the soon-to-be-huge Police, cracks were starting to show. Dammers, whose politics were well to the left, insisted that the band not live too large, so limos were out and the band stayed at dodgy fleapits. When asked by an *Los Angeles Times* reporter whether he was enjoying his stay Stateside, Dammers snapped back how he'd 'had more fun on a school trip to Russia'. And when the band rolled up for a showcase at the Whiskey in LA, Dammers was appalled by the black-and-white checks that had been painted all over the building, an attempt by their US 'people' to spread the 2-Tone message. The writing – or at least the painting – was well and truly on the wall.

However, despite fast-developing tensions between Dammers and gui-tarist Roddy Radiation, the band kept working, even though the dramas continued: there was a stage invasion in Japan, which resulted in a cancelled show, and a brutal race-based attack on Golding, who needed 27 stitches after having his throat slashed. (The attack, however, did lead to another sterling Specials' track, 'Why?', a slap in the face for the National Front thugs who beat him up.) Dammers and Hall were arrested during a gig in Cambridge, after failing to stop another bout of violence that erupted in the crowd. In the midst of all this mayhem, the fragmenting Specials managed to complete a second album – the imaginatively titled *More Specials* – and record the most poignant song of their career, 'Ghost Town', the ultimate soundtrack for both the band's troubled times and life under the iron-fisted Margaret Thatcher. Elbowing aside the likes of Michael Jackson, 'Stars On 45' and Buck's Fizz, the track raced to the pole position on the UK singles chart in July 1981, and sold more than a million copies. In second spot was 'Can Can', from former 2-Tone signing Bad Manners. Dammers, his band-mates and 2-Tone may have seen better days, but if ska had a commercial highpoint, it was right now.

Soon after another tumultuous US tour, however, the wheels fell off. Dammers fired band manager Rick Rogers, and Hall, Golding and Staple split The Specials to form Fun Boy Three. Only two weeks later they dropped their debut single, 'The Lunatics Have Taken Over The Asylum', a song with a message that didn't require a psychology degree to unravel. Dammers lumbered on, renaming the group The Special AKA (for the second confusing time), and eventually completing the madly expensive LP *In The Studio* in August 1984, having eaten up a cheeky £500,000 in the process. (Dammers would refer to it as 'the great mistake'.) Although the truly righteous single, 'Nelson Mandela', did return the band to the upper reaches of the charts, 2-Tone's heady days were well and truly over. And Walt Jabsco was on life support.

But what Dammers and his fellow Specials, plus the many other acts that recorded for 2-Tone – the Bodysnatchers, the Beat, The Selecter, and even Elvis Costello, who cut 'I Can't Stand Up For Falling Down' during a dispute with his own label, and such one-off curios as the Friday Club and the Swinging Cats – couldn't have imagined, was that ska was soon to get a third kiss of life, and this time in the most unlikely location: sleepy southern California.

CHAPTER TWO

The Happiest Place On Earth?

"[Anaheim is] a strange place. It's basically Disneyland and all the hotels and motels, and that's all."

—Gwen Stefani

If there was a part of America that symbolised the nation's post-World War II prosperity – and all its crew cut, apple pie, freshly-mowed-lawn blandness – then it had to be Orange County in southern California. It was the land of Ronald Reagan, Jack Benny and many, many oranges. And if there was a slice of Orange County that captured the region's G-rated, family-friendly dullness, then that was Anaheim. It said multitudes about Anaheim that Walt Disney, America's king of everything squeaky-clean and wholesome, opted to establish his Disneyland empire there.

Anaheim was also ground zero for No Doubt, whose music often maintained a very close relationship with everything that was good and pure and right with the world. This wasn't The Specials' Coventry or The Skatalites' Jamaica, that's for sure.

Yet Anaheim, the 10th largest city in California, has humble roots. While not quite something out of John Steinbeck's *The Grapes Of Wrath*, it was a far cry from the middle-class indulgences of the airbrushed kids in *The OC*. Anaheim was founded in 1857 by German farmers and vintners; it's name was a blend of "Ana", from the nearby Santa Ana river, and "heim", the German word for home. Early attempts to turn the area into a wine region, a la Australia's Barossa Valley, another locale with deep German roots, failed badly, so the local farmers tried their luck with oranges, which turned out to be a much savvier option. Although Orange County would much later be known for producing Tim Buckley and Jackson Browne, writers, painters and musicians settled in the area almost as soon as Anaheim produced Orange County's first commercial orange crop. Anaheim's original public buildings were a school and an opera house, which says something about the arty bent of some of its early settlers.

However, the region's growth was slow. When the city was incorporated in 1876, it boasted a population of 881. By 1920, there were just over 5,500 residents; in 1950, the population had reached a comfortable 14,556. Day-to-day life in Anaheim typified small-town, post-war America; people gathered on the very literally named Center Street (now known as Lincoln Boulevard) to celebrate local events and festivities, such as the annual Halloween Parade, which the city's fathers billed as the "Greatest Night Pageant West of Mardi Gras". This was no idle boast; at its peak, the Halloween bash pulled 150,000 onlookers, yet somehow maintained its down-home character.

As a kid growing up in Anaheim during the Seventies, Gwen Stefani loved Halloween, and even as an adult she was still mad for America's annual night of trick-or-treating. "[It's] my favourite holiday," she declared in 2002, "and in my life I feel like it is Halloween every day."

Gwen, who would become one of Anaheim's most celebrated citizens, typified the city's slightly parochial outlook on the world. "We're proud of being from Orange County," she declared with an unmistakable whiff of defensiveness, as No Doubt's third LP, *Tragic Kingdom*, started to go huge. "[But] it's a strange place," Stefani admitted. "It's basically Disneyland and all the hotels and motels, and that's all."

As she'd prove in her metaphor-free lyrics, Gwen definitely understood Anaheim. Her mother, Patti, was part of the third generation of her family to call Anaheim home. (Gwen's father lived in Detroit – where his parents had moved from Italy – until he was 13.)

Los Angeles, in all its smoggy, seedy funkiness, lay only 40 miles away, but people such as the Stefanis gravitated to Anaheim for other reasons. To the God-fearing, home-and-hearth-loving Dennis Stefani, temperate California must have seemed like the promised land by comparison with the icy winters of Detroit: it was safe, warm and secure. And, as Gwen's bandmate, Tom Dumont, observed, when *Tragic Kingdom* grew like some unstoppable monster, Gwen's lyrics read like a report on life in her back-yard. '[The album] is a snapshot of a suburban female in the Nineties, and there are a lot of honest, heartfelt things she's singing about,' Dumont fig-ured, quite rightly. Gwen Stefani had obviously learned a lot about life in the OC during her days manning The Broadway department store's service desk in the Anaheim Plaza shopping center, and serving cones at the local Dairy Queen.

Given the growth of farming in the area, and a fare war between America's two railroad giants, Southern Pacific and Santa Fe, during the post-war boom – a ticket from Kansas City to LA would set you back all of one buck – Easterners started to head west, with dreams of sunshine and fertile farmland and a comfortable life swimming in their heads. Los Angeles felt the full force of the industrial and economic boom that kicked in after WWII, and once desolate suburban areas were now dotted with signs of life, including new businesses and row upon row of tract homes. Dusty highways and roads were paved, and towns and cities sprang up, seemingly overnight, in spots that were once farms. (The West Coast obses-sion with the motor car grew in tandem with these newly-paved roads and highways.)

But the biggest dreamer of all to cast his gaze westwards was a guy called Walter Elias Disney, who, in a peculiar way, would play a pivotal role in the rise of No Doubt. Born in Chicago on December 5, 1901, to an Irish/Canadian father and a German/American mother, Disney spent his early years in Missouri and Kansas City, and saw a year of action in WWI, driving a Red Cross ambulance in France (he was too young to enlist). By the time he returned to Chicago and started drawing his first, flawed attempt at animation, *The Alice Comedies*, his brother Roy was already in California, so Walt also headed west. They set up shop, first in their uncle's garage and then at the rear of a Hollywood real estate office. When Mickey Mouse made his public debut in *Steamboat Willie*, on November 18, 1928, Disney was truly on his way. Within a decade, Disney would produce the first full-length animated feature, his version of *Snow White And The Seven Dwarfs*, made for a then-budget-busting $1.5 million US. It managed to do what you might call reasonable box office – a cheeky $681 million US, according to 2005 figures – as did such subsequent Disney extravaganzas as *Pinocchio*, *Dumbo*, *Fantasia* and *Bambi*.

Construction finished on Disney's Burbank Studio in 1940, but he had much larger plans. He had his eye on an 11-acre lot across the road from the Disney studio; for years he'd been tossing around an idea for a "family theme park", hoping to improve on the inadequate facilities he'd seen when playing in local parks with his daughters Sharon and Diane. Disney sketched out his thoroughly wholesome dream: Originally called Mickey Mouse Park, the theme park would feature a lake stocked with fish, as well as an island in the centre of the lake where kids could run amok. The park's centrepiece would be Main Street – his own spin on Anaheim's Center Street – where a carousel and a bandstand would offer a flashback to a more quaint way of American life. A miniature train, another of Disney's obsessions, would putter around the park, shuffling happy punters from one attraction to the other. Mickey Mouse Park defined Disney's morally sound take on the world.

With $10,000 in the construction budget and a schematic of the park in his briefcase, Disney pitched his plan to the city of Burbank, but the city fathers rejected the idea, fearing it would turn into a tacky "permanent carnival". So Disney, quite literally, went back to the drawing board. He added a new attraction, "Frontier Land", and quickly came to realise that his 11-acre site in Burbank wouldn't be quite big enough to house his dream. On a drive south along the Santa Ana Freeway, as Disney watched the smog-clogged City of Angels fade in his rear-view mirror, he figured that Orange County would be a much better place for his park. Its comparatively slow pace reminded him of his native Midwest, while its city officials were bound to be more agreeable than the hard-to-please Burbank decision-makers.

But Disney's budget blew out substantially – to complete what was now being referred to as Disneyland was going to set him back at least $4 million, a stiff increase from his original budget of $10,000. A smart businessman, Disney struck a deal with the American Broadcasting Company, better known as ABC. As a partner in Disneyland, ABC would cough up $500,000 and also guarantee $4.5 million in loans for construction costs. Disney, in return, would produce a weekly hour-long TV series for the ABC television network. (The series turned out to be a sensational promotional tool for Disneyland, so everyone was a winner.) As for the site itself, Disney had given Long Beach, Palos Verdes and Canoga Park the once-over, but opted for Anaheim. Disney had designed floats for the city's Halloween Parade and that made his decision a bit easier. It also helped that the recently completed Interstate 5 sliced right through the geographical heart of Anaheim; it was an easy 45-minute ride to Disneyland from downtown LA.

Anaheim's then-mayor, Charles Pearson, remained unsure. How could the city be confident that this Disneyland wouldn't be just another tawdry carnival, employing dodgy characters and drawing a low-rent crowd? Pearson summed up the city's concerns when he told Disney that he "didn't want to see Disneyland as the kind of place where peanut shells littered the ground". (Heaven forbid.) Disney was a very literal man; he assured Pearson that unshelled peanuts (or chewing gum) wouldn't be sold at Disneyland. The deal now in place, Disney announced that his eponymous park – variously known as "the happiest place on Earth" and the "Magic Kingdom" – would throw open its gates to the public on July 17, 1955, which left his staff a few weeks to iron out any irregularities before the month of August, when virtually all of America took its annual vacation.

Disney met his schedule, but the park's grand opening was anything but. A sizeable crowd of 28,000 (including, possibly, more than one member of the local Stefani clan) turned out, many clutching forged entry passes. Rides didn't work. Fantasyland was shut down due to a gas leak. Despite the summer heat, there were no working water fountains. Women screamed as the heels of their shoes got stuck in the hot asphalt. As part of its deal with Disney, ABC had TV cameras everywhere, broadcasting the opening day mayhem to an audience of 70 million – almost half the US population at the time. Future US president Ronald Reagan was one of three celebrities hired to host the live feed.

Deeply disappointed, Disney crowned opening day "Black Sunday". Yet within seven weeks of one of the worst days of his life, the one-millionth visitor had passed through Disneyland's turnstiles and stepped back in time. Within three years it would surpass Yosemite, Yellowstone and the Grand Canyon as America's key tourist attraction. It was a runaway success.

Anaheim, in turn, morphed from ghost town into boomtown. With so many jobs on offer at the park, many of the staff bought homes in the city. Anaheim operated its own utilities, which was another draw, because it meant the residents paid lower utility bills than those in surrounding cities. And the oranges were sweet, juicy and plentiful. As its population increased, the city itself expanded. Roughly 1,500 acres were annexed for new development in 1953; 2,700 more the following year. And in 1955, the year that Disneyland opened, a further 3,300 acres were added. Anaheim was now four times the city that it had been two years earlier. During the 1950s, largely thanks to Disney's family-friendly monument to wholesomeness, Anaheim grew faster than any other city in America. Local officials even updated what was then known as "the worst jail north of Tijuana", so local felons also savoured the good life.

Other facilities would be built in Anaheim, including Anaheim Stadium, home to the Los Angeles Angels baseball team, and the Arrowhead Pond of Anaheim (now the Honda Center), an 18,000-capacity venue that No Doubt would one day fill. Anaheim Stadium, hosted its first rock band, The

Who, in 1970. The volume of the show, however, was so fierce that the city banned concerts for five years, until the less rowdy Beach Boys and Chicago – and, later, the squeaky-clean Osmonds – returned what could loosely be called 'rock'n'roll' to Anaheim.

Yet Disneyland remained the city's defining landmark. Residents such as the Stefanis, who lived only a short stroll away from Dennis Stefani's parents at 1173 Beacon Avenue – which later became No Doubt HQ – accepted it as part of their local landscape. "It was fun," recalled Gwen Stefani, who'd sometimes try to sneak into the park without paying. She'd even spent her prom night there, regally decked out in a homemade outfit based on the black-and-white number Grace Kelly sported in Alfred Hitchcock's *Rear Window*.

To Gwen, Disneyland was simply always there. But her older brother, Eric, wasn't so enamoured of the park, even though he worked there for a while. ("Who from Loara [High] didn't?" quipped classmate, Scot Thiesmeyer.) To Eric Stefani it represented a mundane world, a kind of safe suburban life that was eagerly – too eagerly, as far as he was concerned – embraced by so many Anaheim residents. When Eric used the audio warning from Disneyland's Matterhorn ride – "remain seated please" and the rest of it – at the beginning of a No Doubt track, it wasn't necessarily a celebration of Anaheim's biggest tourist attraction. Eric Stefani dubbed Disneyland the "Tragic Kingdom". Years later, Adrian Young, the future No Doubt drummer, summed up not just Anaheim, but much of Orange County, when he admitted "there's not much culture" in the band's hometown.

★　★　★

Disneyland was a month short of its 12th birthday when Eric, oldest of the four Stefani offspring, was born on June 17, 1967. Along with his brother Todd (born on March 1, 1974), and sisters Jill (born December 15, 1972) and Gwen Renee (born on October 3, 1969), Eric was raised by a staunchly Catholic family. (All the Stefani children were born at Anaheim's St Jude Hospital.)

Speaking with *Vogue* in 2004, Gwen confirmed this. "I grew up, like, a Catholic good girl," she said in her modified Valley Girl style. "Total *Brady Bunch* family."

Gwen's first memory was that of Eric sneaking Oreo cookies from the kitchen, scraping out the white interior and rolling it into a large ball. This established the relationship between these two siblings: To Gwen, Eric was "a nutcase". That might have been so, but she also followed his every move, right down to the point of reluctantly stepping on-stage with him as part of No Doubt, having tuned into the peculiar ska records he'd been soaking up in his bedroom. "I was a really passive person," said Gwen, when asked about her relationship with Eric. "My brother – I was his puppet." (Dancing class, typically a rite of passage for most white, middle-class girls, wasn't so satis-fying for wallflower Stefani. When she was five, too nervous to ask to be excused, she peed on the floor during ballet lessons.)

Gwen may have compared growing up in Anaheim with the all-American life of TV's Mike and Carol Brady, but the Stefanis were actually a little tougher. They were so conservative and super-protective that during No Doubt's early days the band couldn't actually headline a bill, even if the promoter had offered them the gig. Dennis and Patti Stefani had imposed a strict 11 p.m. curfew on their teenage daughter, so she had to be rushed home almost as soon as the band had raced through its final song. (This cur-few even led to the departure of one of the band's original members, and severely hampered their early progress, but more on that later.)

While Patti conformed to the Orange County stereotype, staying at home and raising the kids, Dennis was a marketing exec at Yamaha. That gig would actually lead the teenage Gwen to meet an idol – Sting of The Police – with whom she'd one day share a Super Bowl half-time stage (unlikely as that might have seemed to a starstruck Gwen at the time). Thanks to her father's connections, Gwen also got to meet one-hit wonders A Flock of Seagulls.

Dennis Stefani, whose family was Italian, and Patti Flynn, whose people were Irish/Scottish, were high school sweethearts who married relatively young. The Stefanis may have been strict, but there was a lot of music in their home. Dennis and Patti had performed together in a folk band, called The Innertubes. Taking a page from the Carter Family songbook, Patti played the autoharp while Dennis studiously strummed an acoustic guitar. Both were dedicated Bob Dylan fans, which didn't necessarily rub off on their kids. Gwen disliked the Bobfather – she thought his music was 'gnarly' – and one of her earliest memories was being dragged out of a Girl Scouts get-together to attend an Emmylou Harris gig. But the majority of the music heard in their home was more traditional fare: soundtracks from musicals such as *Annie, Evita,* and *The Sound Of Music* (a huge record for a young, impressionable Gwen Stefani), and Kermit the Frog's 'The Rainbow Connection'. "I was *very* affected by *The Muppet Movie*," Gwen said in 2003, with an impassively straight face. "[It's] probably one of the best films ever made."

The Stefanis were principled people with questionable taste in music, but they were supportive; none of their four children were neglected. "I was very spoiled compared with a lot of people," Gwen said. "We weren't rich, but we definitely had whatever we wanted."

Apart from the Dylan soundtrack, which veered slightly left of centre, life in the Stefani home went pretty much by the Orange County book: It was safe, conservative and protective.

Gwen, the second of the four Stefani offspring, was very much her father's favourite. In a rare interview, several years after his daughter's wholesome image had inspired a legion of imitators – known as "Gwenabees" – you could still sense a certain protectiveness towards his daughter. Was she a sex symbol? "That's a little troublesome," he replied when asked. "I think she's hit on a trend in society where blatant sexuality is really not what's happening." Dennis Stefani preferred to describe his daughter as "healthy, athletic, honest . . . that's why people find her attractive."

As for Gwen's relationship with her mother, it was best summed up by an encounter that took place as *Tragic Kingdom* became one of the mid-Nineties biggest albums. Gwen had reworked the lyric for 'Just A Girl' into a frenzied crowd chant of "Fuck you, I'm just a girl". Her mother had invited another Stefani relative along to a gig and requested that Gwen not use the "F-word" on stage, at least during this one show. When Gwen went ahead and did it anyway, Patti Stefani gave her the cold shoulder for the best part of a week. "That word?" Patti said. "I was quite shocked that she put that in her act. [But] at least she isn't pierced or tattooed."

Years earlier, both Patti and Dennis had given Gwen a serious lecture on the evils of the teen flick *Flashdance*, especially the "promiscuity" of the female lead, so it wasn't the first time Patti had laid down the law. Usually, however, Patti Stefani offered more spiritual advice to Gwen and her siblings during testing times. She'd frequently tell her kids, "pray and you find peace".

Even as an adult, Gwen stuck to this Stefani family adage. "I pray," she told *Teen People* magazine in 2002, "because if you take the time out to be thankful, it calms you down."

Interestingly, as one insider would tell me, this slightly overbearing upbringing would present some problems for Eric Stefani when he took on the role as chief songwriter for No Doubt. Unlike such peers as Nirvana's troubled junkie Kurt Cobain, who'd been bounced between family members like a football, and had lived rough, Eric Stefani had little in the way of life experience to write about. So his early songs would concentrate on such inane subject matter as toothaches, girlfriends and masturbation. "It was hard to take it seriously," said Paul Oberman who, along with Doug

Fatone, briefly co-managed the band in the late Eighties. "Eric and Gwen had all this drive and talent, but they had no life experiences to draw upon."

Long before he threw himself into music, Gwen's "nutcase" brother became deeply immersed in art and drawing, a talent that would earn him numerous awards at school, and also one day provide a very handy career outside of music. His first work of art was an unsolicited scrawl, a smiling sun shooting out rays of light, on the wall of his bedroom. He was two years old at the time.

"My brother was an artist from the day he was born," Gwen has said. As a sixth grader, Eric's habit of drawing everywhere – including on the desk tops in his classroom – meant that he was a regular come detention time, when he was directed to scrub away his doodles. The next day the cycle would continue. Word of his talent spread as far as a nearby junior high. Students there talked him into drawing for their school newspaper.

Gwen's early years took a more conventional path; so conventional, in fact, that she wore white underwear until the end of high school, again on the suggestion of her ever-watchful folks. "My parents were very strict," she said, "but they weren't mean-strict." As for Eric, his way of speaking reflected his straight-laced upbringing: no word stronger than "dang" would ever pass his lips.

By the time of sixth grade, Gwen Stefani – now nicknamed "The Frog" – was a chubby kid and not a big mixer. She tried out for the school swimming team (hence her nickname), but only because she thought it might help her shed some pounds. "I wanted to get skinny," she admitted. "My weight was a struggle for me, like all girls." She also tried water ballet and soccer, again to lose weight. Eventually her mother put Gwen on a strict diet, frightened that she might turn out like her grandmother, who was more than a few dress sizes above the recommended weight. Gwen was all of 12 at the time. "I think that really frightened my mom, you know?", Stefani once said. "It was out of my mother's love for me. [But] I think it's haunted me in a way." Gwen spent a lot of time alone, indulging in youthful fantasies of "dress-up" – she came from a family of seamstresses, a talent that would prove very useful – and imagining herself as "Maria," Julie Andrews' lovestruck character from *The Sound Of Music*.

As charming and quaint as this seems, Stefani's love of that film was more like an obsession. She simply couldn't get enough *Sound of Music*; until her brother turned her on to Madness and 2-Tone, it was her one true love. (In 2007 she finally got the chance to celebrate Andrews in song, riffing on 'The Lonely Goatherd' during her solo hit 'Wind It Up'.)

Boyfriends were definitely not on the agenda, either. Stefani's parents were quite insistent that there were would be no sex before marriage, at least not on their watch. (In a 1996 interview, Stefani echoed her mother's beliefs, although accidentally revealing that she didn't quite live them out. "All I'd say is avoid having sex with anyone until you're married," she warned. "It just brings too many complications." There were some early flings: braces-wearing Brad, from eighth grade, who provided her first French kiss; and a Robert Smith wannabe whom she met in band class (Stefani played the piccolo in her school's marching band) with "an uncontrollable urge" that she successfully repelled. But she was hardly living the life of wild child Courtney Love; instead, Gwen kept a special place in her heart for more G-rated niceties. Furthermore, as Gwen explained, "no boys liked me in high school because I was chubby."

So Gwen was a "girly girl", heavily influenced by *Cinderella* and Julie Andrews. "I wanted to be Maria von Trapp. I even had a dress that looked just like hers," she said. (For serious Gwen-spotters, it's the dress Andrews wore during the 'I Have Confidence' production number. It was the first dress that future fashion designer Stefani actually completed by herself.)

Another of her heroines was doomed Hollywood starlet Marilyn Monroe; an interesting choice of role model, given that Gwen was growing up in the late Seventies era dominated by such steely, "serious" actresses as Meryl Streep and Jessica Lange. Monroe, the star of such glittery affairs as *Gentlemen Prefer Blondes*, was a flashback to a more traditional time, when women smiled, looked beautiful and said very little. "My whole room was Marilyn Monroe posters," she said. A bowerbird of style, Gwen would borrow elements of Monroe's look when she too morphed into a platinum blonde. As one observer noted, Gwen managed to "simultaneously evoke Forties Hollywood and early Eighties So-Cal punk. It [was] quite a trick."

Interestingly, for a woman who would inspire hordes of imitators, who can make any A-list on the strength of a single call from her publicist, the pubescent Gwen was pretty much a loner, living in the increasingly long shadow of her older brother Eric. "I always had my one best friend," she said, "[but] I didn't have a lot of girlfriends. Never have." Her closest ally at Anaheim's Loara High School, whose name has been lost over the years, strayed from their "no drugs, no drink, no sex" policy, leaving late-bloomer Gwen confused and bewildered. "All of a sudden she started partying and doing things with guys," Gwen recalled, "and it was pretty hurtful to me because it was like she was moving ahead of me. She was on a different level. It was a shock — I felt like I was being abandoned." Yet according to Kim Segovia, a Loara High classmate, Gwen was possibly more popular than she let on. "As far as I recall she was well liked, fairly popular, but not a snob.

'I remember the first time I heard "Don't Speak" on the radio and they announced that was Gwen Stefani of No Doubt,' Segovia added. "I told my husband, 'I went to school with a Gwen Stefani'. He said, 'Oh yeah, she went to school in Orange County; it must be the same one.' It was really bizarre: I never even knew she was in a band. It's really amazing to me that anyone can achieve that level of fame. It seems she has dealt with it very well; I know I never would have."

So Gwen retreated into her world of sexually inexperienced nuns and singing Muppets, absently flicking through bridal magazines, humming along to Madonna on the radio, and looking forward to the life of a home-maker, not unlike her mother. Early on, Gwen had none of the natural talent that her brother Eric displayed. She was an average student, at best, who found it hard to maintain the concentration necessary to perform well academically. Sometimes the bell would ring to signal the end of class and she would look down at her desk and notice that she'd spent the entire period doodling the name of whomever she had a crush on at the time "in sketched out, really nice letters". She'd sum up her modest aspirations in the No Doubt song 'Simple Kind of Life', a hauntingly beautiful anthem for those simply seeking domestic bliss (which, ironically, would elude Gwen for much of her first 30 years). "All I wanted was the simple things / A simple kind of life", She sang in her untrained yet beguiling voice, "And all I needed was a simple man / So I could be a wife / I always thought I'd be a mom / Sometimes I wish for a mistake." It was hardly the kind of fuck-the-world sentiment that would kickstart a revolution; it was more the yearning of a typical Anaheim girl longing for a typical Anaheim life.

But Loara High School, which all the Stefanis attended (after Palm Lane Elementary and Ball Junior High), was not a school for under-achievers. Opened on November 1, 1962, with its then 400-odd students decked out in school colours of red, gold and white ("red, white, and gold we honour," declared the school song, "til our dying day"), the ethics of its students, who were known as "Saxons", were spelled out clearly in the stirring poem 'Saga of the Saxon', penned in 1963 by Molly Wampler, one of the school's first counsellors. "In the city of Anaheim / On a street," she wrote, "Where Euclid Avenue and Cerrilos meet / Stood a grove of oranges, bright and green / Just about the prettiest grove you've ever seen / But across the way and behind the trees / Over the highway and thick as fleas / Grew a crop of youngsters, special all through / Who needed a school that was special, too." As the school's Website insists, "once a Saxon, always a Saxon".

Roused by this call-to-arms, Loara High School quickly became renowned, statewide, for its marching band, "the Show Band of the Western

States". The school hit the headlines on October 31, 1987, when US President, Californian and arch conservative, Ronald Reagan, addressed the students of Loara, flanked by secret service agents as his chopper idled on the nearby baseball field. ("President's arrival no secret at Loara", chuckled the local newspaper.) Gwen Stefani, who would graduate that year, was among the many chopper-swept students looking on.

But Loara was better known for the many musicians who would spend their formative years in its student-friendly surrounds. (Loara was so student-friendly that in 1976 the school even set aside a smoking area for pupils, with the proviso: "All cigarette butts must be completely extinguished before they are placed in trash cans." It also offered America's first Family Life and Sex Education class.) Blood, Sweat & Tears' bassist Jim Fielder had wandered the school's hallways, as had doomed junkie-cum-folkie Tim Buckley. Buckley's equally famous son Jeff also attended Loara, and would form a club, of sorts, with other future stars.

No Doubt insider Mike Miller recalled with a laugh, When we went to high school, I was the only one from our lunch-time crew that didn't become a rock star. We'd sit around and there was Gwen and Eric, Jeff Buckley [then known as Scotty], T Bone [aka singer Jeff "T Bone" Gerard], and drum'n'bass guy Q."

Becoming a rock star, of course, seemed about as likely to Gwen Stefani – at least in the mid-Eighties – as hanging out backstage with Police-man Sting. She didn't leave a sizeable impression on too many of her classmates. One member of Loara's Class of 1987, Robert Dagnall, remembers little of Stefani in the classroom or on campus, but vaguely recalled being served by her at Anaheim's local Dairy Queen, where No Doubt's first singer, John Spence, also worked. Another Class of '87 alumnus, Scot Thiesmeyer – who was in Gwen Stefani's English class and on the swim team – remembered the Stefani sisters, Jill and Gwen, as "cute".

"[Gwen was] pretty, shy and quiet if she didn't know you," he said, "and [she had] much darker hair." (Thiesmeyer's friend, Noel Cox, was tight with Eric Stefani and worked alongside him both at Disneyland and on the animated TV hit *The Simpsons*.)

However, Thiesmeyer and many other Loara students got the shock of their lives when Gwen Stefani, the Anaheim wallflower, won a part in the high school musical, *The Lullaby of Broadway*, a sort-of greatest hits of the stage, in which, in order to avoid royalties, director-cum-choral-instructor Ken Tuttle would piece together hit songs from various musicals.

This was most likely held in either 1985 or 1986. (Most histories of the band incorrectly state that she made her debut singing The Selecter's 'On

My Radio'. That came later.) "Gwen did a great job on a solo, 'What I Did For Love' [from *A Chorus Line*]," Thiesmeyer stated. "She had an incredibly unique, sweet voice for someone who had no training and had never been in a musical or a choir. My friend, Dean White, and I sat in the auditorium listening to her at rehearsals and we both agreed that if she pursued singing, she'd go far. Who knew?" (Thiesmeyer has extremely rare video footage of Stefani's performance, that, understandably, he's reluctant to part with.) Despite the urging of Thiesmeyer and others, however, Gwen flat out refused to join the Chamber Singers, Loara's "elite choral ensemble". Instead, it would take a gentle shove in the back from her biggest influence, her brother Eric, to finally get Gwen Stefani on a stage. But first she'd have to undergo a musical makeover.

★ ★ ★

Orange County was the ideal place to live out Gwen Stefani's "simple kind of life", where she'd find the right man, breed a litter of kids and maybe sing the occasional showtune. Or, as the *Los Angeles Times'* Mike Boehm would describe it, she was preparing herself for "the Orange County dream of quiet, well-ordered, economically impregnable suburban living." But the region still had its few moments of pop culture history, even if they were overshadowed by what snickering Los Angelenos referred to as the "Orange Curtain", an invisible, yet seemingly uncrossable Rubicon of cool that isolated the OC from its slick, sleazy neighbour.

Don Snowden, music writer for the *Los Angeles Times* during the Seventies and Eighties, described the gulf this way: "LA vs. OC was like San Fran looking down on LA. OC was like the boring, stifling, sheltered suburban hell you escaped to Los Angeles from, since your parents had probably moved there to escape from Los Angeles. I'm not from So-Cal, but I know boring, stifling, sheltered suburban hell. Hollywood/Hollyweird ruled. And no one in LA necessarily knew what was going on out in the LA hinterlands unless they worked at it."

Even before Walt Disney threw open the doors of his Magic Kingdom, Fullerton luthier Leo Fender had been working on his own visionary statement: the Fender Telecaster and Stratocaster guitars. These six-stringed rock'n'roll icons were weapons of choice for everyone from surf-rock innovator Dick Dale (another OC native, who worked with Leo in developing the Fender Showman amp), The Shadows' Hank Marvin, Elvis Presley sideman James Burton, Bruce Springsteen, Beatles John Lennon and George Harrison, plus Jimi Hendrix, Eric Clapton, Pink Floyd's David Gilmour, Dire Straits' Mark Knopfler and innumerable less notable garage hopefuls. Leo also designed Fender's signature amps and basses.

There was also a healthy number of stars, both one-hit-wonders and otherwise, who emerged from behind the Orange Curtain, well before No Doubt chanced upon their Platinum-plus, ska-pop formula. Silky-voiced duo Bobby Hatfield and Bill Medley (better known as The Righteous Brothers) emerged from the wilds of Santa Ana with such signature tear-jerkers as the Phil Spector-crafted 'You've Lost That Lovin' Feelin' ' and 'Unchained Melody'. Instrumentalists The Chantays were also straight out of Santa Ana; they struck gold with their April 1963 surf-rock standard, 'Pipeline', later covered by everyone from Dick Dale and Hank Marvin to Johnny Thunders and thrash metal marauders Anthrax. Lesser-known, but no less successful, were OC's We Five, who scaled the US Top 20 in September 1965 with 'You Were On My Mind'. And blind soul-pop strum-mer José Feliciano, although he was a native of Puerto Rico, had been claimed by Orange County as one of their own by the time he reworked the Doors' testosterone-drenched 'Light My Fire' into a Latino-tinged, jazz-pop smash in 1968.

There were, of course, more "serious" acts that'd emerged from this fam-ily-friendly slice of Southern California. The aforementioned Tim Buckley, a man with a golden voice and an ultimately dangerous attraction to drugs, was described by *Rolling Stone* as "a sort of late Sixties folkie Coleridge – overwhelmed by the gods with too many gifts". Although born in Washington, DC, Buckley was, like Feliciano, an import claimed by south-ern Californians. Not so singer/strummer Jackson Browne, who effectively defined the sensitive Seventies with such navel-gazing albums as 1974's *Late For The Sky* and 1978's *Running On Empty*. The son of a serviceman, Browne was no import; he was from a solid, comfortable middle-class Orange County family, and honed his craft at the Golden Bear nightclub in Huntington Beach, and the Prison of Socrates in Newport Beach. He then gravitated to such gathering places for tunesmiths as LA's Troubadour, where he'd workshop songs with future Eagles and various other songwrit-ers-on-the-make, in the process helping forge an entire movement (for bet-ter or worse).

However, the scene that would leave a deeper mark on No Doubt and such peers as LA's The Untouchables and San Diego's The Donkey Show – at least in their DIY attitude, if not their dog's breakfast of a sound – was the So-Cal punk scene that emerged, kicking and snarling, from the OC sub-urban wilderness in the late Seventies. Its evolution was as wayward as No Doubt's slow motion rise to the top.

Like most scenes, it took punk rock a good year to head south from Los Angeles, where key UK acts the Sex Pistols and The Clash had helped inspire such bands as X and The Germs (and The Ramones on the East Coast). A bunch of Huntington Beach zeroes – calling themselves The Crowd – were one of the first OC bands to learn that musical chops weren't necessary to start playing punk rock. Guitarist Jim Kaa admitted that "I never felt I was good enough to be in a band," but then he heard The Ramones and changed his mind. They started playing backyard parties and helped instigate a beach-punk scene that would spawn The Vandals (later to feature No Doubt drummer Adrian Young) and TSOL (True Sounds of Liberty).

At the same time, an "inland" OC punk scene was developing in the towns of Fullerton and Placentia. Key bands to emerge from this suburban wilderness included The Middle Class – the first OC band to drop a vinyl 45, the scorching 'Out of Vogue' – and Agent Orange, a gang of 15-year-olds who were set to become Orange County's longest-serving punk act. This underground scene soon coughed up other bands, such as The Adolescents and Social Distortion. All of these groups would congregate at "The Black Hole", a one-bedroom crash pad in a Fullerton apartment complex. Rikk Agnew, from the Adolescents, would immortalise the place in his song 'Kids Of The Black Hole'. Ground Zeroes like The Black Hole would also spring up a few years later in such unlikely spots as Olympia, Washington, as the grunge scene began to take shape.

This being Orange County, not all of the kids playing in these bands had much to rebel against: Agent Orange bassman James Levesque was a star quarterback at Placentia's El Dorado High School, and his mum would come along and play cheerleader at Agent Orange gigs. There were many parallels with the ska-punk scene that would soon find a footing in Southern California: It was often the trappings of the scene – the clothes, the sound, the sense of belonging to a clique – that drew punters, rather than some socio-political agenda or the chance to exact lyrical revenge on "the man". Yet plenty of blood was spilled at many of the punk shows in Orange County, leading a Huntington Beach police sergeant to tell the *Los Angeles Times*: "Basically, they're into violence."

At both Huntington and Newport Beach, local cops would randomly grab punk fans and snap their mug shots for their files. Future No Doubt buddies The Vandals documented one of these skirmishes in their song 'The Legend Of Pat Brown', which spelled out the details of an exchange between a punter and some cops near a Costa Mesa punk club called The Cuckoo's Nest, in late January 1981.

Just as he'd done with the music in his adopted hometown of LA, KROQ

DJ Rodney 'On The Roq' Bingenheimer gave hard-to-find airtime to many of the OC punk bands. He played cuts from such seminal, era-defining albums as Agent Orange's *Living In Darkness*, TSOL's *Dance With Me* and Social Distortion's *Mommy's Little Monster*. This was an invaluable outlet for these bands, because major record labels wouldn't touch them with the longest of sticks — and the suits had no plans, anyway, to venture beyond their Hollywood comfort zone to sniff out these bands. And when you consider that the charts were clogged with the falsetto squeals of the puffy-shirted Bee Gees and the schmaltzy aftermath of the singer/songwriter era (Dan Hill's 'Sometimes When We Touch', the treacly Little River Band, etc), punk rock was hardly the genre of choice for music biz tastemakers.

Robbie Fields, a small-time promoter from the time, summed up the division neatly. "In Hollywood . . . they're thinking about their career," he said. "You go to the suburbs and the kids aren't thinking about that . . . the music was totally uncalculated. Even though they might have been influenced by The Damned or The Clash or The Ramones, they were making their own statements; they were writing about their own lives."

A teenage Bryan "Dexter" Holland, another OC hopeful and later the leader of Offspring, was one of many who listened and learned. (Stone Temple Pilots' Scott Weiland, and Zack de la Rocha of Rage Against the Machine, also did time behind the Orange Curtain, but didn't embrace their outsider status with quite the same gusto as Holland.)

Inevitably, none of these OC punk bands would go on to become million-sellers, unlike some of their admirers in the grunge scene of the Nineties. But what was set in place by The Vandals, Agent Orange, Social Distortion, TSOL and the many others whose names became synonymous with this suburban uprising — including the OC-based Doctor Dream Records — was a grassroots approach that would enable a nascent No Doubt and its peers to make a living, of sorts, without having to bend over for major label dollars. What was the use of a slick promo department if you had a buddy with access to a photocopier, who could help you crank out a few hundred flyers? Telephone poles did an adequate job if you couldn't rent a billboard, and you could always find a community hall to play gigs if some greedy promoter had a monopoly on music venues.

★   ★   ★

At around the same time as the cops were making life hell for Huntington Beach punks, an expat Englishman by the name of Howard Paar was about to introduce the music of 2-Tone to the US West Coast. The "Skalifornia" scene that he'd set in place was an even more direct and powerful influence on Eric Stefani and the original version of No Doubt than the wasters of Orange County. Punk's do-it-yourself attitude may have helped No Doubt stay afloat, but it was the sounds of ska that truly showed the way for the Anaheim upstarts.

Paar was an Englishman adrift on the West Coast, who, as he recounted in 2006, "came for three months and stayed 20 years". A huge fan of punk, Paar was a fish well and truly out of water. He described himself as "typically English – I fry in the sun and I didn't like any LA music. My girlfriend had run clubs and was over it when she was called by someone who had a Vietnamese restaurant that wasn't doing well, and they needed to open a club."

The restaurant was situated at 3037 Sunset – "waaaaay down by the Silverlake area, not a good part of town", in the words of one regular – and was surrounded by Latin American-flavoured markets and liquor stores.

It was a low-rent slice of LA where English was not the first language spoken. "Not a part of town," according to Rick Gershon, an ON Klub regular and now the head of Warner Bros LA promo department, "where you might casually run into mods on scooters."

Paar recalled catching the bus from his apartment in Hollywood to check out the site for the first time. "It felt like we kept riding until the end of the line," he said. When he finally arrived, Paar noticed that the troubled eatery was known as the Oriental Knights Chinese restaurant. Ever the pragmatist, Paar modified the sign outside and the ON Klub was the result. It opened in late 1980.

By this time, Paar had, almost by accident, adopted what would become the official ska wardrobe: braces, Levi's, boots. He'd been listening to all the right records – Bluebeat Records, early ska on Trojan Records, the works. He was also a big fan of vintage soul, especially anything from Stax Records, the label for Otis Redding, Isaac Hayes and many other soul superstars. "Then I saw a picture in the *NME* of The Specials, who'd just released 'Gangsters', and they were dressed the same as me," he recalled. "It was one of those fluky moments; this was what was in my head. And bands such as The Selecter seemed very inclusive, so I was inspired by that."

In LA in the early Eighties there was precisely one reggae band, The Babylon Warriors, and one ska group, The Boxboys. And there were definitely no clubs playing ska or reggae. But Paar knew there was an audience for ska; he'd seen the crowds that groups such as Madness could pull at the Whisky. The problem, as he saw it, was that no tastemakers knew how to capitalise upon the scene. "You'd go to places like the Whisky – and this was a great time for English music fans in LA – and you'd see bands like The Selecter, but the hippie DJ would be playing the Doobie Brothers in between acts," he said. "It was vibeless. They had no idea of a potential audience. So our policy was to have only one band a night, with great music in between. My one rule was not to play stuff you'd hear on the radio. Our intentions were very pure, definitely."

It was during another night in Hollyweird that Paar learned a lesson that would serve him well during the ON Klub's short, fast life: Never let a chance slip by. It was the night of The Selecter gig and he'd been impressed by their choice of an opener for their Whisky set: soulman Geno Washington (immortalized by Dexys Midnight Runners in 'Geno'). This nod to the greats of the past reminded him of the time The Clash had hand-picked Lee Dorsey as their support. Paar was at LA hangout Barney's Beanery when he spotted Joe Strummer holding up the bar. After shouting his hero several beers, he walked to the Whisky with Strummer and asked him how The Clash had managed to hire Dorsey. Strummer turned to him and matter-of-factly replied: "We asked him." That same night, Paar approached Washington and talked him into appearing at the ON Klub.

The club was hardly salubrious. "It was a dump, very bare-boned," said Paar. When he'd arrive to open up the venue most afternoons, he'd throw open the doors and a team of rats would scurry out into the daylight. Although only licensed for 100, Paar found a way to squeeze 300 punters inside the club. And the ON Klub definitely had soul. "At the time," recalled Rick Gershon, "it was the only place that Anglophiles and the handful of mod kids in the area could go. With Howard as DJ . . . it was the only place where you could hear records by The Jam, The Purple Chords, The Merton Parkas, and – natch – The Specials, Madness, The Beat, The Selecter, and even some real Jamaican stuff." The Adapters were booked for the opening night and the gig was a sellout.

According to Paar, "2-Tone was the benchmark; it hit hard and fast at the time." Although KROQ would eventually get on board and start playing the more mainstream-friendly second wave acts from the UK – especially Madness – there were very few other outlets for the music that was invading the UK charts and airwaves, apart from college radio and wised-up LA record stores like Aaron's Records in Hollywood and Westwood's Rhino Records store. (Orange County also had a few worthwhile record stores, as did Long Beach, home to the largest contingent of mods on the West Coast.)

As many of the 2-Tone bands discovered, sometimes the best way to spread the word was to talk up your fellow ska bands from the stage of the Whisky. As for Paar, he could sense the connection between many of the more socially conscious ska acts and the punk bands that he loved. "The Specials meant a lot to me, in the same way The Clash did," he said.

It was truly a grassroots operation – Paar and his friends undertook midnight runs, pasting up flyers; eventually *LA Weekly* took notice and gave it some coverage. So did the *Los Angeles Times*, in which writer, Bill Bentley, christened the ON Klub "The House of Sweat". Despite the occasional flare-up when punk bands played, it wasn't an especially rough venue. "There were a few gang-related things," Paar said, "because of the neighbourhood, but we were very inclusive." Most of the regulars were too wasted on booze and speed – "black bombers" – to become unruly, anyway. And they weren't just LA kids skanking about wildly; ska fans would travel miles to squeeze into the ON Klub.

"There was definitely a connection with OC," Paar said. "Kids would come up to the club, really young kids, all pilled up or whatever. They loved that kind of music." Although no future members of No Doubt actually made it to the ON Klub – and the Stefani family curfew would have ruled that out if Eric had tried to sneak in – the club acted as a conduit, spreading the word of ska way beyond 3037 Sunset.

The so-called third wave of ska, which No Doubt would ride to the top of the charts and beyond, was born here and at LA's Madame Wong's – where West Coast fusionists Fishbone, a huge influence on No Doubt, got their start – and at the A7 Club in New York's Lower East Side, where No Doubt mentors, The Toasters, became the house band.

Early on in the ON Klub's three-and-a-half-year run, Paar was approached by a group of savvy LA kids who'd adopted the place as their clubhouse. He thought they were just punters, but they handed him a rough demo tape and said that they were in a band called The Untouchables. Paar "took a punt" and gave them a Thursday night slot. "I didn't expect much," he recalled, "but when I turned up, all these scooters were parked outside and the place was packed. It was really great, even though, frankly, most of the crowd was kids." (Paar, who was only in his early twenties, would have to re-open the club several times due to under-age drinking busts.)

Like Paar, The Untouchables were dedicated followers of everything 2-Tone, although, as singer Jerry Miller admitted. "I used to be a surfer back in the day, man. When I started buying my own music it was rock'n'roll, basically."

Miller's connection with the ON Klub came via a fellow Untouchable, Chuck Askerneese, who got talking music with a schoolfriend of his, Terry Elsworth. "Terry told him about ska and took him to the ON Klub, and he had such a great time that I had to check it out," Miller said. "And he was right. We all had dance backgrounds; we used to dance in our neighbourhood [No Doubt's original singer, 2-Tone fanatic John Spence, also danced], and everyone was dancing at this club, *really* dancing. And the music was great; it blew my mind. So I brought other friends in to check it out. As soon as I listened to the 2-Tone stuff, I loved it; it didn't have to grow on me. And the ON Klub was the only place in LA that played that stuff. The place only held maybe 200 people, but no matter whether you were a mod, a punk rocker, a rude boy, rockabilly, they catered for all these types of music and you had to hang out together. You had to get along; it felt really special. There was nothing else like that going on in LA."

As for The Untouchables, they didn't actually exist when Miller first checked out the ON Klub. He and his crew became groupies, of sorts, for LA's only ska band, The Boxboys, and would follow them from gig to gig. They were quite a sight. "We'd turn up, five, six, seven of us, all in our suits and parkas and scooters and stuff," as Miller explained. "As soon as we hit the place we'd start dancing, there was no warming up or anything. The bands loved it, the club owners loved it because everyone there would check us out and ask: 'Are you guys in a band? Who are you guys?' We were just fans of music. But after a while we thought maybe we should form a band, just for a giggle. I think two of us actually played music. We played some parties but Howard gave us our first chance." The Untouchables made their public debut in 1981.

The ON Klub, of course, wasn't built to last. Paar started to feel the heat when the gay community began gentrifying the neighbourhood. The last thing they wanted on their doorstep was some rat-infested, multi-racial, super-loud roots music club. It all came undone when a resident filed a police report stating that Paar had robbed their house and disappeared into his club. The cops broke down the ON Klub's door and dragged Paar out. He was only saved by what he referred to as his "wicked" haircut, which surely would have been noticed by the victim, and the simple fact that the club wasn't visible from where the robbery had occurred. "I didn't have enough money to pay the police," Paar laughed, "but I'm sure that would have helped. They only cared when we got successful. But [the club] was done; it had run its course."

Although it would finally close its doors in the early Eighties, the ON Klub, and other venues such as Madame Wong's and even The Roxy, where The Untouchables would become a surrogate house band, had set in place a musical movement that was about to spread into the more comfortable parts of southern California. The third wave of ska had begun, and Eric Stefani was about to become a convert.

CHAPTER THREE

"Yeah, No Doubt!"

"They turned up with seven large pizzas. About an hour after we finished eating, they stopped and went and grabbed mops and did the dishes, vacuumed, cleaned up the whole apartment without anyone asking. I thought, 'Wow, these kids have a good upbringing, man'."

–The Untouchables' Jerry Miller meets No Doubt

While Jerry Miller and his Untouchables were starting to making inroads in LA, their soon-to-be-number-one-fan, Gwen Stefani, was about to make another Loara High performance. But this time she wasn't singing some sappy old show tune, she was belting out a song from her new favourite thing, 2-Tone stars The Selecter, on the recommendation of her brother Eric.

Though the reclusive Eric Stefani has never said it out loud, his ska conversion most likely came via his Loara High School buddy, and future No Doubt singer-cum-showman, John Spence. Spence, according to Gerald Lokstadt, who'd help book No Doubt shows in the band's very early days, embraced the entire ska lifestyle, unlike Eric Stefani. "John was the one who wore braces and Fred Perry and stuff like that," recalled Lokstadt, a keen scooter rider himself and an active player in the early West Coast ska/mod scene.

Paul Hampton, singer of the band The Skeletones, whose career would closely parallel No Doubt's in its pre-*Tragic Kingdom* days, confirmed this.

"They [the Stefanis] didn't go to rallies," he said. "They weren't really into that scene, apart from John Spence, who was a scooter boy."

Loara High's Kim Segovia admits that she didn't know Spence that well, "but I do remember that he was really into ska."

The song that turned Eric Stefani on to ska was Madness' 'Baggy Trousers', which reached the business end of the UK chart in September 1980. Stefani was exposed to an import single of the irresistibly upbeat, slightly goofy ska-pop confection, and he was hooked. Within days it was on repeat on the Stefani household turntable. Eric began to teach himself piano by ear while playing along to the record, which rendered earlier lessons, paid for by his parents, a complete waste of time and money. As for his sister, well, she was about to kiss Kermit the Frog goodbye.

By the time Madness toured the West Coast in the early Eighties, ninth-grader Gwen Stefani was a dedicated fan, who cried herself to sleep when she wasn't able to score tickets for their gig. (Frankly, it's unlikely her parents would have given her the OK to attend the show in the first place). And this wasn't some passing infatuation; in 1996, as her relationship with Bush's Gavin Rossdale took a turn for the serious, she was asked who was sexier: Madness' Suggs or grunge pin-up Rossdale. "Oh God, Suggs," she replied without hesitation. "I have been in love with him for so long." (The video for Madness' 'One Better Day', featuring Suggs' wife, Bette Bright, would inspire another bout of waterworks from Stefani. "I cried for like an hour [after seeing it for the first time]," she said.)

Stefani has always struggled to elaborate on exactly what it was she saw and heard in 2-Tone and Madness in particular that steered her away from the pop confections of Madonna and Cyndi Lauper, although it's clear that she'd listen to anything recommended by her older brother Eric. "I felt like I had discovered the world when I discovered that music. Do you know what I mean?," she said in May 2000. "[It was] from another world away: England. [And] this band was all about this kind of political unity between black and white." Admittedly, Madness, the lily-white, self-proclaimed "nutty boys" from London weren't as overtly political as The Specials or many of the other 2-Tone-era bands – Madness seemed more interested in working on their zany dance moves – but for an Anaheim teenager raised on a diet of Julie Andrews, the Muppets, Disneyland and that "gnarly" Bob Dylan, even Madness, the more acceptable face of the 2-Tone era, would have seemed like apparitions from another planet. ("And where the hell is this Muswell Hill place, anyway?," she must have asked herself.)

Yet the song that the 17-year-old Stefani chose – as always, on her brother's recommendation – to sing in front of an audience of curious Loara

High students wasn't a Madness tune; it was The Selecter's 'On My Radio'. Like Madness' 'Baggy Trousers', it was hardly what you'd call a "pure" ska song: The 1979 hit for the multi-racial, Pauline Black-led Coventry band was ska filtered through the New Wave stylings of Lene Lovich, made complete by Black's quirky vocal tics.

Eric Stefani insists that he didn't force his sister to sing in the talent competition – "I didn't take a whip to her," he once said – but it's clear that she would have sought his approval before belting out 'On My Radio'. "My brother made me do it," she confessed. "Growing up, my brother was the one with all the talent and all the focus. I had him, so I didn't have to do anything, you know?" But Gwen Stefani added her own touches; when she walked up on stage, backed by Eric and a few of his buddies, she was wearing a tweed dress, just like the one Julie Andrews' "Maria" sported during *The Sound Of Music*. She wasn't quite ready to shake off her first love, no matter how much she admired ska. And although it appears that Stefani didn't actually win the talent contest, her fate was sealed: Within months her brother had talked her into joining a band. Admittedly, it didn't take a lot of effort on Eric's part; not only did his sister agree to pretty much everything he suggested, but she'd developed a taste for performance.

"She's always been a big stage ham," a No Doubt said.

"She was always destined to do this," added another.

If nothing else, her love of ska-pop gave Gwen "The Frog" Stefani some kind of identity, even if it heightened her reputation on campus as a loner. "I was the only ska girl at my school," she has said, "as far as dress went, anyway." And Stefani finally moved on from the faux Julie Andrews look when she spotted what she'd describe as "the cartoon girl" on the cover of an English Beat album. She made a key decision on the spot: "Maybe I'll get an outfit like that." No Doubt, in their own stop-start kind of manner, were on their way, as was Stefani's reputation as the "Betty Boop" of ska-pop.

★   ★   ★

Few of the 2-Tone-generation acts actually generated chart action in the US. In fact, Madness were the only band to score airplay *and* mainstream success when 'Our House' – clearly not a ska song in any shape or form – peaked at Number 7 in the Billboard chart in July 1983. But bands such as The Selecter and The Specials were huge influences on what would become known as ska's third wave, a movement that started to gather momentum in tandem with the baby steps of No Doubt. Like punk, ska–punk established footholds on both coasts, thanks, primarily, to the grassroots success of The Untouchables in California and The Toasters in New York.

Apart from a change of locale, there were other key differences between the second and third waves of ska. The leading 2-Tone acts had chanced upon a way to blend pop smarts with the authentic sound of Jamaica, but these third wave groups also looked elsewhere, drawing on the red-hot energy of punk, amongst other things. And they weren't as blatantly politicised as such 2-Tone figureheads as Jerry Dammers – although the multiracial blend remained prominent, even with such straight arrows as No Doubt. If there was some kind of credo that unified the third wave bands, it was simply about having a good time, all the time.

"When I first started I thought it was a cool thing to do in my spare time, in between school," said Eric Carpenter, a key member of the No Doubt horn section during its tough pre-*Tragic Kingdom* era. This echoed the admission of The Untouchables' Jerry Miller, who said his band formed "just for a giggle". Aaron Barrett, of the OC ska-punk band Reel Big Fish admitted to not even knowing what ska was. "I grew up on MTV in the Eighties, so I got a lot of new wave and hair metal and pop," he said. "I also listened to a station called 91X from San Diego, and they played all the cool stuff like The Smiths and The Cure and The English Beat. I loved bands like Madness and The Specials but I had no idea it was called ska. I didn't even realise there were different categories of music until I was in high school. Before that I thought it was all just called music."

At roughly the same time as Eric Stefani was going through his 2-Tone makeover – and force-feeding his sister Gwen this "new" music – such key third wave bands as Fishbone were undergoing their own conversion. Angelo Moore, who led the LA band and would form a bond with Gwen Stefani that would still be going strong when she started making solo records, discovered ska while riding on public transport with his buddy Walter A. "Dirty Walt" Kibby II, another future member of Fishbone. "It was on the bus that he let me listen to The Selecter," Moore told journalists, ska scenesters, and broadcasters Albino Brown and Tazy Phyllipz, key chroniclers of the third wave era. "I said, 'What are they playing?' He said, 'They're playing the ska'. I said, 'Fuck, yeah'. I've been gettin' down and gettin' funky with it ever since." But Fishbone, like No Doubt and so many other acts from the time, could hardly be called a "straight" ska band. Brown and Phyllipz got it right when they described the band as a "junkyard ska, punk, funk, metal outfit from South Central".

According to Jon Phillips, who would manage Sublime and drift in and out of the No Doubt world for more than a decade, Fishbone's influence was massive. "There wouldn't be a No Doubt or Sublime if it wasn't for Fishbone."

ON Klub regulars and 2-Tone purists such as Rick Gershon weren't turned on by Fishbone, but he could recognise their appeal. "Fishbone were not to my liking, but they were certainly an anomaly at the time, being one of the few black bands to incorporate punk rock with jazz, funk, ska – and be embraced by a primarily white audience due to their constant support from The Red Hot Chili Peppers [whose bassist Flea would become another early champion of No Doubt]. Their decidedly wacky live stage show, weird look and goofy attitude were perfect for dopey white kids who did not know anything about jazz, funk, etc. Having said that, they were quite good live and worked very hard."

Fellow West Coasters Operation Ivy took a more direct route than Fishbone, lifting a lot of its musical cues directly from The Clash (even down to the jarring, faux-Cockney vocals of Jesse Michaels). In Long Beach, Sublime – yet another band from this time to give No Doubt a leg up – could have passed as a straight punk band, operating on pure energy and adrenaline (at least until it broadened its repertoire, just like No Doubt, and were "discovered" by a much bigger audience). Other West Coast acts, including Hollywood's Jump With Joey, Ocean 11 and LA's Hepcat – whose members included Alex Desert, from the TV sitcom *Becker* – took a more trad approach, faithfully mixing such Jamaican standards as 'Rub Up, Push Up' and 'Rocksteady' with their originals. Persephone Laird, vocalist for Ocean 11, summed up the attitude of these "new traditionalists" when she admitted that a lot of the original ska songs reduced her to tears. "When the Ethiopians hit those awesome vocal harmonies . . . it's a music of mixed emotions, of joy, of happiness, and of sadness," she said.

Other bands, including San Francisco's Undercover SKA, Santa Cruz's Square Roots, the aforementioned Untouchables and The Schmedleys, who, like No Doubt, came from behind the Orange Curtain, looked directly to the 2-Tone bands for their skankin' sound and their Fred Perry/Doc Martens look. Although not heard on mainstream radio, 2-Tone even reached into such country music strongholds as Nashville, Tennessee, where Freedom of Expression formed. "I came out of a mod band without any real sense of musical direction," one member admitted. "Then one day someone brings in this album, *I Just Can't Stop It*, by The English Beat. I went crazy over that album. That did it for me; I was going to play ska in the country capital of the world."

On the East Coast, the conversion of The Toasters' mainman, Rob "Bucket" Hingley, took a more global route. "I moved to Kenya at an early age," he told Brown and Phyllipz, "and [so] I always felt close to the African and world beat rhythms. After my family moved back to England, I remember being taken in by Millie Small's 'My Boy Lollipop'. It was the ska that moved me." Hingley's Moon Records would be the principal ska label in the US, at least until the time that the major labels started zeroing in on such acts as Sublime, the Mighty Mighty Bosstones and No Doubt. Moon was the first label to release anything from No Doubt, a song called 'Everything's Wrong', on 1988's *Skaface* compilation. Proving that serious third wave fans had an elitist streak, like any other musical movement, the album was a vinyl-only release. Of course.

"It's like this," said Tazy Phyllipz, when asked to describe the musical milieu from which No Doubt would emerge, "third wave ska, for the most part, is a hodge-podge of musical styles that incorporates the ska as an element." It would form the ideal musical backdrop for No Doubt, a band that would always be frowned upon by the ska purists for taking a few too many liberties. But the reality is that No Doubt was merely reflecting the current dog's breakfast of a musical climate – and if the band hitched a ride on the slipstream of ska's third wave, then more power to it for its impeccable timing. As Paul Oberman put it: "No Doubt put a twist on it, even from the start. They had a lot of good pop influences – Gwen had the right kind of voice and they weren't so immersed in the subculture that they couldn't afford to offend the purists. They're from Orange County, so they're inherently part of that OC suburban culture." Oberman's business partner and friend, Gerald Lokstadt, had a similar recollection. "[Gwen] had a bob at the time but never wore traditional ska stuff. After [getting some recognition] she didn't want anything to do with the scene at all – and I thought that was better because if they wanted to be seen as more than 'that ska band from LA' and make it big in the music scene, they needed to broaden their horizons. They weren't like The Skeletones or Hepcat, which were way more traditional ska bands."

★   ★   ★

In the beginning there was Apple Core. Or, at least, that was the name that Loara High classmates John Francis Spence and Eric Stefani kicked around when they decided to take their love of ska one step further and actually form a band. By 1986, Eric knew his way around a keyboard and had even tried writing his own songs. Spence had no formal musical education, but what he did have was a wild, untrained voice and a showman's presence – and an incredible ability to pull off gravity-defying backflips and various other gut-busting moves without, seemingly, breaking a sweat (or tearing a muscle).

"Now that guy, he was a real bundle of energy," recalled Untouchable

Jerry Miller, who'd headline the bill at No Doubt's first official gig on March 12, 1987. "He was one competitive guy, too, a joy to watch and full of energy. He was always joking around, in a good-natured way – it was almost like sports. He'd say, 'We're gonna go out and do our thing and then you better do yours', that kind of thing."

"John was a super cool dude who everyone liked," said Alan Meade, Spence's bandmate in No Doubt Mark 1. "I remember his way cool personality and his explosive stage presence. And he taught me how to do backflips!"

Although people such as Meade and Miller considered themselves friends of Spence's, he remains the most elusive figure in the world of No Doubt, even to those especially close to him, including Skeletones' guitarist Rick Bonnin (aka Spyda).

"I'd never been to his house – he lived off Lincoln close to Loara High School – even though I'd dropped him off there a few times," Bonnin said. "Then I read that the No Doubt guys had never been to his house, either."

This is especially curious, because not only did Spence attend Loara with the Stefanis, but he and Gwen worked together in Anaheim's Dairy Queen. They were by no means strangers.

What is known about Spence is this: The wild-man persona he adopted as soon as he hit the stage was his way of expressing admiration for Bad Brains' singer-cum-maniac, HR. African-American punks were as rare as African-American ska fans, so it's understandable that Spence adopted HR as a role model. And Spence wasn't alone; HR was also a huge influence on Skeeter Thompson, the charismatic black bassist for Washington, DC, punks Scream, a band for whom Dave Grohl would drum in his pre-Nirvana/Foo Fighters days. Thompson, like Spence, saw the light when he witnessed HR throwing himself around on stage (and into the audience) like some kind of black Iggy Pop. "That's definitely where I want to be," Thompson said after seeing Bad Brains carve it up – and Spence felt exactly the same.

Spence wore a hat that he fondly referred to as his "fuzzy furry", which one friend recalled as being made of bicycle seat covers "sewn shut at the top". Spence's hat was as big a part of his make-up as the expression that he uttered constantly: "No doubt!" As the idea for the band came together between classes at Loara, Spence and Eric Stefani figured, wisely, that No Doubt was a far more attention-grabbing band name than Apple Core, a tag they'd borrowed from an old Warner Bros cartoon featuring Bugs Bunny and used for a few covers-only gigs. "He used to say, 'Yeah, no doubt'," confirmed Gerald Lokstadt, "that's how they got their name."

The youngest of three Spence sons, John was much deeper into ska than either of the Stefanis. The Skeletones' Rick Bonnin recalls spotting him in the mosh at shows in 1986. "He used to roll out to the early Skeletones shows; I think he was at three or four of the early gigs," Bonnin recalled. "And when we saw them [No Doubt] we knew we had to step it up." Spence's relationship with Bonnin came about through a mutual friend. "Before the whole rude boy thing I was into breakdancing [as was Spence, an accomplished athlete at Loara, hence his dynamic stage moves]," Bonnin said. "It turned out that my best friend's sister was also a friend of John's. Sometimes we'd stay with mutual friends in Orange County; that was our stomping ground."

Bonnin knew about as much as anyone else of Spence's family situation, but that wasn't a hell of a lot. "I knew through my best friend and his sister that the situation with his parents was kind of strict." Spence certainly wasn't about to invite Bonnin, or anyone else, for that matter, back to his family house for milk and cookies. Spence's home, and that part of his life, was strictly off limits.

Gerald Lokstadt said that the off-stage Spence was noticeably different from the ball of fire that would briefly front No Doubt. "He was a very quiet person, kind of introverted. He kept to himself a lot," he said. Lokstadt first met Spence on Lambretta rides for Club Impact, LA's largest scooter club, of which Lokstadt was president; Doug Fatone was another active member. "That's how we knew each other; John would come out for rides with us and stuff," said Lokstadt. (Spence rode a P200 Lambretta, which, significantly, he would sell along with his prized record collection, only weeks before he killed himself, These two acts suggested his suicide was planned well in advance.)

Spence and Eric Stefani, of course, did not an entire band make, although between them the fledgling No Doubt had a songwriter and creative director in the latter – Eric told Fatone that his influences for the band were "Madness and cartoons" – and a dazzling showman in the former.

Fresh from her few minutes in the spotlight singing The Selecter's 'On My Radio', Gwen agreed to share the microphone with Spence, although she'd blend into the background when Spence started pulling off backflips and other stunts. "John would always jump in the crowd with his mic," said Lokstadt. "[But] Gwen would never do that.

"I remember Gwen being very shy on stage," Alan Meade recalled. "She slowly blossomed into what you see today, but she was so different, looking back on tapes of our shows."

The other members of No Doubt Mark I included the lanky Jerry McMahon, guitarist and Jerry Dammers-wannabe, who helped Eric Stefani write some of the band's first songs. McMahon was the cousin of Chris Leal, No Doubt's bassist from the time of their first gig in 1986 until Kirk Hofstetter joined the band for its first 'official' gig on March 12, 1987. (Tony Kanal replaced him within weeks.) Their drummer, at least until 1989, was Chris Webb, who co-manager Paul Oberman remembered as "the punk rock guy" in the line-up. Whereas McMahon and Spence, and trombonist Paul Caseley would dress the part in ska-inspired gear, Webb typically rolled out in jeans and a T-shirt.

Eric Stefani knew that any ska band worth its porkpie hat needed a horn section, so he roped in brothers Tony and Alan Meade – "the only other Panamanians I know in the United States", said The Skeletones' Rick Bonnin – on sax and trumpet respectively. The Meades would be important members of the band, at least in the formative years of No Doubt. Alan Meade said, "My brother Tony and I were friends with Mikey Miller, as well as the whole OC crowd. The Meade brothers were always seen together; I was like my brother's shadow."

Paul Oberman, however, remembers the Meades being "a little problematic; they were a little younger [than the rest of the band] and immature." A suggestion that Alan Meade was dating Gwen Stefani didn't make inner-band relationships any easier to cope with, either, although he downplayed this later. "Offstage, we were how any normal friends would be," he said. "We were all good, good friends."

Oberman said that they did date for a time, although the band's management insists that this suggestion is blatantly false. Doug Fatone recalled that Gwen "flirted with everybody", and said that Meade was a "smooth talker", but added that he "didn't really notice" if they were together.

The Meades had shifted to Orange County when Alan was in fourth grade. Like the Stefanis, they lived within walking distance of Disneyland. "It was awesome to be living across from the Happiest Place on Earth," Meade said. "I remember the fireworks every night – they were so loud. OC was cool; there was always something to do." The Meade brothers had musically curious parents; most Saturday mornings they'd wake up and their father would be playing salsa records or the sweet Motown soul of Stevie Wonder and Marvin Gaye, usually at maximum volume. "There was always music in the house," Alan Meade recalled. Although Alan liked all kinds of music, his first pop hero was Michael Jackson. "I wanted to be a singer and performer for as long as I can remember," he said. "Whenever I got the chance, I would sing or put on a talent show for the family or at school – and it was usually a Michael Jackson tune."

It was his brother Tony who inspired Alan to start blowing his horn in junior high. Soon after, he played covers with Eric Stefani in the fledgling Apple Core, again on the recommendation of his big brother. "Looking back," he says, "I was so horrible at playing the trumpet, but I guess no-one is that good at 13." Through his friendship with John Spence and Eric Stefani – and, you guessed it, the influence of his older brother Tony – Meade was weaned off Wacko Jacko and steered in the direction of "the ska".

"I especially loved Fishbone, The Specials, and Madness, because of my brother. Then I started dressing the part when I got into No Doubt and started hanging out with John and Eric. I loved skanking and the whole ska sound. It was so wild and so much fun – and that was me, fun and wild." Meade's one regret was that he didn't own a scooter, unlike some of his new ska buddies.

The third member of the horn section was trombonist Paul Caseley, who in his post-No Doubt life would set up a music school in Seattle. His one lasting legacy with the band was the trombone solo in early live favourite 'Total Hate', a stop-start, funk-punk fusion that owed a hefty debt to The Red Hot Chili Peppers. (As would the haircut and slap-bass style of future No Doubt-er Tony Kanal, but more on that later.)

"I remember he was good," Alan Meade said of Caseley, "and we loved his [English] accent." Caseley also sang the lead vocal on the band's cover of Madness' 'Baggy Trousers', after co-managers Oberman and Fatone rejected Eric Stefani's suggestion that they get up on stage and sing that one song. "Not a good idea," laughed Fatone, who later achieved some notoriety as a member of skinhead band the Boot Boys. Despite the band's rejection of their hardline ideals, the members became poster punks for West Coast neo-Nazis.

Eric Stefani took the lead with the horn section and pushed them especially hard; he knew that a punchy horn sound was essential when playing ska. "Eric would make sure we were all tight," Meade confirmed. "I loved Eric's drive; it gave me something – practices and shows – to look forward to. It's what I loved, and we were all so into it."

The fact that guitarist McMahon most likely got the gig purely because of his family ties to Chris Leal showed just how incestuous the No Doubt universe was. And that extended beyond life in the band: The Meades once considered forming a group with Chris Leal and Alan Meade would make on-stage cameos with No Doubt years after he left. Doug Fatone had No Doubt connections of his own; his then-roommate, Jahn "Boxer" Hardison, was a band roadie for years. Another insider, photographer/videographer Eric Keyes, who caught No Doubt's first backyard show in 1986, was still documenting their career two decades later. Because of contractual restrictions, Keyes was unwilling to be interviewed for this book. "I've known these guys for 20 years and although I've documented a lot of the band's life through pictures and video, our main tie is one of friendship and family," he explained via e-mail. "To do an interview without their consent in my opinion is wrong. For me anyway, it would be like talking behind their backs and I respect their privacy too much for that."

By the time that No Doubt made its backyard debut in late 1986, Eric Stefani had been steadily working on a catalogue of original tunes. His first composition was hardly auspicious; it was a throwaway called 'Stick It In The Hole', a song ostensibly about a pencil sharpener but with a certain unmistakable nudge-nudge subtext. But it was an original, and it fleshed out a set that included covers of The Specials' 'Gangsters' and The Selecter's 'On My Radio'. Interestingly, in an effort to keep their daughter under close supervision, the Stefanis allowed Gwen to rehearse with the band at her paternal grandparents' Beacon Avenue home. (The Anaheim home of Gwen's maternal grandparents would feature in the video for their song 'Sunday Morning'.)

Backyard parties were an ideal introduction to the world of playing live; if and when No Doubt screwed up, their friends were there looking on, shouting encouragement, helping them get it back together. One of the earliest bashes they played was Lokstadt's 24th birthday party. He was especially impressed by manic frontman John Spence. "On stage he used to shine; he had a great voice," he recalled, "and most ska bands' lead singers don't have to have a great voice; it's more about the energy and the horn lines and dressing well. But he did have a great voice." Even then the idea of managing the band – or at least helping them organise some real gigs – was foremost in the mind of Lokstadt's friend and partner Paul Oberman.

The Skeletones' Paul Hampton was also amongst the faithful at one of the earliest No Doubt gigs. "My keyboard player and I heard about this ska party that was going down in Orange County and we decided to go," he said. "We got there and this band called No Doubt were playing – I think it was their first show. They were doing Selecter covers, lots of 2-Tone covers. Damn they sounded good. This was when they had John Spence singing."

As mentioned earlier, Hampton immediately knew that his own band had to crank it up a notch to keep pace with these Orange County upstarts. "There was always a little bit of rivalry between us and No Doubt," Hampton added. "We always wanted to be as good as them; they've always been an amazing band. They inspired us; they were responsible for lighting a fire under our arse, so we always wanted to be as good as them. We tried to impress them as much as the audience."

The healthy sense of rivalry that existed between many of the So-Cal bands from that era was now well and truly in place. As green as its members were, No Doubt was leading the way, even though it drew a slightly different crowd than The Skeletones. "We'd have more scooter people coming to our shows," Hampton explained, "people from the scooter clubs."

John Spence became especially tight with the guys from The Skeletones. "We all hung out," said Hampton. "We were all rude boys in the scene, going to scooter rallies, gigs, all the same places all the time."

Hampton and his fellow Skeletones – like The Untouchables – shared a love of 2-Tone with Eric Stefani and Spence. "I was really into all the 2-Tone bands and collected all the Madness records on Stiff, plus the Chrysalis records," Hampton said. "In a scene like that there are always the purists, the guys who have to have the Fred Perrys and the Lonsdales and the right record labels – Trojan, Stiff – and I wanted to be that guy."

Eric Stefani, however, wasn't as gregarious as Spence, according to Hampton. "Eric was more the animator," Hampton said. "He did a lot of their art. And he didn't hang out as much; he wasn't the party type."

Skeletone Rick Bonnin was overwhelmed by the chemistry between Spence – who onstage was part toaster, part MC, part stage diver – and the more reserved Gwen Stefani. "John and Gwen were awesome on stage together," he said. "I hope I'm doing Gwen justice, but back in the day, John kept people on their toes. He was doing backflips, rocking all over the place. At the same time I knew Gwen was going to be huge; but I don't think they knew how big they would become."

★ ★ ★

The healthy vibe created by these Orange County backyard bashes was all the validation that Oberman needed; he and his friend Lokstadt approached the band and offered their assistance as surrogate managers, with a vague plan of helping them score proper gigs. "Paul O and I wanted to manage No Doubt," Lokstadt insisted, "because we felt they had something big in their music and stage presence."

"They blew us both away," Oberman said, simply enough. It was a move that both men – only in their early 20s at the time – would view, many years down the track, with a mixture of joy, regret and despair.

Interestingly, while the band acknowledges the role Oberman – and his other business partner, Doug Fatone – played in its very early days, the members have no recollection whatsoever of Lokstadt, apart from a sighting in a group photo from Palm Springs in early 1988. "Well, they must have selective thinking or something," Lokstadt countered. "I was involved, and more so behind the scenes; Paul was in their face weekly – daily, sometimes – I, on the other hand was making the phones calls, co-coordinating gigs, publicity, etcetera. I was not so much in front of the band, except at the concerts."

"You know," added Doug Fatone, "it's not too surprising that the band doesn't remember 'Spot' that well. He was more the promoter of their early shows, rather than working directly with them. [But] I'm sure if they saw Gerald they would recognize him straight away."

Lokstadt and Oberman operated under the name Spot Productions, a shortening of G Spot, Lokstadt's college nickname. ("A long story," the amiable Lokstadt laughed, without giving too much away.) This pair of ska-lovers and scooter-riders had a very dilettantish approach to booking gigs. Essentially, they did it because they enjoyed the music and wanted to spread the word. Turning a profit wasn't their number one priority.

Of the two, Lokstadt was, in Oberman's words, "the more musically proficient guy; he's a collector, a record nut." They didn't know much about concert promotion, but they knew they faced some stiff opposition trying to book No Doubt, or any other band for that matter, in southern California.

"It was tough," Lokstadt recalled. "In LA, the [agencies] Avalon, Nederlander and Goldenvoice [who promoted more No Doubt shows in Southern California than any other organisation] have everything sewn up; they have a monopoly on it all. They have exclusive contracts on The Roxy, the Hollywood Palladium – it's all booked up. As an independent concert promoter you couldn't do jack. Everyone wanted to play for me because they liked me, but then Goldenvoice or whoever would overbid on the bands. [Goldenvoice's] Paul Tollett would say, 'Well, if Spot Productions are going to pay you $2200, we'll pay you $2500.' And I couldn't afford to lose money on a gig; I was only doing a couple of shows a month but they were booking enough shows to make up for any losses on some ska gig. It was cutthroat."

Oberman added that they were "tight" with Paul Tollett early on, "at least as tight as you could be. That was a love/hate relationship, us and Goldenvoice."

Spot did manage to secure the early gigs of a few bands that would go very large, include Long Beach's Sublime and some wannabes from Seattle calling themselves Nirvana, who did a show with Spot in mid-1989. "Nobody knew who they were," Lokstadt said, "They were selling their own [concert] tickets. I thought they were fantastic. Then they'd come down and do a show every three or four months; they just did it themselves after I first booked a place for them."

Because the larger agencies had a stranglehold on the key venues, Spot had to look elsewhere, so they booked reggae and ska gigs in a club called the Egyptian Ballroom, which was situated in the basement of an Orange County Masonic temple (the same room used for the roller-skating scene in the Goldie Hawn flick *Swing Shift*). They would also book bands into the Dominion, an OC-based British pub.

Like *the Ska Parade*'s Albino Brown and Tazy Phyllipz, the men of Spot had nothing but respect for the founders of ska. Accordingly, they booked several West Coast shows for Skatalite Rolando Alphonso, who was backed by the more '"trad" third wave groups like Let's Go Bowling and San Diego's The Donkey Show, a band that would often be likened to the John Spence-fronted No Doubt. (And, later on, would be one of many bands thought unlucky not to rise to the top alongside No Doubt.)

The comparisons between No Doubt and The Donkey Show were fairly obvious: they both shared a multi-racial line-up (The Donkey Show featured a charismatic "toaster", Ray Campbell, their very own John Spence) and an attention-grabbing, eye-catching female (their Kym Clift was referred to as the "Peggy Lee of ska"). And, as bassist Tom Zambrano would tell Albino Brown in an unpublished article, they also shared No Doubt's 2-Tone obsession. "In junior high, we all caught the last breath of the 2-Tone movement," he said. "The members of The Donkey Show pretty much got into the same bands at the same time: The English Beat, Bad Manners, Madness, The Equators, The Specials, The Selecter. And most of us were influenced by our older siblings and friends who were into the mod scene." Zambrano's personal ska conversion was not unlike that of Eric Stefani; but whereas Eric got hooked on Madness' 'Baggy Trousers', Zambrano fell hard for the nutty boys' instrumental hit 'One Step Beyond'. "I flatly fell in love with ska music," he confessed. His first move was to buy a copy of Bad Manners' 1983 LP *Klass*. His next step was to procure the right wardrobe. "I bought a thin tie, some winged-tipped shoes and some pegged pants." He also mastered the bass by playing along to records by his new 2-Tone heroes.

Even then, Paul Oberman could see the similarities between the two bands, but he could also spot the differences. "There was that whole purist rivalry thing with The Donkey Show," he admitted. "People said there was some kind of rivalry, but Donkey Show were really part of the whole sub-culture, whereas No Doubt liked Fishbone, the Chili Peppers and The

Untouchables. They were suburban Orange County kids who just liked some of those 2-Tone bands [amongst others]. But No Doubt were a better band than The Donkey Show. And they evolved, unlike some of those bands from the time. When it came down to it, they were one of the best bands out there."

According to Gerald Lokstadt, there were some connections between the two bands. "They did have a female lead singer," he said. "I wouldn't say her and Gwen looked the same but they were playing the same kind of music and they were about at the same time – maybe it was just the milieu, the environment. There was a rivalry for a while, but it wasn't bad. They weren't street fights or anything like that."

The Donkey Show, like No Doubt, got its start by playing what Albino Brown referred to as "weekly rendezvous, band practices [and] parties" before taking on its first show before a paying audience, in 1986 at San Diego's Ballroom Dance Studio. Soon after that The Donkey Show's path would intersect with No Doubt's for the first time, at No Doubt's maiden public gig. And if there was ever a venue that least matched the Stefani's G-rated upbringing, it was Fender's Ballroom in Long Beach, where No Doubt stepped out for the first time on March 12, 1987. The venue would become a second home, of sorts, for the band, who played there six more times before the end of the year.

★   ★   ★

Like the residents of the senior citizens' home that was located nearby, Fender's Ballroom had seen much better days. Built around the time of WWI, it was on the site of what was originally a Hilton hotel that had gone condo in the Seventies and been converted into a 20-storey beachside high rise. Its occupants were mainly blue-rinse retirees. The venue itself was formerly the car park of the Hilton, which had been remade into a ballroom. As salubrious as that sounds, Fender's Ballroom was anything but. The 800-capacity club filled with as many as 1,600 punks, according to one report, when The Ramones played there in 1986. Its ceilings were barely 10 feet high and there was no air conditioning. Two unfortunately positioned pillars (they were on the stage) made it hard to actually see whatever band was playing. And the venue's sound system was rubbish, according to Ken Phebus, who booked acts into Fender's Ballroom for many years. "It was just a bunch of old stuff that they blasted out as loudly as possible," he recalled. Inside the room, conversation was impossible because the music was cranked to such intense volume. "You could see people's lips moving, but you couldn't hear anything," Phebus said. (Doug Fatone recalled seeing

Motorhead at Fender's Ballroom and not being able to hear for days after-wards.) On some nights, when the volume was particularly excessive, club owner John Fender would lock the exit doors, in an attempt to keep noise pollution levels at a minimum. To keep costs down, there was only one burly guy at the door in charge of security (at least theoretically). "It was pretty wild," Phebus said. "We didn't try to control it; we just tried to keep the vol-ume down. There'd be broken legs and arms in the moshpit and blood everywhere. It was wild, it was simply nuts, and it's a miracle that it lasted that long, especially in such a conservative town." (Long Beach was the hol-iday venue of choice for many mid-westerners, whose conservative politics had taken hold there.)

If the ON Klub was the House of Sweat, Fender's Ballroom was surely some kind of Punk Rock Hell, although Lokstadt felt that the club "was good for Long Beach. It was the only thing happening at Long Beach."

Phebus recalled one night when The Untouchables' drummer passed out mid-set, a victim of heat exhaustion. "We thought they guy was dead," he said. "We called 911, the whole bit." On another occasion, Phebus was approached by some local vice cops – Fender's regulars – who told him that there was a situation that he had to fix right away. They led him to the venue's ticket window, which was clouded in thick and pungent dope smoke. Inside was Gary Tovar, Paul Tollett's partner at Goldenvoice, which provided most of the bands for Fender's. When Phebus approached him, Tovar was "puffing away on a huge spliff with some friends, oblivious to the rest of the world. And this occurred almost every night." (Tovar would even-tually be busted for dealing in what Phebus referred to as "Maui carpets" and did some hard time in the late Eighties, which forced him to sell Goldenvoice to Tollett. When he was released, Jim Guerinot – now No Doubt's manager at a company called Rebel Waltz – organised a fundraiser on his behalf.)

The nearby residents empathised with the local vice cops: they weren't too thrilled by Fender's Ballroom, either. They'd stroll back to the condo after another slow day, look up at the marquee and note that Love Canal and Doggy Style would soon be appearing, the night after The Righteous Brothers, Ricky Nelson and Ray Charles. (Phebus was very open to more mainstream artists; the first act he booked for Fender's was Joe Cocker.) "Surprisingly," Phebus said, "there were never that many problems with the police, apart from noise complaints. But that was understandable – you'd have these senior citizens living 50 feet away from this venue where bands played at ear-piercing volume."

As for the owner of the venue, the enigmatic John Fender, Phebus remembered him as "a real estate guy; a real wheeler-dealer – and a shady character." In order to run Fender's Ballroom as a live venue he'd applied for a dance permit, which stated that he'd host "seniors' swing nights'". With such bands as The Ramones, The Untouchables, The Donkey Show and a fledgling No Doubt providing the music, apparently.

Gerald Lokstadt had a much more explicit memory of John Fender. "[He] was a big coke addict," Lokstadt said. "You'd come in and ask if you could book a gig on Friday or Saturday and he'd look at his calendar and go, 'Yeah', and then offer you this big ol' pile of coke. That's all he did, day and night."

According to Doug Fatone, there were strong rumours that Fender sometimes even paid bands with Bolivian marching powder.

Ken Phebus readily admits to partaking in the lifestyle; he said that Fender's was a place that was crawling with drugs and undercover cops "trying to mingle. Anything that you could ingest that might open your mind was being taken there." The local authorities were always hoping to shut down Fender's; eventually the venue was wiped out after an unsolved, and highly suspicious, arson attack.

The members of No Doubt weren't all straight arrows like the "conscientious, well-educated, hard-working, drug-free" Stefanis, according to Oberman. "John [Spence] might have smoked some pot and I wouldn't have been surprised if Alan and Tony [Meade] smoked some pot, too."

The debauchery that was on nightly display at Fender's Ballroom must have shocked No Doubt to their OC core. Although it's never been confirmed, it was suggested that the band, during its sort-of-residency at Fender's, may even have chanced upon heroin-addicted members of The Red Hot Chili Peppers spiking up backstage. It wouldn't have been out of character – it was just another night at Fender's.

"I'd call it a dump," said Mike Miller, the Stefanis' Loara High buddy and life-long friend. "Originally it must have been really nice, but by the time No Doubt were playing there, it was a dump. There was bad sound, bad security."

In spite of all this illegal activity, No Doubt's debut at Fender's Ballroom was done with the best of intentions: The gig itself was a fundraiser, organised by Oberman and Lokstadt, going by the name of Scooter Aid.

"The Vespa/Lambretta shop [in LA] burned down," said Lokstadt, "so we did this fundraiser, with The Untouchables headlining. No Doubt were the opening act. There were 10 bands for 15 bucks – the UTs and all these power-pop and ska bands in between." The line-up was set in stone – other bands on the bill included The Key, The Standards, Sold, The Crooks, The

Subway, Instep and The Upbeats. And it was agreed that The Untouchables would be the only band getting paid ($1,000). The day before the gig, Lokstadt and Oberman got a call from the managers of The Donkey Show. "They asked if they could also play," said Lokstadt, "so they opened the show. It was the first time that No Doubt and The Donkey Show actually met each other."

"There was no rivalry as far as I recall," said Alan Meade. "Everyone got along great and we had many shows together with the same bands. We just had a blast."

The madness in the moshpit at Fender's that night was the same as any other, except this time it was one of the men from Spot who was actively involved. Midway through the set, a drunken Oberman decided to get in on the action, as Lokstadt recalled. "Fender's had these beams which held up the ceiling, so there's these two freakin' beams right in the middle of the stage. [During No Doubt's set] Paul Oberman jumped up on one of them, hanging upside down. He's wearing these 12- or 13-hole Docs and he decides to take a jump into the crowd. But they didn't catch him – they just parted – and he headed right onto the dancefloor, ankles first. His ankle was swollen up to the size of a watermelon. It was crazy."

Jerry Miller of The Untouchables also recalls No Doubt's debut fondly, if not quite as painfully as Paul Oberman. "I do remember that gig, although some of them are a bit foggy," he told me. "I think there was a wedding reception going on in another part of the building. So there was a wedding happening and then all these people turn up on scooters and stuff. That place had some wild gigs – reggae shows, punk rock shows – with a bunch of disrespectful kids doing what they do, having a good time."

Scooter-aid was no windfall for the band and Spot Productions, financially-speaking. After graduating high school in May 1987, Gwen Stefani manned the counter at The Broadway department store. Oberman held down a job in a Cash & Carry warehouse, and at night, fuelled by acid, would attend gigs. All the time everyone involved with No Doubt was aware of Gwen's 11 p.m. curfew, which hung over the band like a long black cloud.

Now a parent himself, Oberman has finally come to understand this restriction that the Stefanis placed on their daughter at the time. "They were very protective," he said. "I don't think they ever took the band too seriously, no matter how big the shows got. Their position was: 'Your future comes first, the band is a nice hobby'. We couldn't convince the parents to allow them [to tour]."

According to Doug Fatone, the Stefanis were "really nice, conservative

No Doubt's Tony Kanal, Tom Dumont, Gwen Stefani and Adrian Young (from left). "They're like pop culture engineers," said friend and collaborator Dave Stewart. "They live it, you know?"

(PAT POPE/REX FEATURES)

Gwen Stefani, just a girl from suburban Anaheim, before her brother Eric enticed her into joining No Doubt. "I wanted to be [*The Sound of Music*'s] Maria von Trapp. I even had a dress that looked just like hers," Stefani admitted. **(WENN)**

A keen swimmer while at school, Stefani was nicknamed "The Frog", in part because of her prowess in the pool, but also due to her size. "My weight was a struggle for me," she said, "like all girls." **(WENN)**

Stefani made a big impression with her singing debut in a Loara High school production. "She had an incredibly unique, sweet voice for someone who had no training and had never been in a musical or a choir," said a classmate. **(WENN)**

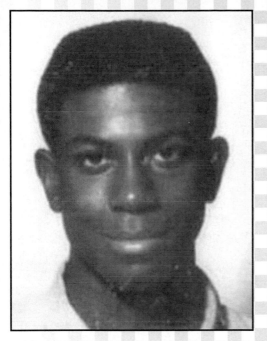

John Spence, No Doubt's first, doomed lead singer. Of the original band, he was the guy who totally embraced the 2-Tone lifestyle. "John was the one who wore braces and Fred Perry and stuff like that," said one insider.

No Doubt at the Clean & Sober beach party, Newport Beach, 1989. **(BARRY KING/WIREIMAGE)**

Stefani with Young and Kanal at the Clean & Sober gig. When wild boys The Untouchables invited them to a house party, they did the housework afterwards. "I thought, 'Wow, these kids have a good upbringing, man'," said Untouchable Jerry Miller. **(BARRY KING/WIREIMAGE)**

Stefani at the Clean & Sober gig. "She would cartwheel and bounce around and dance so much that she basically was a sweet ball of sweat by the third song – and we all loved that," noted an early follower of the band.

(BARRY KING/WIREIMAGE)

A flyer for a very early bill that No Doubt shared with like-minded ska freaks The Skeletones. "They were all business," said Paul Hampton of The Skeletones. "We'd drink, smoke, hang out; we were a bunch of hooligans. But they were real conservative, real strict."

At The Roxy in Los Angeles, September 1989. "Gwen and I would do little dance routines and dance steps in sync, to make the shows look more fun," recalled Alan Meade (far right), who shared the mic for a time with Stefani. **(BARRY KING/WIREIMAGE)**

Gwen Stefani at The Roxy. At the same venue, almost two years earlier, the band's showcase became a tribute to John Spence, who had just killed himself. "Everyone in the audience was crying, and we were really depressed on stage," admitted Tony Kanal. **(BARRY KING/WIREIMAGE)**

Angelo Moore of LA fusionists Fishbone. "Angelo Moore was a huge influence on me," Stefani said in 2002. "He just had a sparkle to him. And that was always my goal, to give off that kind of energy." **(JEFF KROLL/LFI)**

Ska-punks The Untouchables, another band idolised by No Doubt. "We were just fans of music," said their leader Jerry Miller. "But after a while we thought maybe we should form a band, just for a giggle. I think two of us actually played music." **(PETER MAZEL/LFI)**

"Finally it's here!!!," screamed the flyer talking up No Doubt's self-titled debut LP of 1992. But if they could, Interscope "would have signed Gwen to a solo deal in a second," according to Dito Godwin, who produced the album.

Another shared bill, this time with Xtra Large and Swim Herschel Swim, at Anaheim's Inn at the Park Ballroom, March 1993. "Eric mainly does all the writing," Gwen said of her brother. "He's really creative." He also designed the artwork for their flyers.

Packing Crawford Hall, at the Irvine campus of the University of California, December 11, 1993.
"[Interscope's Tony] Ferguson loved the record and I was told that Jimmy Iovine liked it, too," Dito Godwin
said of their debut. "Then Nirvana came along and fucked my whole thing up." (KELLY A SWIFT/RETNA)

Eric Stefani at the same University of California gig.
"The [early] songs were great," said Paul Oberman, their
first manager, "but the lyrics were too goofy. You know,
Eric describing his trip to the dentist, things like that.
It was hard to take it seriously." (KELLY A SWIFT/RETNA)

Dumont, Stefani, Young and Kanal, just as *Tragic
Kingdom* fever started to break. "If *Tragic Kingdom* didn't
sell, they'd likely have to go back to finish school and
move on with their careers," said former member Eric
Carpenter. "I laugh at that now." (PAUL BERGEN/REDFERNS)

Stefani backstage at the Pond, Anaheim, March 12, 1996, a pivotal hometown show in the band's rise. Stefani, noted one writer from the time, "Looked like a cross between Jessica Lange and a naughty cheerleader." (JOE GIRON/CORBIS)

people who thought the band was just a phase." And while Gwen may have given the impression that she toed the family line, her performance that first night at Fender's suggested otherwise. "I always thought of her as this quiet, shy Catholic girl," Fatone said. "And then at the Scooter-aid show she flashed her bloomers at the crowd. She really belonged on that stage."

No Doubt gigs followed in the wake of Scooter-aid: a month later they played Gino's in Hollywood, a club that Oberman used to frequent. They returned to Fender's Ballroom on April 25 and June 12, 1987, and played an OC house party in early June. After their debut at The Roxy in Hollywood on June 19, they re-united with The Untouchables for a gig at Santa Monica's legendary Madame Wong's West on June 28. Run by the revered Esther Wong – who was then in her late sixties, and would often patrol her club, trying to sniff out dope smokers – the venue has hosted everyone from Oingo Boingo to The Police, X to The Motels and The Knack. But for Jerry Miller, the gig was more memorable for what occurred before the bands actually reached the venue.

Miller had reached out to the Orange County novices and invited them to a pre-gig get-together, to be held at his friend's house in Santa Monica. In attendance was all-girl group Rebel Pebbles, who were also on the Madame Wong's bill. "It's kind of a cute story," he said. "It was real early on in No Doubt's career; they were youngsters. [Gwen Stefani was still a few months shy of her 18th birthday.] They drove up from Orange County and came to a friend of mine's house to hang out before the show, and they turned up with seven large pizzas. So we're hanging out, drinking Cokes, listening to music, and about an hour after we finished eating, they stopped and went and grabbed mops and did the dishes, vacuumed, cleaned up the whole apartment without anyone asking. I thought, 'Wow, these kids have a good upbringing, man'. I'd never really experienced that. It was their way of sharing their gratitude. I thought that was cute. They have manners; so many people come through and have a good time and party, but this was different."

No Doubt was also starting to develop the musical chops to accompany their good housekeeping skills. Clearly, the band's relationship with The Untouchables – and, soon after, Fishbone – was based on more than manners. Were they good openers?, I asked Miller. "Oh yeah, definitely," he replied. "Our bands were similar in that respect; we both had lots of energy and fed off the crowd. And we were both fans of ska music; we came straight off the dance floor, basically, and we brought that attitude to the stage. It was important to give to the crowd and they would definitely get the crowd going." Paul Oberman could also see the development in the band, after only a handful of live gigs. "With John and Gwen as lead singers," he said, "well, they were very dynamic, they just had great chemistry."

"John didn't really sing," Gwen Stefani said, when asked about her former bandmate. "He yelled and screamed and did these backflips, and I was like his little sidekick. Originally [No Doubt was] just a bunch of people that didn't know how to play their instruments trying to imitate the music they loved, which was ska. I never wanted to be a rock girl." What Stefani and the band couldn't have known was that they were about to be hit right between the eyes by the type of tragedy that would kill most bands stone dead.

CHAPTER FOUR

Losing A Friend And Moving On

"I really credit Tony [Kanal] with keeping the band together and helping it move forward. At times, that was tough. As a friend, there were times when you wanted him to just take it easy and enjoy the moment more."

–former No Doubt–er, Eric Carpenter

For the rest of 1987, No Doubt began to establish a following, as they wore a path between their Orange County base and LA clubs The Roxy (where they played on June 19) and the Whisky, where they plugged in on August 1. Unlike most of the more pure ska bands, No Doubt had something going for them from the get-go; namely, the shapely figure of Gwen Stefani, who was gradually moving out of the shadow of her co-singer, John Spence. And there was no doubt that this band could play.

"When I first started singing, there weren't many female singers in the scene," Stefani said upon reflection. "Whenever we went to a club, I would always be looked upon as a tagalong girlfriend – 'Where's your wristband?' But as soon as I finished a show, the same people would be like, 'Ooh, I can't believe you were up there.'"

Sexism wasn't the only issue Gwen had to confront; the response from other women could sometimes be frosty. "The attitudes of the girls in the beginning – [it was] like, 'Bitch, who does she think she is?'" So she had plenty to prove.

"Gwen's talent and stage presence was always a huge plus for making an impression with a new audience," said Eric Carpenter, who played with the band from 1988 to 1994. "As for those shows at Fender's, they're hard to describe," he added. "They were an event. We looked forward to the concerts for weeks. Eric [Stefani] usually drew up original artwork with the show's date and other bands that were playing, and we'd go to the print shop, then hand out flyers around school and to friends. The bill often included five bands or more. It was just non-stop music and the challenge was always to make an impression, to stand out among the parade of other bands playing. We'd try to plan the set list so that there were very few lulls in the set, keep the energy high and leave them wanting more."

Carpenter accepted that most of the fans' attention was directed towards their livewire singer. "Of course they loved Gwen," he said. "They loved her stage presence. I remember a guy running up to me after a gig and saying, 'Hey, I have a question for you: why aren't you guys huge?' We had a lot of people rooting for us, but I think they also enjoyed the feeling that we were under the radar, that No Doubt belonged to them."

To preach the ska according to No Doubt, the band again took their cues from ska-punk groundbreakers The Untouchables, whose policy was essentially to play wherever, and for whoever, would have them, as Jerry Miller explained, "We must have played every club in LA, lots of clubs in Orange County, Long Beach, basically up and down California, spreading the word. We distributed our own flyers, did it real grassroots. The Roxy was our only real residency. Otherwise we'd play wherever they had us – lots of colleges." No Doubt Mark I did likewise, playing sets at house parties in Sunny Hills in Fullerton ("Rob's house", according to the band's well-maintained show archive), and at Santiago High School in Garden Grove. The band also played two shows on the campus of Cal State Long Beach. (Upon her graduation from Loara High, Gwen Stefani would enrol and study art at Cal State Fullerton.)

Gerald Lokstadt was one of many people who observed how No Doubt was already developing a following; there were many familiar faces in the moshpit at these shows. "They had the same people; a lot of people were coming to all the gigs," he said. "It wasn't super-trad ska; Eric wrote what I thought was quite pop-ish ska music, so it was pretty accessible, even then."

The No Doubt crowd was a mirror image of the Stefanis: white, middle-class kids who were out for the best possible time. Nothing too risky, mind you, just good clean fun.

Amongst the band's true believers was Mario Artavia II, whose attitude typified that of their earliest fans. "I used to be a 'Gwen Groupie', so to speak, in those days," he said. "'Every time I saw them, I had to be right in the front just drooling over her and her athleticism. She used to be a quite different performer on stage. She would cartwheel and bounce around and dance so much that she basically was a sweet ball of sweat by the third song – and we all loved that. Too bad folks these days don't get to see a dripping wet and wild Gwen on stage!" It was clear, even then, that Stefani was learning how to get physical from John Spence.

As enjoyable as these early gigs clearly were, the band was already stuck in a rut: They were a hometown hit, at best. Alex Henderson, who was to become No Doubt's trombonist in 1991, was amongst those who could spot the band's potential, but couldn't work out why they weren't bigger. "People would come from Orange County and Santa Barbara to the shows; it was a loyal following," he said. "I remember thinking, 'How could this not be big?' But it just wasn't catching on outside of California."

The Stefani family curfew, of course, played a role in the band's inability to secure gigs beyond southern California, and when they did play outside of the OC, Gwen would inevitably return home late and end up grounded, which further delayed the band's progress. "They were protective," said Paul Oberman, "and it was a pain in the ass. They wanted to make sure that [the band] didn't trump educational and family goals."

Inner-band relations were also less than rosy. First, there was trouble with the Meades – the so-called "Alan and Tony Show" – who took a very liberal approach to rehearsals. And Alan Meade didn't have the best of relationships with the men from Spot, especially Oberman. "There was tension between Alan and me," Oberman confirmed. "One time he even bumped the back of my car with his. I wasn't super happy with the guy, and I knew he had something going on with Gwen." ("I don't recall a lot about Gerald and Paul," Meade replied. "I just handled the practice and performing parts on my end. I didn't get involved with all the specifics. I was so young.")

Oberman (and possibly Gerald Lokstadt) had also invested some band money in singing lessons for Stefani, but she seemed reluctant to show up. "I am not sure why Gwen wouldn't do them," Oberman said. "Maybe it was ego. Maybe she was starting not to take us [No Doubt's surrogate managers] seriously." Oberman also had his own demons to deal with at the time, although he added that he didn't let his usage and abusage impede on his responsibilities. "I had a lot of frustrations with the band – and I started taking a little too much acid."

The band would rehearse on Thursdays and Sundays at a space called The Stomp Box in Anaheim. But money was very tight. "I remember having to ask my Dad for money every time [the band rehearsed]," Gwen Stefani recalled in an interview with *The Hub*. "I also remember John Spence having a plastic bag of pennies and counting them out every week . . . We used to pay two dollars for a mic. We'd be like, 'Do we really have to get two mics? We could share'."

While the approach of some of the band was casual at best, Eric and Gwen Stefani took a more professional attitude (with the exception of Gwen's singing lessons, perhaps). That professionalism increased significantly when the stone-faced Tony Kanal joined the band in early 1987.

Kanal had looked on from the Fender's Ballroom moshpit at an early No Doubt show; he'd been talked into attending by Andrew Stanley, a fellow member of the Anaheim High swim team. Stanley was a friend of drummer Chris Webb, who'd suggested that he bring Kanal along to the show. They weren't happy with their bass player; maybe Kanal would like what he saw and consider joining. Webb had also approached Eric Carpenter, who recalled, "Chris Webb knew that I had played bass at the same junior high school [as Kanal]. He asked if I wanted to play bass and I told him I only played sax now, but I knew this guy who did play bass and might be interested – Tony."

It's not possible to overstate the importance of Tony Kanal's recruitment into No Doubt. Firstly, unlike many of the others in the band, he approached music with a deadly earnest sense of conviction. Lokstadt explained, "Tony and Gwen were serious and everyone else wasn't that much. So they got themselves other musicians, a new guitarist and drummer, and then they got real serious."

Kanal had boundless enthusiasm for No Doubt; not too long after joining he'd become their surrogate manager as well as their bassist. Although his chops paid a sizeable debt to such musical heroes as Chili Pepper Flea, Fishbone's John Norwood Fisher, Mark Bedford of Madness and The Specials' Horace Panter, Kanal would eventually bring his own distinctive bottom end to the band's sound, helping them shake off the ska-punk straitjacket. And, crucially, his lengthy and sometimes rocky relationship with Gwen Stefani would provide just the right subject matter for her when she took on the role of the band's sole lyricist. Their career-making hit, 'Don't Speak', was essentially a valentine-cum-kiss-off from Stefani to her bandmate and former lover.

Being of Indian descent, Kanal was an anomaly at Anaheim High, which he attended with future No Doubt saxophonist Eric Carpenter and Eric's brother Dave. It was a mix of mainly white students and Hispanics. His classmates also included Michelle Sharples, who was Gwen Stefani's first cousin, and Shawn Nourse, who sat in with Kanal for the high school talent show, playing in a one-off outfit they called "Secret Colors". Nourse was another person to steer Kanal in the direction of No Doubt. "Chris Webb said the band was looking for someone to replace the current bass player," he recalled. "I'm pretty sure I told him about Tony − or told Tony about Chris and his band. [The] band [at that time] was very different than what it came to be."

Christine Becerra (nee Van Steenwyk), a classmate of Kanal's from Anaheim High, confirmed that Kanal was the only Indian on campus. "The school was mostly white, yes − Tony was, for sure, a minority," she said. According to another Anaheim High alumnus, Sean Jones, Kanal adapted pretty well to life there, regardless. 'There were minor racial problems, but the people were mostly tolerant of each other," Jones said. "Tony being Indian didn't appear to matter that much. Of course, he also acted and talked just like anyone else around him."

Yet another Anaheim High classmate of Kanal's, Brian Elledge, recalled being approached by Kanal to join No Doubt as a guitarist. "Do I ever regret not following through with that," he wrote via e-mail. "My most vivid memories of Tony were that he was very friendly, cheerful and down to earth," Elledge continued. "Tony was in the high school band and he seemed to hang out mostly with fellow band students. I remember he had braces on his teeth back then − he was kind of a small guy, not very big or muscular. Tony and I did share similar musical tastes: Depeche Mode, U2, The Cure, Oingo Boingo, Duran Duran, The Smiths, The Cult.

"His hair and dress styles reflected the new wave culture a bit," Elledge continued. "I don't remember Tony ever being a troublemaker or anything like that. I wouldn't consider him a 'popular' kid at school, nor was I for that matter. The jocks and cheerleaders seemed to be the most popular. Anaheim High was somewhat arts-oriented, and there were many aspiring artists and musicians. However, I would say that 'Anahi's' culture was more sports-focused."

Elledge also had another curious connection to the No Doubt world: His cousin, Matthew Elledge, was Gwen Stefani's high school sweetheart (something Kanal would soon be able to relate to on a very personal level).

Elledge said, "[Matthew] was always in love with Gwen up until the day he died. [By his own hand, a few years ago, after a battle with drugs.] I never did get a straight answer from Matt as to why she broke up with him; he really didn't like to talk about it." Elledge, however, plays down any notion that the break-up with Stefani caused his cousin to kill himself.

The older of two sons – his brother's name is Neil – Tony Ashwin Kanal was born in Kingsbury in northwest London on August 27, 1970. His parents, Gulab – a big music fan and a major influence on Kanal's future career – and Lena, had emigrated there from India. In 1981, the Kanals shifted base again, this time moving to Anaheim and then, seven years later, to Yorba Linda, probably best known as the birthplace of disgraced US President Richard "Tricky Dicky" Nixon. (For years afterward, Kanal was an Anglo/Indian living in California and travelling under a British passport.)

The Kanals opened a shop called Kanal's Gifts and Fashion on Harbor Boulevard in Anaheim. As for life in Yorba Linda, it was the usual Orange County fare in a comfortable, safe, conservative city of 50-odd thousand, once rated by CNN as the "21st best place to live" in the US.

Prior to Anaheim High, Kanal attended Anaheim's Benjamin Franklin Elementary school and South Junior High. John Pantle, who years later would book No Doubt shows, was a classmate of Kanal's, blowing alongside him in South Junior High's school band. "He played in the jazz band," Pantle said. "He was a good musician; a good guy."

Kanal met his future No Doubt bandmate, Eric Carpenter, on the first day of "band camp" in 1984. "He was an honour student kind of kid," Carpenter recalled. "Obviously intelligent, with a great sense of humour – and a really good alto saxophonist. We both learned to play tenor sax our freshman year, in order to be in the jazz band. Tony was first chair, I was second. He was just a naturally talented musician and a smart kid – whatever instrument he picked up, he learned fast. We played mostly standard tunes, swing, salsa, jazz. Neither of us liked marching band; we were in it for jazz band. That's where we really developed chops and learned how to improvise and write music."

Kanal switched from the sax to the bass when he befriended Eric and Dave Carpenter. Dave Carpenter had been playing professionally since he was 16, mainly in a punk band that played Damned covers, opening for such bands as the Chili Peppers. When Dave graduated, the school band needed a new player. No fool, Kanal noted that Dave Carpenter never seemed short of female attention. "He was a cool guy and all the girls liked him, so I put my hand up," said Kanal.

Dave Carpenter and Anaheim High band teacher, Mike Stopher, put Kanal through a summer crash course. As recently as 2000, Kanal would return to Carpenter – who introduced him to the work of jazz giants Jaco Pastorius and Stanley Clarke – for lessons and guidance.

"Dave was the one who taught me how to play bass," said Kanal. "I wouldn't play the bass if it weren't for him."

Kanal's first four-string was a Rickenbacker; soon after he bought a Yamaha BB1600, which he'd continue to use for many years. However, the humble Kanal admitted that he struggled through the jazz band, because he "wasn't a great sight reader". He was also spread pretty thinly; Kanal was on the school swim team, spent four years writing for and editing *Anoranco*, the school paper, and played in No Doubt. It was a heavy load for a teenager, but typical of his attitude to work.

Kanal didn't have older siblings to expose him to new music, so the Carpenters acted as his musical guides. Until then, he'd been the biggest Prince fan in Southern California – "Tony was definitely a Prince fanatic," said Anaheim High buddy Shawn Nourse. (The first album Kanal actually bought, however, was Men At Work's *Business As Usual*, which influenced his choice of the sax for the school band.)

It was Prince's *Purple Rain* that really made Kanal see stars; he'd use it as motivation for swim training, which necessitated a 6 a.m. wake-up most days. "I became obsessed with Prince," he said. "There's an instrumental part on 'Computer Blue' that I'd keep rewinding to get the adrenaline flowing."

On some school days, Kanal would actually dress in purple, as a nod to his diminutive hero. According to Gwen Stefani, "Tony thought he *was* Prince."

The first rock show that Kanal attended was a Prince concert The Forum in LA on February 23, 1985, as the man in purple toured his *Purple Rain* album. Kanal's thing for Prince would prove handy when he joined No Doubt, because Gwen Stefani was also a major fan; they'd bond over this shared love. "He makes the sexiest music," she once said of the artist formerly known as The Artist Formerly Known As. "Total make-out music."

The Carpenters also took Kanal to see Bruce Springsteen & The E Street Band's *Born In The USA* show at the Los Angeles Memorial Coliseum, and U2's *Unforgettable Fire* tour at the Los Angeles Sports Arena. Soon after, Eric Stefani, Webb, Spence and Tony Meade would continue the Carpenters' good work as Kanal's musical gurus and introduce him to Madness, The Specials, The English Beat, The Selecter, Bad Brains and Fishbone.

Kanal went through a few other curious musical phases before his close encounter with No Doubt and ska-punk. During the summer break between ninth and tenth grade, the Kanals underwent a pilgrimage, of sorts, returning briefly for a vacation in India and the UK. Kanal went record shopping and snapped up a copy of Sigue Sigue Sputnik's *Flaunt It*, mainly because he loved the cover. ("And it was on the front rack of the store.") But he also developed a taste for their smart-assed sounds, which he'd describe as "sophisticated new wave". When he started playing the bass, he became a dedicated follower of The Cure ('Boys Don't Cry' was the first song that he mastered on his Rickenbacker). He admired the simple, minimalist bass lines of The Cure's Michael Dempsey and his successor, Simon Gallup. (In the mid-Nineties, with No Doubt mania in full swing, Kanal admitted to frequently having sex to a soundtrack of The Cure. "The girls liked it, too," he said.)

And, like John Spence, Kanal was a fan of Bad Brains, talking up the "amazing metal grooves" of their *I Against I* album. He was also a big admirer of Bob Marley & The Wailers, citing bassman Aston "Family Man" Barrett as a major influence on his early playing style. The group's 1983 album *Confrontation* would become a key record for Kanal soon after joining No Doubt (the first and only band he has ever played in, incidentally).

But above and beyond Prince, The Wailers, Bad Brains and the rest of them, Kanal regarded one group – and one bassist, in particular – as God-like: Californicators The Red Hot Chili Peppers and bassist Flea. Soon after joining No Doubt he'd follow these LA contenders from club to club, digging their funk-punk grooves and, especially, the frenetic slap-bass style of Australian-born wild child Michael Balzary (aka Flea). Of the band's early records, Kanal fell especially hard for *The Uplift Mofo Party Plan*. "I'd go to see them just to see Flea, who was such a huge influence on me as a bass player," he admitted. "To be 16 or 17 and hear 'Fight Like A Brave' – the world seemed so fresh and exciting."

It didn't take long for fledgling bassist Kanal to adopt Flea's very upright, very fast and extremely physical style of bass playing. "Back then, as a young man, it was all about the energy. At the time, his slapping blew me away." Like the man he so admired, it would take Kanal several years and a couple of records before he worked out that it's sometimes what you don't play that adds so much to a song.

As much as he loved slapping away at his bass, Kanal never envisaged a musical career. This well-adjusted, if somewhat austere, son of hard-working immigrants thought that his life would take a more traditional path: graduation, then college and "becoming a doctor or something professional". He even studied psychology for a time.

So Kanal didn't have great expectations when he turned up to the band's Fender's gig, but he was turned on by what he witnessed.

Eric Carpenter felt exactly the same when he first saw No Doubt. "I was blown away," said Carpenter. "I still remember the heat in the club and the sheer volume. I think there were nine players on stage, including John Spence. It was just mayhem. And at the centre of it all was Gwen, like a mother hen just trying to keep everything under control, smiling and singing in this sweet voice that cut through all the snare drum, bass and horns. It was like a cartoon with everything in the background at a hyper pace and her at regular speed. She was captivating."

When Kanal turned up to the Stefani family garage in Anaheim for his audition, he was decked out in baggy pants and Mexican sandals. After playing a couple of songs with the band, two key things happened: Kanal was asked to join and he had cast a spell, albeit unintentionally, over Gwen Stefani, although it took her a few months to work up the courage to put a move on him. (Famously, she said, "Dude, are you going to kiss me or what?" With that, their lips, and to some extent the band's future, were sealed.) Kanal's more careerist approach to the band fitted well with the outlook of the Stefanis – in time, he'd also become the band's historian.

"One thing I do know," said Paul Hampton of The Skeletones, "is that they were all business. We were the party guys; we'd drink, smoke, hang out; we were a bunch of hooligans. But they were real conservative, real strict, very business-like."

According to Oberman, "Tony was like Switzerland. He was a very smooth guy, he never made trouble; he was very competent. He put a lot of work in, as did Eric."

"I can't overstate how important Tony's skills were to the band early on," said Eric Carpenter. "He believed in No Doubt and its potential long before anybody else. It truly baffled me sometimes, the kind of knowledge he had and how [he] got things done. He had a knack for finding the right people to help the band. And if he couldn't find somebody to do it, he'd do it himself. I'm sure he had doubts and fears, but they weren't obvious. He inspired confidence. I really credit Tony with keeping the band together and helping it move forward over the years. At times, that was tough. As a friend, there were times when you wanted him to just take it easy and enjoy the moment more." Kanal may have kept the band moving forward, but to many of their original fans, John Spence was the heart and soul of No Doubt, which makes what happened next all the more poignant.

The band had the chance to start making real waves in the music industry when they were offered a showcase on December 30, 1987 at The Roxy in LA, opening for The Untouchables. This wasn't just another night at Fender's Ballroom; this was a genuine opportunity to stir up some interest from the music biz. But John Spence had other plans. In mid-December, he went to the local DMV with the Meade brothers and passed his driving test. ("He was so happy," said Alan Meade.) Then, on December 21, Spence drove into the parking lot of an Anaheim building, turned off the engine of his blue VW "square back", pulled out a shotgun and shot himself in the head. The force of the blast was so severe that it ripped a hole in the roof of his car. He was 18.

★　★　★

No one in No Doubt's inner circle really understood why Spence killed himself. But it seemed as though the 18-year-old Spence had clearly thought it through, selling off his beloved scooter and his record collection and giving away all his clothes in the days leading up to his death.

"I met his parents afterwards," said Gerald Lokstadt, "and it turns out that he'd tried suicide once before, eight or nine months before, but I didn't know him then."

The existing members of No Doubt have always paid due respect to Spence's role in the band, but have never mentioned this earlier suicide attempt. Paul Oberman said, "Everyone I spoke to said that they had no idea that he was thinking of this. And if they knew, no-one in the band let on to me that they did. I believe they didn't."

Doug Fatone was one of the first people outside the band to get the news; as soon as Eric Stefani called him, he and Oberman dashed over to the band house. "No-one had any idea what was going on," Fatone said, still saddened by the recollection almost 20 years on. "The band was John and Eric's baby, and they were doing well. That's what shocked me the most. But I don't think John's home life was that great."

The shockwaves of Spence's suicide hit his bandmates and friends hard; many years down the line Gwen Stefani still had no idea what led him to kill himself. "I couldn't answer that question," she admitted in 1996. "Obviously he was in a lot of pain, [but] it's really hard to understand why anyone would commit suicide. Mostly I have happy memories of him; he was a very important part of the band. He was the one who used to say, 'No doubt.' And that's where we got the name. It still haunts us in a way." She revealed just a little more in an interview with the *Los Angeles Times*. "He was the one who was so happy all the time," she said. "I knew he had problems with his family, I knew he had problems with depression in high school. But when it happened, things were so normal. It was awful. It was horrible."

Spence's friends, including his buddies in The Untouchables and The Skeletones, were as bewildered as Gwen when they got the news of his death. "None of us expected what happened with John," said Paul Hampton of The Skeletons. "No-one had any idea. It was pretty mind-blowing." Jerry Miller of The Untouchables was equally stunned. "I was kind of shocked. When I saw him he was always happy, always joking around, smiling. He was a real bundle of energy. I thought that he must have had some serious troubles to do that. Everybody was really sad. I saw Tony [Kanal] a couple of months ago and I mentioned the guy's name, and you could see it still hurt. They're still real passionate about the guy." So passionate, in fact, that Kanal and many others, including Alan Meade, do their best to gather at Spence's gravesite every year on the anniversary of his death, to pay their respects.

Meade was as devastated as the other members of No Doubt when he heard about Spence's suicide. He and Spence had become especially tight during their time together in the group; Spence had been teaching Alan Meade how to pull off those amazing on-stage backflips. "It's so difficult, still to this day, to believe that someone who was so cool, and well loved, who was a big part of your everyday life, left us in this way," Meade said. "I cried my eyes out. I knew through my best friend and his sister that the situation with [Spence's] parents was kind of strict. There was a break up with his girlfriend, he'd crashed his Dad's car – it all happened at the same time. [But] I had no idea he was down – you couldn't tell from his attitude, which was always fun. It was a huge shock. It's probably the most shocking memory of my life. When I'm in town [Meade now DJs and plays in the band Starpool with ex-members of Orange County ska-pop contenders Save Ferris] and I have the opportunity, I will stop by his gravesite, just to reflect on the fun times we had."

"To go out the way John did; I couldn't have imagined that in a million years," reflected Skeletone Rick Bonnin. "He never spoke bad about anybody; he was just an awesome guy." To his regret, Bonnin was out of touch and didn't hear about Spence's death until after his funeral was held. (Spence's mother has since east to Ohio.)

Paul Oberman learned a few more half-truths about Spence after his death, but nothing that made the reasons for his suicide any clearer. "Some stories emerged afterwards that he had a bad relationship with his father," Oberman said, "and that he'd been writing some poetry, indicating how he was feeling. But, still, it came from 100 miles out of left field." The band and the men from Spot now had to make a serious decision: should they somehow deal with their grief and continue with The Roxy show, as a tribute to their dead friend? Or did Spence's death signal the end of the band that he'd help form? They had less than a week to make up their minds.

★   ★   ★

The band and management got together soon after Spence's funeral and agreed that No Doubt should carry on. Alan Meade would back up Gwen Stefani, who would now be the band's lead vocalist, and Eric Stefani would re-write some songs to accommodate Gwen's voice. Gabe Gonzalez would take over Meade's trumpet gig. To avoid losing the chemistry that existed between Spence and Stefani, Meade would attempt to replicate this, at least to some extent. Nonetheless, it was a tearful meeting.

"We all stood around, looking at each other, and said, 'What do we now?'," said Doug Fatone. "We decided to keep going was what John would have wanted." As a memorial to his bandmate and buddy, Eric Stefani pieced together a video montage of Spence.

Alan Meade recalled that Eric Stefani approached him with the idea of moving into the co-vocalist's spot. "We felt that John would have wanted the band to keep going, so Eric said, 'Alan, why don't you sing with Gwen?', and that's what I did. I was a singer at heart, anyway. I felt privileged, yet I knew I had a job to do and I was so into it – I was serious about [the band]."

During the Roxy show, which was dedicated to Spence, Meade decided to make his own statement. "On stage, I kept a part of John with me because I wanted to give the audience what he gave them," Meade recalled. "John had taught me how to do backflips, so I pulled one off there in memory of him."

A fan of the band expressed the feeling of many in the crowd when he stepped on stage at The Roxy and announced that it was the end of No Doubt – and it was, at least to their more diehard followers. "Everyone in the audience was crying, and we were really depressed on stage," Tony Kanal would later tell the *Los Angeles Times'* Mike Boehm.

Alan Meade did his best to capture a little of his predecessor's magic, but he was fully aware that Spence was a particularly hard act to follow. "Gwen and I would do little dance routines and dance steps in sync, to make the shows look more fun, and I remember being reminded to play to the audience," he said, adding that this was exactly what Spence would do.

But the band's managers felt that Meade simply didn't have Spence's "man of the people" appeal. Oberman considered Meade an accidental frontman, at best. "He didn't have the charm, or the charisma, or the voice." Fatone agreed. "He just didn't have the on-stage personality [of Spence]."

Eric Carpenter, however, felt that Gwen generated sparks with both Spence and Meade. "Gwen worked great alongside John and later alongside Alan," he said. "She was the calm presence to their amazing high energy. I think she was influenced by John, but also by the frontmen she admired, like Anthony [Kiedis] from the Chili Peppers and Angelo [Moore] from

Fishbone. When that happened we saw a whole new side to Gwen: she was more aggressive, more in charge. I think that's when No Doubt really started to appeal to an audience beyond the ska scene."

The beginning of No Doubt Mark II also marked the decline of the relationship between the men from Spot and the band. Although the band would play a support slot for The Untouchables at the Riviera Hotel in Palm Springs on April 1, 1988, while Spot was involved, Oberman was losing patience with some of the band, and with the stunts pulled by promoters. Often they'd be short-changed after shows. "Magically, there was never enough money to pay us what they promised," Oberman recalled. [Goldenvoice's] Paul Tollett was a real pain in the ass on that issue." (Fatone backed this up, adding that No Doubt were always Tollett's "pet band", and that the promoter was making life difficult for Spot so that he could start booking the band's shows.)

The division within the band between the less-than-serious Meades, the super-dedicated Tony Kanal and the Stefanis was quite clear by this stage. "It was a pain in the ass," said Oberman, "and we didn't have the managerial chops to wrangle them in. Sticking it out wasn't an option, though. They outgrew us and Paul Tollett started directly booking them on much larger shows. After that we were out of the picture."

Fatone left when he realised that he'd rather be booking shows for his own band, The Boot Boys, than No Doubt. "And we didn't know what the hell were doing," Fatone added.

The Palm Springs show with The Untouchables, however, was a genuinely upbeat note for No Doubt. The band's part-time managers knew that in order for No Doubt to become anything more than hometown heroes, they needed to travel outside of Southern California. The Stefani curfew was addressed by having the band take the stage at 9.30 p.m.; No Doubt played for an hour and then Gwen was driven home at breakneck speed, just beating her 11 p.m. deadline. Despite her hasty departure, the band still managed to leave an impression on the 1500-or so liquored-up students in the crowd. "It was a great show," recalled Untouchable Jerry Miller. "Palm Springs was a real popular place for the spring breakers, the college students. It was all set up when we got to the hotel; we didn't have to do anything but play. And No Doubt was kind of competitive with us, in a fun way."

More gigs followed, as the band played every few weeks: at the Variety Arts Center in LA on April 23; the Numbers Club in Long Beach on May 6; a club called Joshua's Parlor at Westminster on June 3 and the Elks Lodge in Pomona on June 19, followed by a return to The Roxy on July 16. But the band had to undergo another recruitment drive when guitarist Jerry McMahon left during that summer. (When last heard of by the band, McMahon was practising law.) McMahon's successors in the band, however, didn't stay long. Shane Ries from the band The Key played one show; then a guitarists simply known as "Todd" filled in for a few nights. However, Tom Dumont, who would join No Doubt soon after McMahon left, was a keeper.

★ ★ ★

In his own way, Dumont would play as important a role in No Doubt's future as Tony Kanal, just without the romantic entanglement. Unlike many of the group's early members, Dumont wasn't passing through; this wasn't some dalliance while waiting to get on with the more serious business of life. Playing the guitar was the most crucial thing in his world. And his versatility on the axe – Dumont was schooled in metal, but knew a great pop lick when he played one – was another essential part of the No Doubt signature sound. His hard-rock past also meant that he added some much-needed sonic muscle when No Doubt started to rock the stadiums. And he'd take on a very necessary role, further down the line, when he became the band's on-line blogger.

Born on January 11, 1968, in LA, Dumont was adopted early on by Fred and Ellen Dumont; he was one of three Dumont children (along with brother John and sister Gina). There was definitely music in the Dumont homestead: Gina Dumont would earn a degree in classical guitar from the University of California Irvine. John (aka "Bert") Dumont, meanwhile, was a multi-instrumentalist who would play in such bands as The Dead Hensons and Baby Snufkin. (The latter, now called Snufkin, opened for No Doubt during the European leg of their 1997 world tour.) The Dumont brothers didn't just share albums, they shared obsessions: George Lucas' *Star Wars* meant almost as much to them as rock'n'roll. (No Doubters Tony Kanal and Adrian Young were also huge fans of the sci-fi saga.)

Dumont's musical upbringing echoed that of the Stefanis: Living in Irvine, California, his first records were Disney compilations; his father played the piano at home. By the time he reached grade school, Dumont was a huge Beatles fan. His first guitar, a 12-string acoustic, was a gift from his Aunt Ruth (a former nun); he pared it back to a regulation six-string and strummed diligently while tuning in to the sensitive tunesmithery of such acts as James Taylor. "My dad paid for lessons at the local music store," the lanky, soft-spoken Dumont said in 1997. "I learned regular chords and finger picking patterns; I picked it up pretty quickly. From there on I was self taught."

72

But like so many American teenagers of the Eighties, Dumont under-went a metal makeover – a relative slipped him a copy of Kiss' *Destroyer* and his teenage life changed dramatically. Iron Maiden, Black Sabbath, AC/DC, Judas Priest, Canadian prog-rockers Rush and, especially, fire-breathing car-toon rockers Kiss, were among his new metal/hard rock heroes. By the time he was 13, Dumont owned his first electric guitar, a black Les Paul copy, selected primarily because it was just like the guitar wielded with menace by Kiss' Ace Frehley. Before he moved on to Hamer axes in 1996, Gibson guitars would become the weapon of choice for Dumont. And he wasn't the type of player who'd complicate his set-up with too many effects, as he explained in a one-on-one with *Guitar Player* magazine. "I love players who can pull out all the effects and do it really well, like [Rush's] Alex Lifeson and [Bowie sidekick] Reeves Gabrels. But for me, it's pretty much just gui-tar, wah-wah and amp." Dumont's first band, Northeast, pulled off an ambi-tious take on Rush's 'Jacob's Ladder' – Dumont was in 8th grade at the time.

Dumont's close encounter with No Doubt came about purely by chance. In 1988, in between classes at Cal State Fullerton, Dumont was bending strings in his sister's hard-rock band, Rising, whose set included a cover of Judas Priest's 'Desert Plains'. Rising happened to rehearse at Anaheim's Stomp Box, the same space used by No Doubt.

Dumont, who was growing increasingly dissatisfied by his band "and the whole direction of the metal scene in general", would sometimes look on while the Orange County band rehearsed. "It was fascinating," he admitted, "because this was different from any kind of music I'd heard before. Ska music – I was pretty unfamiliar with it . . . [but] their scene seemed so much healthier to me."

A few days after quitting Rising, Dumont was idly glancing at the "muso wanted" ads pinned to the notice board at Stomp Box when he spotted a flyer from the Orange County contenders. It read, simply: "No Doubt needs a guitar player." One audition later, Dumont realised two things: No Doubt were the right band for him, despite their vastly different musical backgrounds; and he was done with music theory. All he had to do was tie back his hard-rock mullet and own up to his "lack of fashion sense" and he was in the band.

"Eric [Stefani] was breaking all the rules I was learning," Dumont recalled. "He came up with the greatest, most fucked-up chord progres-sions." At the same time, the rules of Cal State Fullerton specified that, in order to get a degree, Dumont had to specialise in one of their instruments. "Classical guitar was the closest to what I played," he said, "but I felt like I was starting over. I'd much rather have an amp and crank power chords, so

I dropped out." Nonetheless, Dumont's classical training would come in handy when a solo was needed for the breakthrough hit, 'Don't Speak', even though purists would have choked on their 12-strings if they'd known that the maverick Dumont played the solo with a guitar pick. Dumont knew that, too. 'As I recorded it,' he admitted, "I was thinking about how any true classical players would've hated the way I did it. [But] I hated the anal sitting position and the fingering positions."

While hiring Tom Dumont was a step in the very right direction, No Doubt was about to experience yet another shake-up in the ranks. The 18-year-old Alan Meade had taken up with another woman – Gwen Stefani now had eyes only for Tony Kanal – and Meade soon had some heavy news for the band: His girlfriend was pregnant.

This was at a time when No Doubt was starting to become a regular name on the southern California live circuit. Meade knew that he had to advise the band of his plans, and very quickly.

Even today, Meade draws a deep breath before explaining how it played out. "I was so young and my then-girlfriend got pregnant," he said. At the time, No Doubt was so busy playing that I couldn't perform full-time and work *and* be a daddy. My hormones were way out of control and it got me in trouble, but also, I had to be responsible and take care of my kid." To his credit, Meade took the responsible path and married his pregnant partner; they moved to Truckee, California, near Lake Tahoe.

"When I look back to that whole part of my life," Meade added, "I think, 'What the fuck was I thinking!' I wish I had not gotten married, of course – even before the band made it big – because my marriage barely made it to one year and the band was my life. I could have worked and stayed home and been in the band. I was faced with such a life-changing decision at too young of an age and was too scared to make the decision that I *really* wanted. I get asked all the time if I have any regrets, and I say that I would be lying if I said no, but the truth is that our lives are pre-planned out for us. We have many open doors to walk through and none of those doors guarantee success. Had I not gone through that difficult part of my life I would have never met my current wife and her beautiful family who I'm truly thankful for." (Meade added that he now has a "great and close" relationship with his teenage son, although they live in different states.)

With Meade now out of the picture, Gwen Stefani took the logical next step and became the band's lead singer. According to Lokstadt, it was only a matter of time before Gwen stepped out front of No Doubt; her idiosyncratic fashion sense and on-stage confidence seemed to be developing in tandem. "She was a natural," he said, "she always got the crowd going."

Jerry Miller agreed. "Having Gwen as the front person didn't hurt; the girls liked her, but the guys were drooling over her." However, the Stefani family curfew was about to lead to yet another departure.

By April 1989, the band's dance card was pretty damned full: they'd played yet another show at Fender's, followed by a well-received set at the John Anson Ford Amphitheatre on April Fool's Day, again with The Untouchables. Miller has vivid memories of the gig and the venue itself: "That's right across the street from the Hollywood Bowl; it's like a mini Greek [Theater], a little amphitheatre that holds around 1,200 people. It doesn't get used much; I think when we played there with No Doubt was the first time we'd stumbled upon it. It was a great show; I remember they were so happy."

There was definitely growing interest in the band – according to Lokstadt, "within six months of that Palm Springs gig people really started to dig them."

The band's next key gig was opening for the up-and-coming Red Hot Chili Peppers at Cal State Long Beach on April 19. No Doubt were keen on hooking up with the Chili Peppers – especially hyperactive bassman, Flea, who'd soon produce some rough demos for the band. But to really move forward, No Doubt's surrogate managers knew that the band needed to play dates outside California. "It was getting stagnant, so we came up with the idea of getting them on the road," Oberman recalled. "But Gwen's parents said no. Chris Webb, who was more of a punk-rock guy anyway, had had enough, and he left." Or, as spelled out on the website of Webb's former band, One Hit Wonder: "Drummer, Chris, was in No Doubt but quit because Gwen wasn't allowed to tour, and he didn't see it going anywhere."

But Webb's departure was a minor setback. The next man to stroll through the No Doubt revolving door – greenhorn drummer Adrian Young – would turn out to be just as vital an acquisition for the band as Tony Kanal or Tom Dumont. The "classic" No Doubt line-up was gradually falling into place.

★   ★   ★

It all started with a white lie. Young had been a fan of No Doubt for some time, often checking them out with a bunch of his running buddies from Long Beach. And the band knew of Young. They'd spotted him getting physical in numerous moshpits. They also knew that he played the drums.

When Webb left, No Doubt roadie Rob Cummins called Young and asked if he'd be interested in trying out for the vacant spot.

"How long have you been playing?," the Stefanis asked Young, who was just out of his teens, during the audition. "Six years," he shot back.

It typified the cocky spirit that the diminutive, hard-partying drummer would bring to No Doubt.

The truth, of course, was slightly different: Young had been drumming for little more than 12 months at the time he auditioned for the band, but there was no way that was going to stop him joining his favourite group. (Young played down any crush he may have had on Gwen – he thought she was "cute" – but the predominantly male population at No Doubt shows spoke volumes about her pin-up status at the time.)

Adrian Samuel Young was born in Long Beach, California, on August 26, 1969, and has lived there ever since. (For years he lived within walking distance of Tom Dumont.) Like his fellow No Doubters, there was plenty of music in his home while he grew up. Young has often spoken of how he and his brother Damian were "the children of hippies", who put them through a crash course of classic Sixties and Seventies rock'n'roll – everything from the Doors to Jimi Hendrix, Deep Purple to Led Zeppelin was on high rotation in the Young music room, with the occasional Bob Marley album thrown in. They may have been ageing hippies, but life wasn't all peace, love and understanding at the Young household; Adrian's mother left when he was very young, leaving the brothers with their father Sam.

The start of Young's life as a drummer almost co-incided to the day with John Spence's suicide: His first drumkit was the pick of his gifts on Christmas Day 1987. That was when Young, like so many other southern Californians, fell for ska in a big way. Yet he was also mastering the moves of hard-rock drumming, closely studying every fill and paradiddle of such renowned time-keepers as Deep Purple's Ian Paice, Neil Peart of Rush and The Police's Stewart Copeland. At the same time he was buying his first album with his own money: The Ramones' warp-speed *Road To Ruin*. Like No Doubt's other recent recruit, Tom Dumont, Young had a broad musical vocabulary that would help him add some much-needed grunt and diversity when the band graduated from The Roxy/Fender's/Fullerton campus circuit and started playing the concrete bunkers of America.

"It was a big deal when our original drummer left in '89," Tony Kanal would admit in an interview with *Bass Player* magazine. "Adrian was a bundle of energy when he auditioned, a true California kid we had seen at shows." (Young, who studied at Cal State Fullerton, like Gwen Stefani, still owns a No Doubt T-shirt he acquired at a 1987 show.) "He told us he'd been playing for years," Kanal continued, "but in fact he had learned every song – every beat and every hit, part for part – from our five-song demo tape."

76

Young was obviously a fast learner, because, according to Kanal: "At his audition he played them perfectly. We said, 'You're in', but very quickly we learned that he'd been playing only a few months. He tricked us."

Young, like Kanal, hadn't played in a serious band prior to joining No Doubt, although he had spent some time in the little-known metal outfit Echostar, and also played in The Naked Postmen, which was appropriate, given Young's love of streaking. And his attempt, while in the ninth grade, to drum to Doggy Style's 'Bend Over' at a school talent comp, didn't go over that well.

Kanal and the Stefanis, of course, weren't fools; they could see in Young's eyes just how much the band meant to him when was hired in 1989. (The band's logo is now proudly tattooed on his leg.) If Dumont was the group's quiet achiever and Kanal the tightly wound careerist, then Young was the energetic core of the band, a guy who could drum like a human tornado, lose his clothes in an instant (often on stage) and party like David Lee Roth when the time was right. (When asked about groupies, Young admitted to indulging generously, while his favourite off-stage trick was a move known simply as "the turkey". Enough said.)

"Both Tom and Adrian played key roles in the band," said former No Doubter Eric Carpenter. "Tom had such a heavy metal background that I didn't think it would mesh with the band at first, but I think helped take No Doubt's music in a new direction.

Adrian's musicianship was not as sharp in the beginning," he added. "He told the band he'd been playing drums longer than he actually had when he joined just to try to get the gig. But the great thing about Adrian is that he learned quickly and there was no matching his enthusiasm. He was a huge fan of the band before he was in the band. He was a breath of fresh air [and] kept everybody smiling – [even] making fun of himself by dropping his drawers just to lighten the mood."

In mid-1989, the core of No Doubt – the Stefanis, Dumont, Kanal and Young – was finally in place. And it wasn't long after that line-up was established that the band ventured outside of their So-Cal comfort zone, playing in Arizona during July 1989. Saxophonist Eric Carpenter recalled the road trip as a key moment for the band; maybe there was life beyond Fender's, after all. "That whole experience was like a scene from a movie," he said. "We piled in and 'caravanned' in three cars, I think. We met at 3 a.m. at a Denny's restaurant and headed east. It was this little union hall in Arizona that was blistering hot, on a stage that I was convinced would fall over. But the experience bonded us.

"The road trip was great fun," he continued. "It was in the days before cell phones, so I remember Eric and Gwen would be working on song ideas, then would pull over to the side of the road. The entire caravan of cars would pull over in the middle of the desert and we'd all get out of the car and start adding parts to the song. I think it was key to us considering that there was life for the band outside of just southern California. It sparked our interest in touring and fed the excitement of trying to win over new audiences."

At the same time, No Doubt was about to finally shrug off the men from Spot who, by their own admission, had done all they could for the band. By this time, there'd been some major label interest in the band. Eric Stefani's 'Everything's Wrong' was included on a vinyl-only compilation called *Skaface*, released by New York-based Moon Records (later called Moon Ska Records, a label operated by The Toasters' Rob "Bucket" Hingley).

"I have doubts I could have got them to another level," said Lokstadt. "Interscope, and another label I can't remember, were already interested." Spot had shopped the band's demo – which included 'Paulina', which would make their debut album, and 'Your Lovin' ' – to a few labels, including Chrysalis, which passed. "[They] said, 'We just released The Specials, that's enough'," Lokstadt recalled.

The split with Spot occurred soon after Oberman spoke, once again, with Eric Stefani about his lyrics, which he felt lacked substance. "The songs were great," Oberman said, "but the lyrics were too goofy. You know, Eric describing his trip to the dentist, things like that. It was hard to take it seriously." Oberman decided that he'd attempt to re-write the lyrics to 'Ache', Eric's ode to a toothache. (Sample lyric: "Oooo ahhh / the pain is tremendous / why can't I take it like a man? / Oooo ahhh / the pain is horrendous / why don't you lend a helping hand?") "So I sat down and rewrote the lyrics to the song," Oberman said. "I called Eric and read him the lyrics and he was like, 'OK . . . ' By the end of it I knew it was a bad idea. He was polite, he wasn't mean. But he was just too quiet. I said, 'OK, forget about it, I know this is a bad idea, so let's hire someone to work with you on your lyrics.' I never did that again. Our relationship . . . they were outgrowing me and Gerald [and Fatone]. We'd done as much as we could."

On the same night as this fateful phone conversation, Oberman got a call from the band, who advised him that Spot's services "were no longer required". Neither Oberman nor Lokstadt was surprised. "Despite managing to the best of our abilities, Paul O. and I were overwhelmed," said Lokstadt. "We wanted to help, but 22- and 24-year-olds only know so much. And headlining and going on the road were out, thanks to Gwen's parents."

"Some people say to me, 'You must be so upset; they did so well'," Oberman added. "I just don't understand that. The way it worked out is the way it worked out. Some big record company was bound to come along and appoint a big manager. Am I disappointed? Not at all." Although Oberman would continue to work with the band for a while, co-managing them with Doug Fatone, No Doubt's fortunes improved significantly when Paul Tollett's Goldenvoice started booking their shows. "I sensed that once Gerald and I were out of the picture," Oberman added, "they were opened up to bigger things with Goldenvoice. We didn't talk [with the band] after that; we didn't run in the same crowd."

Fatone, however, looked back fondly on his stint with the band. "It was a blast," he said, "a lot of fun. I was in my early twenties, I had no responsibility, I was working with bands, travelling." Yet despite his continued involvement with promoting shows — he'd tour manage The Selecter and Bad Manners, an experience he compared to "baby-sitting a 300 pound skinhead" — Fatone never saw No Doubt again.

Lokstadt, however, would hear just once more from No Doubt. He and Oberman had registered the name "No Doubt" as a DBA ("doing business as"), and when the band finally signed with Interscope, they tracked him down. "Interscope wanted us to sign a release giving them the rights to the name," Lokstadt recalled, "but we never saw the paperwork and it [the DBA] expired after five years. I didn't pursue it; I didn't want anything from them."

Oberman, who now works in the film industry, would have a more personal final encounter with one of his former charges. He was on a film set — "it was maybe '97 or '98" — when he thought he saw Gwen Stefani. "It was a really weird situation. This woman looked so much like Gwen — idiot that I am, it took a good few minutes for it to sink in that it really was her. I walked over, she looked at me, we looked at each other. She said: 'Paul Oberman, holy shit!' It was cordial, very nice, but we simply didn't have anything to say to each other. It sums up our time, really." By this stage, of course, No Doubt were platinum-plated superstars, but in the early Nineties, what lay before them was a seemingly endless stretch of gigs, inner-band turmoil and record label frustration.

CHAPTER FIVE

Trapped In A Box

"[Kanal and Gwen] were clearly very in love. But they also respected the band and knew that it wouldn't go over well that they were dating. Beyond that, it was like having seven other brothers because the entire band was protective of her."

—Eric Carpenter

Dennis Stefani may not have approved of his daughter's involvement with what Jerry Miller described as "the seedy people" who gravitated to such clubs as Fender's Ballroom, but he did play a vital role in No Doubt's history. He'd often film their shows, usually from the relative safety of the back of the room, on what could best be called "unsteady cam". These raw documents, heavy with audience noise, muffled live sound and Dennis Stefani's unimaginative camera technique, paint a vivid picture of the live world of these hometown heroes. No Doubt was definitely a band undergoing a "makeover" by the time they hit Spanky's Café, in Riverside, on January 6, 1990.

Although small, Spanky's was a good venue for No Doubt to play – not only was it a few steps up the ladder from the decaying Fender's Ballroom, but many other ska-loving bands had played there, including The Angry Samoans, The Voodoo Glow Skulls and Bostonians The Mighty Mighty Bosstones, who would grow into one of the more successful third wave acts.

The opening stage announcement revealed plenty about No Doubt, even at this developmental stage of the band's career: "Ladies and gentlemen, please welcome – GWEN STEFANI!", bellowed pint-sized MC Tony Kanal, as the band got nice and loose. Even back then, No Doubt's lead singer's star was rising and she was being treated accordingly. A smiling Gwen obliged, bouncing on-stage like a wind-up doll, part ska-pop Madonna, part Pauline Black of The Selecter, dressed in a sensible (rather than sensuous) sleeveless, knee-length dress.

Once the applause – and this was a very full house – died down, the eight-piece band stopped on a dime and launched into the jaunty, sonically schizophrenic 'Trapped In A Box'. Probably the best example of Eric Stefani's anything-goes songwriting style from the time, the live version of 'Box' is anchored by the rock-steady drumming of Adrian Young —virtually invisible behind his elevated kit – and is spiced considerably by a scorching solo from the bespectacled, floppy-fringed Tom Dumont that draws heavily on the warp-speed riffing he learned during his metal apprenticeship. Then the song takes a sharp right turn and explodes with a totally unexpected Dixieland shuffle, which the band pulled off surprisingly well live. In true No Doubt style, the band had somehow managed to throw several musical styles at the faithful within the first number of their set.

That, of course, would be one of No Doubt's biggest dilemmas, back in the days before they zeroed in on a sound and a look that suited them: This was not an easily defined band. It's likely that they weren't quite sure where they were going stylistically, either, as Adrian Young admitted in an interview. "Even in the beginning," he said, "the music . . . was all over the map. We're going a mile a minute, from punk to ska to Dixieland to I don't know. I think it took us a long time to get signed because our songs were all over the place."

One thing that and was clearly demonstrated by this 1990 live set was Eric Stefani's well-defined sense of musical democracy. Thanks to their nights in The Stomp Box, No Doubt was a well-oiled machine, and Eric gave everyone the chance to demonstrate their chops. The band's three-man horn section – Eric Carpenter on sax, plus Gabe Gonzalez and Don Hammerstedt (who was a good five years older than the rest of the band) – got the chance to stretch out and play during 'Get On The Ball'. This was another herky-jerky grab bag of musical styles, part ska-punk frenzy, part something else altogether, which followed swiftly on from 'Box'. (Most of the songs from this live set would end up on their Dito Godwin-produced debut album, almost in the same running order.) Throughout the set, the moshpit found it impossible not to bounce around like human Jack-and-Jill-in-the-boxes.

'Let's Get Back', the next number, was another showpiece for the horn

men, who all blared out solos, as did guitarist Dumont, blazing his way up
and down the fretboard like a So-Cal Angus Young. Gwen let her hair
down, literally, during 'Let's Get Back' as she untied her mousy-blonde locks
and let them fall down over her shoulders, much – it must be said – to the
exhilaration of the many males throwing themselves around giddily at the
front of the stage. She also busted some moves, belting out the we-are-one
chorus of "let's get back together" with enough gusto to pop a lung. The
song, like so many in their set list from the time, may not have meant much,
but that didn't stop her singing every lyric as if it had all the gravitas of
Sinatra's 'My Way'. And Gwen Stefani truly knew how to work the stage
and the crowd, flexing her slight body sensually, as if she were on the yoga
mat, and rolling her eyes lasciviously at the full house. Hardly the Anaheim
wallflower.

The band's individual roles were becoming well defined: Gwen Stefani
was the flamboyant frontwoman, sexy enough to excite the men in the
moshpit, but not so provocative or sluttish that she'd alienate the band's
many female fans. She was also coming into her own in matters of on-stage
fashion: It's safe to say that no other singer in their third wave world dressed
as distinctively as Gwen Stefani.

Her brother Eric had also found his place; buried away in the background, playing piano, directing the musical traffic but keeping well out of
the spotlight – literally. (Well, at least until he stepped forward, mid-set, for
a faux mariachi throwaway – cleverly titled 'The Matador' – that included
some half-assed cape-waving and general mayhem. All it proved was that
the band needed better filler and that centrestage was best left to his sister.)

As for Tony Kanal, he was behaving like some lost kid brother of the
Chili Peppers: His frantic, hyperactive on-stage bouncing owed plenty to
Flea, while his tied-back mane suggested Anthony Kiedis on a bad hair day.
And the buttoned-up jumpsuit that he was sporting at the time – well, who
knows? The matching gold hoops in his earlobes gave the Indian bassman
the appearance of a dark-eyed gypsy, something that wasn't lost on the ladies
up front of the stage. No Doubt clearly had sex appeal, albeit in a G-rated,
"don't-offend-the-parents" kind of way. In between laps of the stage, his
head bobbing to the insistent rhythms, Kanal acted as on-stage MC, while
keeping a watchful eye on his girlfriend and bandmate.

Guitarist Dumont, as much the quiet achiever of the band as Eric Stefani,
preferred to stay one step back, peeling off skyscraping riffs and just as
quickly reverting to the requisite 'ska-ta-ta' rhythm work needed to keep
this ska-punk-rock show on the road. His live stringwork was invaluable; he
filled the flat spots in Stefani's songs with urgent, muscular riffing and

soloing. Producer Dito Godwin, who was soon to connect with the band, recognised that Dumont was a "hot" guitarist and ensured he had plenty of solos on their first album. "I didn't want to lose it; I wanted him to play," Godwin said.

But this was Gwen Stefani's show: during 'Total Hate' – their live centre-piece at the time, complete with blasts of horn, stop-start rhythms and another explosive burst of guitar fire from Dumont – she prowled the stage, totally in control, occasionally launching herself into an athletic drop-kick that John Spence would have found hard to beat. During 'Paulina', a mid-tempo song as close to trad 2-Tone ska as the band came, Eric Stefani enjoyed a rare few moments on the mic, trading vocal lines with his sister, yet refusing to emerge from the rear-stage shadows. Once again, each member of the brass section was granted a solo, wrenching surprisingly clean notes from the venue's murky mix.

'Paulina' was a particular favourite of the crowd, as was 'Brand New Day', the band's signature song. This set-closer sent the moshpit into convulsions: Kanal's jackhammer riffing on the bass had spines shuddering from one end of the room to the other. Yet while Kanal may have looked after most of the introductions, Dumont may have been the man with the chops, Young may have kept the beat and Eric Stefani pumped out the tunes, all eyes were on Gwen.

That was most definitely the case, however, when No Doubt made a rare TV appearance on short-lived LA cable show The Tube. They performed another track that would make their debut LP, 'Big City Train', as well as 'Up Yours', an Eric Stefani tune that would turn up two years later on another Moon Ska Records compilation (entitled *California Ska-Quake, Vol. 1*). The band, with Hammerstedt notably absent, was wedged onto a tiny sound stage – at one point, Kanal and Dumont (both clearly in the middle of their long-haired, big-shorted period) almost bumped heads as they did their best to claim their own six inches of space. Carpenter and Gonzalez, meanwhile, were squeezed shoulder-to-shoulder in the background, rubbing elbows with the boyish, fair-haired Young and his ever-expanding drum kit.

Gwen was now sporting roomy orange dungarees, a look the ever-alert singer-cum-designer had 'borrowed' from the video for Dexys Midnight Runners' 1982 smash, 'Come On Eileen', and would eventually force on the horn section. The camera showed some fleeting interest in the stark, Eric Stefani-designed, 2-Tone-inspired No Doubt logo splashed all over Dumont's T-shirt, but kept flashing back to the human live wire fronting the band.

During the clumsy, nervous interview that followed, Gwen took the lead. "We've been together about three years now," she stated in her immediately recognisable chirp. "We have a demo tape but we're in the middle of recording right now; we're probably going to be putting it out on a CD, but we're trying to get signed right now." Very much the band's head of propaganda, Kanal interjected briefly that Flea helped with the demo, while Fishbone's Angelo Moore sang some back-ups.

When asked who wrote the songs, all fingers pointed in the direction of Eric Stefani who, as always, lurked on the edge of screen, almost out of shot. "Eric mainly does all the writing," Gwen says, "He's really creative."

The trouble, of course, was that Eric's songs about dental pain, self-abuse and break-ups were a tough fit. While No Doubt was raising the roof at Spanky's, the US charts were clogged with the big-haired balladeering of Michael Bolton, who squeezed out the treacly 'How Am I Supposed To Live Without You' as if someone were removing part of his large intestine. His chart-mates included the bland mainstream blatherings of sometimes Genesis timekeeper Phil Collins ('Another Day In Paradise'), Foreigner belter Lou Gramm ('Just Between You And Me'), Cher ('Just Like Jesse James') and Rod Stewart (a mediocre cover of Tom Waits' 'Downtown Train'). Swedes Roxette were 'Dangerous', New Kids on the Block were insisting that 'This One's For The Children', the Amazonian Taylor Dayne was over-cooking 'With Every Beat Of My Heart' and ageing rockers Aerosmith were reinventing themselves with 'Janie's Got A Gun'.

The UK charts, meanwhile, had a similarly bland outlook, with Oz soapie stars Jason Donovan ('When You Come Back To Me') and Kylie Minogue ('Tears On My Pillow') cashing in on their crossover appeal, and Jive Bunny & The Mastermixers insisting 'Let's Party'. Elsewhere, Black Box, Lisa Stansfield and Mantronix were cranking out Eurovision-standard dance pop.

Stuck somewhere between the spandex and priapism of hair metal and the simmering grunge underground, the mainstream was a creative wasteland at the turn of the decade. The simple fact that the miming, mincing Milli Vanilli would scam a Grammy for Best New Artist – only to subsequently have it rescinded, in one of the institution's biggest scandals – proved just how desperate the state of pop was in 1990.

There was a similarly vacuous quality to the year's highest-selling songs: Two of the top five ('Love Takes Time' and 'Vision Of Love') were squawked by Mariah Carey, a small woman in an even smaller dress. Irish firebrand Sinead O'Connor had been tamed, crooning Prince's 'Nothing Compares 2 U' with sufficient meekness and surrender to reach the

Number two spot on *Billboard's* Top 100 songs of 1990. It was also the year of Vanilla Ice, Paula Abdul, Bell Biv DeVoe, Janet Jackson and Stevie B. It was impossible to imagine how songs like 'Paulina' or 'Trapped In A Box' fitted with such slick chart fodder, or how a band such as No Doubt – all, bar Gwen Stefani, looking every inch a stylist's nightmare – could insinuate itself into the mainstream or onto MTV. The situation didn't improve when Nirvana, Pearl Jam and No Doubt's role models The Red Hot Chili Peppers started to emerge from the underground in the early Nineties. How the hell did No Doubt fit in a world of brawny riffs, flannel shirts, funked-up rock and existential angst? Did this band actually belong anywhere?

Interscope's Tony Ferguson read the situation pretty clearly; he understood that No Doubt was a live sensation but not necessarily a natural fit on the all-important airwaves. "At the time," he said, "Pearl Jam and Nirvana [who Ferguson, unwisely, had passed on, albeit without hearing 'Smells Like Teen Spirit'] were breaking and nobody wanted to hear an eight-piece horn section [sic] with a girl from Orange County doing ska retro-disco-metal-funk. But the kids did. I would go to the shows in Orange County and up here [LA], and they were selling out. Kids were stage-diving to this with Pearl Jam and Pantera T-shirts on." Ferguson, who was to play a pivotal role in the rise of No Doubt when he signed the band in August 1991, simply had to work out a way to make Middle America understand.

Saxophonist Eric Carpenter was as surprised as the rest of the band by Ferguson's enthusiasm. "We had played so many "showcase" shows where record companies either passed after seeing us or never showed up at all," he said. "Personally, I wasn't convinced it would ever happen. But Tony Ferguson saw something in the band. And when he arranged for us to play for [head of Interscope Records] Jimmy Iovine, we started to understand, hey this might just happen this time. The musical atmosphere was not ideal for the time we signed, but I don't think we let that influence us too much. We never talked about trying to sound more like Nirvana or Alice In Chains. It just wasn't a possibility. We admired those bands, but knew we had to stay true to our sound, and people would find us."

Expat Brit Ferguson was a good man to have on the band's side. He understood ska-pop and punk, having worked with Stiff Records, the label of Elvis Costello, Ian Dury, the Damned and Nick Lowe, during the late 1970s. As a sound engineer, and then a tour manager-cum-sound guy, Ferguson helped these English acts find their feet (and their sound) during their early tours of America. But Ferguson's connection with music ran deeper than that. Like another successful expat Brit, Peter Asher, who'd struck A&R gold with many of the West Coast singer/strummers of the

Seventies, Ferguson was originally a musician. In his late teens, during the 1960s, Ferguson had been a member of the band Unit 4+2, who had a worldwide hit with the easy-listening singalong 'Concrete And Clay', which reached the UK Top 5 in 1965, and the more soulful 'You've Never Been In Love Like This Before', which peaked in the British Top 10 during June 1965. The band's star started to fade when they dabbled in psychedelia with 1966's 'I Was Only Playing Games' and they split in 1969. But, as the All-Music Guide would note: 'Unit 4+2 was a one-hit wonder that probably deserved better.'

By now, Ferguson had a taste for the pop life; he tried to replicate Unit 4+2's brief success, this time as a guitarist with the band Christie, which was fronted by the Leeds-born Jeff Christie. Touted as the Limey Creedence Clearwater Revival, Christie, like Unit 4+2, started with a flurry, charting highly in the UK with its 1970 debut, 'Yellow River', and then almost repeating the effort with 'San Bernardino'. Yet despite the recruitment of another Unit 4+2 alumnus, Howard Lubin, and the support of Columbia Records prez Clive Davis, Christie slipped into obscurity in the early Seventies.

With the 1974 oil crisis hitting the European circuit especially hard, Ferguson looked Stateside. "I decided that I had had enough of England," Ferguson said in an interview with www.taxi.com. "The music business was getting really stale over there and America was just like this wealth of possibilities. [And] I always loved America."

In his mid-thirties, Ferguson established himself in New York during the early Eighties, doing time as a road manager for re-formed suburban rockers Grand Funk Railroad. He also road-managed saxman Clarence Clemons and the various side projects of other members of Bruce Springsteen's E Street Band. This is how he met Jimmy Iovine, who'd helped engineer and mix the working class hero's immortal *Born To Run* album, and produced long-players from such stars as Tom Petty, Patti Smith, Dire Straits and Bob Seger.

Working in tandem with Iovine, for the best part of three years Ferguson co-managed Lone Justice, a band led by the hugely under-rated Maria McKee. During that time, Iovine had shifted coasts to LA. "He called me up one day when the Lone Justice thing was petering out and not happening anymore," Ferguson recalled. "He said, 'There's a plane ticket for you to come out to LA.' I said, 'What for?', and he said, 'I don't know. Just come out. LA is great.'"

Ferguson took the plunge in the winter of 1985, when Iovine had been hired as a consultant to upgrade A&M's West Coast studio. Straight away,

Ferguson noted something curious: While the music business may have remained in New York, all the talent had headed west. He moved his family to the West Coast, and decided to stay.

Iovine was a savvy player, who, in Ferguson's words, "knew that the power of the music industry was basically at the labels. He wanted to form a label for the longest time." Iovine was also a shrewd businessman, according to Linda Perry, who'd recorded for Interscope as part of 4 Non Blondes before falling out with the label. She would later freelance for Interscope as a songwriter on Gwen Stefani's first solo LP.

"You don't have to like people, but I definitely respect him," Perry explained. "And I might not like Interscope as a label but I respect him as a businessman. I always admired him; he's definitely someone who has done a fucking lot of shit, especially in his producer years. He's made some great music."

However, Iovine early attempt to set up a boutique label with Ferguson failed, despite an injection of cash from A&M. Their fortunes changed when Ted Field, best known as the producer of such Hollywood hits as *Revenge Of The Nerds*, *Cocktail* and *Bill & Ted's Excellent Adventure*, got on board, and Interscope Records was born. (Interscope was the name of Field's holding company.) Ferguson recalled, "Jimmy said, 'Well, what do you want to do?' I said, "' don't know. A&R sounds fine.' And that's what I ended up doing." The label was established in 1990, with the help of some serious dollars from Atlantic Records, who held a 50 percent stake in Interscope.

In some ways, Interscope's success echoed Ferguson's days as a performer: They hit hard and fast, although not necessarily with the coolest act on the planet. The label's first release, 'Rico Suave' from Ecuadorian-born rapper-cum-beefcake Gerardo, went Top 5 in the US in the spring of 1991. But Gerardo quickly learned, as The All-Music Guide astutely noted, "dance-pop and teen-pop audiences can be incredibly fickle" and he fell from favour, the limelight and the charts. Nevertheless, the hits continued for Interscope: Marky Mark (aka future Hollywood hunk Mark Wahlberg) and his Funky Bunch's debut LP, *Music For The People*, went Platinum in early 1992, proving that fluff sells. (*The Rolling Stone Album Guide* summed up the record perfectly: "[It's] an album of innocuous white rap ... unexciting stuff, but harmless." The kids of America clearly agreed.)

Iovine wanted to prove that there was more substance to Interscope. Said Ferguson, "Jimmy always had this affiliation with black music ... [and] saw a great opening for rap." Iovine figured that if he could find an outfit that could grab the attention of both white suburban teens and black kids from the 'hood, he'd have an act that could be bigger than Guns N' Roses. Accordingly, Interscope set up a distribution deal with Death Row

Records, the creation of Dr Dre, hip-hop's very own Phil Spector, and Marion "Suge" Knight. (If Dre was the brains of Death Row, the often-violent Knight was definitely the brawn – his frequent stretches behind bars proving that beyond any doubt.) Despite the monumental sales of such records as Snoop Doggy Dogg's *Doggystyle* and Tupac Shakur's *All Eyez On Me*, the association between Interscope and Death Row was incredibly volatile: Iovine and his people were dragged into an altercation with the DC-based National Coalition of Black Women, while Time Warner put pressure on MCA not to distribute such hardcore hip-hop. The vitriol directed at Death Row (and, by association, Interscope), blew up into one of the biggest music industry controversies of the Nineties.

At the same time, Ferguson, in his A&R role, was eyeing "this little Orange County band . . . called No Doubt." Although No Doubt seemed a very uncomfortable fit for Interscope, especially in the midst of the whole Death Row imbroglio, Ferguson could sense that the band had commercial appeal. And he had his own reasons for eventually signing them. "I grew up with ska . . . I loved ska," he said. But he knew it was a sizeable risk; as he saw it, "I was in the wrong place with the right band."

Ferguson had checked out many of the third wave bands, including The Mighty Mighty Bosstones and Let's Go Bowling, and felt that they shared one thing: "Zero songs. . . All of them were about the beat and the fun. They were like frat party bands," he explained. "They could pack out a club on Saturday night, and you'd have one hell of a time dancing your ass off, but I could never see radio catching on." But Ferguson sensed that there was more to No Doubt than the soundtrack to another liquored-up weekend free-for-all. He also saw the potential star-power of Gwen Stefani.

Before signing on to produce the Orange County hopeful's first album, producer Dito Godwin, a colleague and long-time friend of Ferguson's sat in on numerous No Doubt/Interscope meetings, and got a feeling that "they would have signed Gwen to a solo deal in a second" if the "band thing" didn't pan out (pretty close to the way things happened, when viewed from a 2007 perspective).

Interscope chief Jimmy Iovine was more direct. He took Gwen Stefani aside and told her that within six years she'd be a "huge star". Stefani's stunned response showed just how green she was when it came to the business of music. "I was like, first of all, who the hell are you? And second of all, I'm not going to be in this band six years from now. I'm going to be having 14 children and be married," she said.

★　★　★

In the lead-up to the Interscope signing in August 1991, No Doubt continued to do what they did best, playing live, despite their ongoing difficulties in hanging on to horn players. Gabe Gonzalez departed in 1990; leaving a brass section of Eric Carpenter, Don Hammerstedt and trombonist Alex Henderson – the ensemble that would blow together on the first No Doubt album.

Each had come to the band in their own unusual way. Hammerstedt answered an ad that was posted in Bionic Records, the local music store in his home city of Cypress, California, and was asked to join at his audition. He was something of an anomaly. Several years older than the rest of the band, he was the only member not living at home. Prior to No Doubt, Hammerstedt had played trumpet for Argentinean Latin rock ensemble Harry y Sus Palangas (later shortened, thankfully, to Bersuit).

Carpenter was the brother of Dave Carpenter, both friends of Tony Kanal since their days at Anaheim High. "The band didn't pay full-time wages but required full-time commitment," Carpenter, now a staff writer at the *OC Register*, wrote in a 1997 reflection on his time in the group. "I was one of several members throughout the band's history who needed to find other avenues when things got tough. In my case, it was a return to journalism school." He had grown up in a housing development that he later learned had once been the family farm of legendary guitar-maker Leo Fender. Although his parents weren't musical, they appreciated music, taking Eric and Dave to the annual Playboy Jazz Festival and escorting them to a lot of rock shows. "Santana was my first real concert at age 11," Carpenter said. "They took us to The Who, The Clash, U2. They really supported our interest." His early musical heroes were jazzmen: Branford Marsalis, Joe Lovano, Michael Brecker. "Tony [Kanal] was the one who turned me onto bands like Fishbone and The Specials and The Beat. I loved the raw energy of that playing. [But] it wasn't until I joined No Doubt that I found people like Desmond Dekker."

As soon as Carpenter joined the band, Eric Stefani put him through a crash course in ska, often passing along CDs. "[It] was almost like homework," Carpenter said. It quickly became clear to the saxophonist why ska was leaving its mark in southern California. "I think a couple of things about So-Cal culture made it a fertile place for appreciation of 2-Tone. One, it's a very culturally diverse area and the message of 2-Tone appealed to a lot of people of my generation. And secondly, I think the Jamaican origin found a home in the beach culture of So-Cal – the sound was something different, more upbeat than the punk music that was out there." Carpenter made his No Doubt debut on July 16, 1988, at The Roxy, opening for Fishbone.

As for Alex Henderson, he joined the band as a result of pure serendipity. He'd been playing trombone since elementary school because, as he said in early 2006, "they needed tall kids with long arms" for the school band. Like Hammerstedt, Henderson had a musical history that was a world away from the 2-Tone/Disneyland roots of much of the band. "I was more like a jazz instrumentalist guy," he said, "and I played some bass in a pop band." Henderson's record collection was littered with older, classic jazz records and Latin jazz albums, but at the same time he had a muso's natural curiosity towards 2-Tone and the sound of Madness and The Specials.

He'd seen No Doubt open for Ziggy Marley at the Irvine Meadows Amphitheatre show in August 1990, one of the band's most high profile supports to date. "I'd never heard of No Doubt," he admitted, "but I thought, "Wow, these guys are great"." Henderson knew Don Hammerstedt, who he recalls was wearing "loud, baggy pants" at this gig and was easy to pick out of the after-show crowd. He wanted to ask about No Doubt, but just when he spotted Hammerstedt, Henderson had to answer the call of nature – "I was busting for a piss" – and when he returned from the bathroom, Hammerstedt and his loud trousers were gone.

Henderson finally got lucky a few months later at The Stomp Box. He was rehearsing with his own band, when he caught a glimpse of Hammerstedt wearing those very same trousers. He offered his services to No Doubt on the spot and the band agreed, but only if Henderson would play an upcoming LA showcase for free, as a trial run. The showcase was a success and Henderson was in.

"The cool thing about No Doubt," Henderson said, "was this blending of styles they had going on. It wasn't all ska."

To Eric Carpenter, the band's mix-and-match style didn't mesh with what else was happening in the live scene at the time. "The band's upbeat ska-influenced rock-pop sound was a risk in the late Eighties in Los Angeles," he said, "where leather and hairspray were as mandatory as guitars and drums. [But] the musical gamble paid off with a loyal following in Orange County and Los Angeles."

The downside was that the band barely generated enough cash from shows to cover essentials. In all his time with No Doubt, Eric Carpenter's greatest backstage indulgence was occasionally receiving "dry towels and a six pack of beer. We all had other jobs when I was in the band," he said. "Playing gigs was our hobby; we did it because we loved it, not because it paid a damn." But according to Alex Henderson, the hired men of the horn section fared better than the rest of the band. "We were actually on a weekly salary on the road," he recalled. And the nights that the brassmen spent at

Motel 6 while on the road did its bit to bring the horn section closer together. Henderson recalled that on most nights it would typically be "two guys [sleeping] in one bed and one on the floor."

When Carpenter completed his 1993 tax return, he realised that he'd accumulated a grand total of $905 from working with the band; yet at the same time he relished the challenge that came about from playing to unfamiliar audiences, or the thrill in packing small rooms. "When we played sold-out shows, we played to 500 people in intimate clubs, where you could see all the faces in the crowd," Carpenter stated. "[And] while touring we could walk into a new town and sight-see without being hounded."

He did, however, have some trouble being known as a "hired hand"; his role in the band changed considerably once they signed to Interscope. "The label asked, "Who is the band?" And the guys in the band – Gwen, Tony, Tom, Adrian and Eric – decided that the horn section was ancillary. We'd never faced these decisions before, and it was difficult to face being on the outside," he said. "We'd be signing band photos after gigs and people would be asking, "But where's the horn section?""

With Gwen Stefani now in her early twenties, the family curfew had been lifted and the band was able to play gigs without having to race her home immediately afterwards. However, all of the 28 shows they played in 1990 were in their Californian safety zone. Spanky's in Riverside and The Roxy in LA became regular gigs, and the band returned to other such familiar haunts as the Elks Lodge in Orange, Pomona College in Claremont and the campus of Cal State in Fullerton. Their set lists were also becoming well established, as the band began to understand what songs worked best live. 'Trapped In A Box', 'Brand New Day', 'Get On The Ball', 'Paulina', 'Let's Get Back', and, inexplicably, 'The Matador', were all live standards.

The core members of the band were also starting to stake out their territory. Gwen Stefani was becoming more and more involved in the band's on-stage look; she even inflicted her faux-Dexys threads on the horn section. "[The] funny overalls [were] not particularly my style," Henderson said diplomatically. For one gig, Stefani dressed as Little Bo Peep; Kanal played an entire set wearing a tiger outfit; Young wore less and less the more established he became. "They were more like events and less like regular gigs," Henderson figured.

As one of the band's hired hands, Henderson was sufficiently removed to see how the band operated. "Gwen was the central figure on stage," he said. "She had a bunch of different outfits that she had made and wore on stage. She really had an eye for that." Henderson also felt that she had the ideal voice for her brother's songs; interestingly, he recalls her doing vocal exercises before most shows, on the suggestion of Eric (maybe they'd learned something from their time with the guys from Spot, after all). "I thought she had a great voice," Henderson said. "She could belt out songs but she also had this high vibrato."

As for the rest of the band, their roles were also clearly defined. "Tony was the business guy," Henderson recalled. "He was signing the cheques and paying the sidemen. And Eric [Stefani] did a lot of the creative stuff, writing the songs, designing the logo, coming up with the artwork. Eric seemed in charge of things; I got along with him, he's a cool cat."

Henderson willingly took on a role as the band's funny bone, often cooling down tense moments with his catalogue of jokes and impersonations. Then he'd step forward for his big musical moment, the solo during 'Paulina', which he'd improvise most nights. He found it peculiar, however, that the Stefanis "were always worried about what their parents would think", often changing lyrics and not swearing when their folks were in earshot. "Yet that song "Paulina" is about masturbation," he pointed out.

★ ★ ★

Looking back, 1990 was a year of stabilisation for No Doubt. They'd further established their rep as a dependable live band – within the radius of a few hundred miles of the Californian coastline, that is – and had built up a reasonably large catalogue of original tunes, which were now well and truly road tested. And just around the corner lurked their much-hoped-for major label deal, thanks to the enthusiasm of Tony Ferguson.

They brought the year to a close with another full house at the Whisky. Looking on at the gig was Dito Godwin, who had been taped produce their debut album. He knew straight away how the record should sound. "These were, and still are, great players," he told me. "I looked at their chops and [decided to] step back."

It was still a long eight months between their blazing set at the Whisky, signing up with Interscope and then recording with Godwin. Uncharacteristically, after the Whisky show the band took a three month break from gigging, returning in March 1991 for the usual rounds of college shows (University of California Santa Barbara; Cal State Northridge) and such familiar venues as Hollywood's The Roxy and La Palma Park in Anaheim. But it was all a prelude to sessions for their first "proper" recordings.

As helpful as it was in getting the band signed to the William Morris Agency, the "Flea tape" – two tracks, 'Big City Train' and 'Doormat' (featuring Angelo Moore) produced by Flea – was not much more than a way to introduce No Doubt to the few labels who showed any interest in this "little band from Orange County". Recorded in January 1990 at Santa Monica's Ground Control studio, with money borrowed from Goldenvoice's Paul Tollett, they weren't release-quality recordings. As Kanal would tell *Bass Player* magazine, "It was when Flea was on the cover of *Spin*; I was 19, and it was a really big deal for me. It was Adrian's first studio experience and it was just horrendous. It wasn't Flea's fault; we just weren't ready – I remember Flea trying to show Adrian how to play beats. But that experience helped make Adrian the great drummer he is today."

Eric Carpenter, however, was surprised by the bassman's work on the demos. "I only knew Flea as this party guy, but I couldn't have been more impressed," he said

What No Doubt needed was a professional producer. But the path that led Dito Godwin to the band was just as long and winding as Tony Ferguson's journey from one-hit-wonderdom to No Doubt cheerleader at Interscope. Godwin had been formally trained on violin, and was part of a duo, called Touched, formed with a high school buddy. They renamed themselves Atlantis, were signed, briefly, to RCA and then, after another name change (this time to GCB), they signed to London Records. Despite support slots with such high-profile acts as Supertramp and Deborah Harry, "a Yoko broke up the duo", according to Godwin. At the age of 28, he gave up performing and shifted to LA to sniff out production work.

Godwin had worked with Interscope and Tony Ferguson before producing the No Doubt debut, recording a band called Newton's Law, who were led by a talented, volatile African-American named Tony Newton. Godwin saw the potential in an all-black hard rock band, a la Living Colour, but Newton proved too hard to handle. "The leader of the band was completely insane," Godwin laughed. Jimmy Iovine signed them, attempted to produce the album and backed off. Peter Frampton, of all people, did likewise, but ended up in the studio carpark with Newton, slugging it out. Godwin was then called in to finish the LP and along the way found the perfect remedy for Newton's volatility: high-grade pot. "He was a hothead guy but an incredible musician," Godwin recalled, "and he didn't pull any of that crap with me." However, despite sinking thousands of dollars into the project, the album stiffed and Interscope dropped the band. "It went nowhere on the nowhere express," the colourful Godwin said. It wasn't Interscope's finest hour.

Soon after, possibly as payback for his perseverance with Newton, Ferguson called Godwin from the road and offered him the No Doubt job. Godwin's original mandate was pretty simple: Ferguson only asked him to "repair" Gwen's vocals, because the band had already laid down serviceable tracks by themselves at South Coast Recording in Santa Ana.

There are two versions of what happened next: Godwin today insists that he worked on Ferguson and got him to OK re-recording all the tracks bar Young's drums. In 1995, however, Gwen Stefani said that the band "begged [Interscope] to let us re-record it, and we wanted to go in a better studio." (Curiously, in the same interview, Stefani stated "there was no real producer" for their debut LP, something Godwin hotly denies. His co-production credit alone is proof enough.)

Godwin and band set up camp in Hollywood's A&R Studios, but he split his time between two projects: during the week he'd record with a "prototype grunge" band called St Thomas, cutting tracks for an album called *Electric City*. He'd give No Doubt his full attention on Fridays, Saturdays and Sundays. Godwin's two bands would sometimes pass each other in the corridors of A&R. "[These were] very different bands – and everyone was just staring at Gwen. It was interesting," he chuckled.

Helping Godwin out behind the desk was renowned engineer Michael Carnevale, a portly fellow dubbed "the round mound of sound", who had first met Godwin many years earlier in Toronto. According to Godwin, Carnevale was a legend, who'd learned his trade under producer Tom Dowd, who was himself "in every single way a genius". And Dowd's CV is remarkable; he had produced enormous hits for everyone from Rod Stewart to Eric Clapton, Cream to Booker T & The MGs, Aretha Franklin to Meatloaf. Carnevale's credits, which included Tom Petty & The Heartbreaker's *Long After Dark*, the *Grease* soundtrack, various soft-rock hits from Chicago and Eric Clapton's *Money And Cigarettes*, were equally impressive. In short, studio royalty was working on the No Doubt LP. Godwin knew that, too. "Carnevale took the steam out of my game; he showed me true studio etiquette, which he'd learned from Tom Dowd."

Despite his best efforts, Godwin only managed to squeeze $15,000 US from Interscope for the sessions, even though "we wanted at least double that". But apart from this conflict, his rapport in the studio with Ferguson was solid. "Tony was pretty cool; he was definitely not a pain in the ass. He would come down to the studio a lot but would spend time making calls. I tried to be Captain Kirk at the bridge, but he was the record company and I appreciated that."

The only person that Godwin clashed with was Tony Kanal. "We locked horns in the first week," he recalled. "It was not pleasant; not pleasant at all. [There] was too much testosterone; a power struggle ensued. I was the guy hired by the record company, I'd made a lot more records than anyone in the band, so I exerted a sense of confidence. But I was always open to ideas, especially from the creators of the music. I tried to make that clear early on."

As Godwin read the situation, he needed to win Kanal's approval before they could work together comfortably. And this did eventually happen – they're still friends some 15 years later. "Winning Tony Kanal over was my acceptance to the band; we became very tight. Tony's not a follower," he added. "He's been in charge of that band for a long time and this was their first opportunity to make a record for a record company." After a while, Godwin would refer to Kanal as 'Blue Sky'. "He filled the space in each song, in a good way." And interestingly, despite the clandestine way that the Kanal / Stefani romance was handled at the time of *Tragic Kingdom*, they were very public with their relationship in 1991. "And Eric [Stefani] was very cool with it, too," Godwin recalled, which shoots down many subsequent reports that Gwen's big brother felt uneasy with their inner-band romance.

"I had an interesting vantage point to Gwen and Tony's early relationship," added saxman Eric Carpenter. "Tony was my good friend, so he confided some in me early on. They were clearly very in love. But they also respected the band and knew that it wouldn't go over well that they were dating. So Tony was anxious about that. He didn't want to ruin the relationship with Gwen or with the band, so he found himself walking a tightrope. Gwen's whole family was protective of her and Eric, and beyond that, it was like having seven other brothers because the entire band was protective of her."

Obviously Kanal didn't realise it at the time, but his tug-of-love with Stefani – his first "real" girlfriend, a fellow member of his first "real" band – would provide juicy subject matter for some of No Doubt's best songs. And the "tightrope" that Kanal was walking surely contributed to his decision, a couple of years later, to end their romance. It must have made for some uncomfortable times, having his private life put on full display by his lover – not that the poker-faced Kanal gave too much away, of course.

It also didn't take Godwin long to work out that the elder Stefani was the brains of the operation. "He managed the music; he was wild," Godwin said. "He was the guy with most of the sounds. He was the heart and soul of the band, absolutely."

Carpenter agreed. "Eric was definitely the creative force [of the band]. His artwork defined the style of the band, and he had a great mind for music."

Although he'd only see the band play once, at The Roxy, Godwin knew that all of their songs had been well and truly worked out. So his job during the sessions was fairly simple. "[There were] not a lot of takes," Godwin recalled. "My job was more about creating the atmosphere and saying the right words. It was partly motivational, like using keywords in an Internet search." And despite the hiccup with Kanal, group and producer developed a strong connection. "There was a very warm rapport between the band and myself," Godwin figured. "I don't want to pound my chest too much, but nobody except the band, the engineer and myself know the shape I put this band into compared with how they were when they came in[to the studio]. They could play their asses off, with really good material and a phenomenal lead singer, but musically it wasn't together. I think they took some of the good habits they learned from me and went on and had a successful career. I'm certainly not the only person responsible for their rise to fame, but I'm one of the guys who helped. A first album should be like deflowering a band and I feel like I accomplished that."

Looking back, Godwin's only lingering beef is the co-production credit that was given to the band (despite Gwen Stefani's suggestions that Godwin "just sat back" during the sessions). He said, "Should they have [that] credit on the album? Hmmm, I don't know. They came to the table with a lot of parts, but I changed a lot of the parts and produced the record like I always have and have continued to do. [But] they showed up ready, willing and able and took direction quite nicely. Tony Kanal and I bumped heads a couple of times within the first week but that smoothed out and we were on the same page for the rest of the record." Kanal, however, did impress Godwin in two ways: with his rock-solid playing and his sheer bloody-minded devotion to the band. (Kanal would become a regular face in the Interscope mailroom, using the company's resources to update the ever-expanding No Doubt mailing list. "[He] would come in here with boxes of flyers to mail out for their shows," Tony Ferguson said. "The mail-room guys would cringe . . . there were literally hundreds and hundreds and hundreds of these mail-outs.")

"Personally," Godwin said, "I would have made him the head of the band's promotion. He's quiet and unassuming but very pushy, very intelligent. He'd be cracking the whip at Interscope. [He and the band] were amazingly diligent about the business of No Doubt. They ran it like a business and they did not fuck around. I've used their attitude as a business model ever since; up-and-coming bands could take a lesson from the organisational skills of No Doubt. I haven't seen anything like that since."

This business-first approach extended into band downtime; Godwin recalled that the sessions were powered by "the occasional beer and lots of

Chinese". And his stimulant of choice? "I'm not going to get into that," he chuckled enigmatically. The band did not imbibe, of course.

★ ★ ★

As in so many of their shows, No Doubt opened their self-titled debut long-player —dedicated to their fallen frontman, John Spence – with the blink-and-you'll-miss-it instrumental 'BND' (as in 'Brand New Day'), which was basically an opportunity for the band to kick out the jams, all in the space of 45 seconds.

They then slipped comfortably into the New Wave-flavoured groove of 'Let's Get Back', and straight away Godwin's plans to get the brass section front and centre became very clear – he's convinced that this track was the best example on the record of the punchiness of the horns. Don Hammerstedt's trumpet, in particular, ruled the mix, while the interplay between Dumont's funked-up guitar, Kanal's sinewy bass and Young's dependable time keeping made this live favourite even more of a pelvis grinder on record. As for the lyric, well, Eric Stefani had little of substance to say. Regardless, Godwin knew that the band should lead with their musical ace. "What makes a long song great," he explained, "is when it feels like it flies by – and that song does. It's an excursion of musical styles, all kicking my ass one at a time. Everything that the band could do was happening there. There's a jazz trumpet solo in there, there's a steaming guitar solo in there – people don't know how good Tom is as a player until they listen to my record, where he played his ass off."

'Ache' was the next track, Eric Stefani's ode to dental pain, the same song that hastened the end of the relationship between the guys from Spot and No Doubt. Godwin pulled another top-shelf performance from the band – almost enough to overlook the eminently disposable subject matter. Even with additional lyrics from his sister Gwen, 'Get On The Ball' suffered the same shortcomings – in the pantheon of lost-love lyrics, "Don't wait too long or she'll be gone fast as a blink" wasn't going to change the world. Again, Godwin cranked up the brass section, especially during the helter-skelter outro; this added sonic muscle elevated what was a decidedly pedestrian track.

Interestingly, despite the very horn-heavy end result of 'Get On The Ball', and the album itself, producer Godwin found that recording the brass section was the most challenging few days of the entire process. Even though they'd played the parts dozens – maybe hundreds of times – the players had trouble reading the charts; they came into the sessions massively unprepared. So Godwin was forced to break down each player's parts and then stick with them "until they were fucking perfect.

"They were great players," he recalled, "but it was a real hair-puller."

One of the men in the midst of that huddle, Alex Henderson, had a slightly different take on the situation. Recording the horns was "challenging," Henderson agreed, "and they were long, long days, analysing each note. What made it harder was that they [Interscope] wanted it to sound like a pop record. I think the horns sound fine; they're pretty tight. But it was a very revealing exercise, with everything under the microscope like that." (The long hours took their toll on the brass section; Eric Carpenter, who held down a day job in a tomato-canning factory, recalled turning up late for a shift after another lengthy recording session. "I raced to work back in Orange County and apologised to my boss as I ran to relieve the guy who worked before me," he said. "When he came down later, over the roar of machines, he asked why I was late. When I told him, he just laughed and said, 'You're not my typical employee. Good luck with that.'")

Tom Dumont was given centrestage for 'Move On', a co-write among all five band members. No Doubt's quiet achiever opened the track with 30 seconds of butt-ugly metal guitar, before the band settled into a more familiar ska-punk groove, only to drop back into a middle eight that was a blast of pure arena guitar from Dumont. But unlike 'Let's Get Back', a live favourite that was improved upon in the studio, 'Move On' dragged its feet for almost four tiresome minutes. Respite, however, was in sight, with the bleakly beautiful piano ballad, 'Sad For Me', another co-write from the Stefani siblings, written about Eric's former girlfriend, Jennifer Fried. One of the few songs on the album that simply doesn't try too hard, this is a showcase for Gwen's agile vocals and her brother's sometimes-astute sense of melody. Unlike 'Move On', it's over far too soon.

"Gwen was way confident as a vocalist, even then," Godwin insisted. "She knew exactly what to do. She was the MVP of that record – and her range was killer, absolutely killer. I wanted to make sure she performed the shit out of those songs, and that wasn't difficult." Of all the parts that Godwin produced for the record, Gwen's vocals needed the least work. "She had her shit together and flew through her tracks. I liked her very much; by the end of it we were all very close."

The band settled back into another hyperactive groove with 'Doormat', in which Kanal slapped his bass as if it had done him wrong – he even took the time out for a passable solo – while the horn section kept it tight and funky. Proving that the band wanted to structure the album tracklisting to replicate one of their gigs, the energy was kept on the boil with 'Big City Train', the next track, another live party-starter, although Gwen didn't deliver her best vocal (she slips in and out of the song as if she can't quite work out whether Godwin was recording).

'Trapped In A Box' followed, which was definitely the most interesting song the band had in their bag. Based around a taut guitar line from Dumont – who wrote the poem that inspired the "TV is messing with my head" lyric – 'Trapped' bounces between styles and sounds: while Dumont delivers another fretboard-burning solo, and the instrumental break is pure metal fury, there's also a Dixieland jazz fade out, which Godwin edited and mixed to sound as though the horns were emerging from a megaphone.

As quirky as the song was, to this day Godwin remains uncertain why it was chosen as the album's lead single. "[It] was never my pick, but it was certainly the label's. But grunge had appeared by this time and anything we released would have been a disaster. [But] it just didn't strike me as the magic tune."

Like 'Sad For Me' earlier in the record, the mid-tempo ballad 'Sometimes' is a showcase for Gwen's fast-improving vocals, but it just isn't as interesting or melodic a song. Instead, it veers gloomily towards the middle of the road. Her brother's muddle-headed lyric doesn't help any, either; Gwen sings as if she's reading from a cue card. The record then heads for home with another upbeat firestarter, 'Sinking', in which Godwin, searching for a little sonic colour, recorded the ringing of a buoy at sea, mixed with the sound of a jackhammer, taken from a library of sounds. This curiosity piece was followed by the gorge-yourself-until-you-drop nonsense of 'A Little Something Refreshing' – original guitarist Jerry McMahon received an arrangement credit, which showed how old this song was – and the faux 2-Tone sweetness of 'Paulina', Stefani's masturbatory valentine to Czech-born supermodel and not-so-super actress, Paulina Porizkova (whose husband, The Cars' Ric Ocasek, would work with No Doubt on *Rock Steady*). No Doubt then closed with the complete version of 'Brand New Day', the band's "people-together" anthem, a final opportunity to throw everything at the studio wall: Kanal's frantic slap bass, Dumont's blazing guitar work, some blaring horns, and the rest of it.

According to its producer, *No Doubt* wasn't purely a ska record, despite the band's strong links to the third wave scene (and the heavy 2-Tone influence of the album's artwork). Said Godwin, "It's beaming with a Latin feel, it's got jazz, it's got rock, although some of the parts are pure ska, especially that upstroke guitar stuff. But the music is multi-faceted. And it's the only album they ever recorded where the players really go off. I got a great performance from every son-of-a-bitch in that studio. There's not one bad song on that record," the garrulous

He added. "I can still listen to it. And it continues to sell, it's still in the stores, and I have no problem with that, either. Those royalties will keep coming in when you and I are tripping over our big white beards."

"I think our biggest frustration was trying to capture that live energy on tape," recalled Eric Carpenter. "At times it worked, but other times it fell short. My most vivid memory is the entire band setting up in the studio and playing together through professional microphones and earphones. We felt like, finally, here's our shot. In an ideal world, I think we would have had more studio time and more lead time to get to know Godwin. But in the end, we were happy with what we got on tape. It captured where we were musically at that time."

What Godwin, Interscope, Carpenter and the rest of band couldn't have predicted, of course, is that on its release on March 17, 1992, this "multi-faceted" record would become an ugly stepchild in the new musical world order. "[Tony] Ferguson loved the record and I was told that Jimmy Iovine liked it, too," Godwin said. "Initially everyone was in puppy dog heaven. Then Nirvana came along and fucked my whole thing up."

CHAPTER SIX

The Beacon Street Blues

"It would take an act of God to get this band on the radio."

–KROQ programmer, 1992

Generation grunge may have been about to wipe the smile from the face of No Doubt and Interscope, but that didn't mean that the band was dissatisfied with the end result of their debut LP. In fact, on January 27, 1992, two months prior to its official release, Eric Stefani wrote this gushing letter to Dito Godwin:

"Dear Dito, All of us in the band want to give you our thanks and appreciation for producing our first record. We all feel you blew away the tapes that we were going to originally re-mix; thank you for letting us re-record the entire album. You really captured the sound that we were looking for; your selectivity of each performance gave this album a certain perfectness, without sounding over polished. Personally, I was particularly happy with the way "Trapped In A Box" and "Sinking" came out, although I think all the tracks sound great. Everyone says that every time they listen to it, it sounds better and better. Thanks for putting up with Adrian's free-form drumming ["I had trouble keeping him in metre," Godwin explained], all the horn problems [Godwin: "Which were a fucking nightmare, pardon my French"] and all of my pinkies ["when Eric played the piano he would have sloppy finger posture and his finger would drop onto a key it wasn't supposed to, so there was a rotten chord that I had to catch each time"]. After recording with Michael and yourself I think we all found some areas that we need to concentrate on. I can hardly wait until we get the first copies printed up. Thanks again for making our dream come true and we hope to be working with you again in the future.

Sincerely, Eric Stefani and No Doubt"

This letter, which Godwin still has framed on his wall, contradicted Gwen Stefani's earlier comments about the producer being a virtual non-presence in the studio, and makes her comments all that much harder to understand. But, of course, by the time she made that observation the band were defending themselves against allegations that their party-hearty mix of styles was seriously out of touch with grunge's flannel-clad, life-sucks moaning. On more than one occasion, the band would accuse Interscope of failing to get behind the record. It seemed as though they wasted a lot of energy blaming others for bad timing, when they clearly should have sucked it up and started again.

"Looking back, we were naïve," Gwen Stefani said of their debut LP. "It was almost like an independent release, anyway – there was no push for the record [by Interscope] and no kind of support at all."

Tony Kanal had a more diplomatic take on the album's mixed fortunes, when he spoke to the *San Diego Union-Tribune* a few years after its release. "It's safe to say that the album was released into a radio environment that was not friendly to the kind of music we were playing," he understated neatly. "What we had to offer was not welcome." This was a fair call, given that the top five tracks on KROQ's Top 106.7 Countdown of 1992 came from The Red Hot Chili Peppers ('Under The Bridge'), Pearl Jam ('Jeremy'), The Cure ('Letter To Elise'), Nirvana ('Come As You Are') and U2 ('One').

Producer Godwin had a different spin on the indifferent response to the album and the band's blame-the-record-company attitude. "I think they were not happy with this record because it didn't happen [commercially]," he said, "But, quite frankly, other than *Tragic Kingdom*, none of their records have really exploded. The band probably does very well on the road financially, but in terms of record sales, well, this is not AC/DC. These guys had one album that absolutely exploded, and the others have sold a couple of million each."

It's also worth noting that in light of the success of *Tragic Kingdom*, sales of *No Doubt* also spiked considerably. It sold around 25,000 copies soon after release, mainly in southern California, yet currently sits at around 600,000 units shifted, according to Godwin's estimation. Not bad for an album with a $15,000 production budget.

Trombonist Alex Henderson recalled that Interscope did cough up the cash for a three-week road trip supporting the album. "The tours were fun," he added, "even though it was hard driving all day in a small van. They were bittersweet times, I guess, but it was an interesting way to see the country." After that first tour, however, Henderson sensed that Interscope started to look elsewhere, especially as *Nevermind*-mania was breaking out all over. Henderson felt that the label "had shelved [us]. I got the feeling that they couldn't tell if this band was popular or not. They were definitely out of step during grunge. You know, "Who is this crazy, eclectic band?" "

"We didn't spend a lot of money on the band," Tony Ferguson admitted, "but we kept their touring base. We kept the band on the road touring all the time." Ferguson also acknowledged that No Doubt was a self-sufficient band; they didn't need too much label input to keep moving (apart from unlimited access to the Interscope mail room, that is.)

"They are the smartest people I know," Ferguson continued. "They took care of themselves. They put their own merchandising together. They got their website together. They got their fan base together. I mean, they were very, very motivated. [And] it was growing all the time."

Promoter John Pantle, Tony Kanal's schoolfriend, who was now helping the band book gigs, noted how self-reliant the band was. "They read audiences and markets well, and they worked hard to reach their fans," he said in 2006. "In order to have a fan base before radio [support], before MySpace and the Internet, you had to send out thousands of flyers and mailers. So the band would have flyer and mailer parties at Gwen's house, and everyone would mail flyers and postcards while eating pizza."

Media response to the *No Doubt* album may have been thinly spread, but what did come through was mainly upbeat. (It didn't hurt that Prince declared himself a fan, which must have extracted a rare smile from Tony Kanal.) One of the most comprehensive reviews of the album came from the *Sunday Telegram* in Worcester, Massachusetts, way over on the East Coast. Music writer Craig S Semon was seriously smitten. "Combining elements of dance, ska, funk and rock," he wrote, "*No Doubt* is like a loony tooney musical ride, where anything can happen." He gave most of the kudos to the Stefanis, drawing a strong link between Eric's "parallel" career – having been an animator – on the Saturday morning kids show, *The New Adventures Of Mighty Mouse*, then Matt Groening's hugely popular *The Simpsons* – and the band's day-glo sounds. Semon also sensed the connection between Disneyland, "the happiest place on Earth" and the album. "After experiencing *No Doubt*," he wrote, "it's hard not to have a childish grin on your face."

Semon was also one of the first writers to get a handle on Gwen Stefani's grab bag of influences. "With sassy, fast-paced vocals," he noted, "Stefani captures the listener's attention instantly with a voice that sounds like a combination of Madonna and Dale Bozzio of the now-defunct Missing Persons." (Other writers would later describe her as "a cross between a Forties pin-up queen and a Marine sergeant", "a Forties starlet dressed in baggy skatepunk clothes", "Betty-Rubble-meets-Marilyn-Monroe" and a woman "who could be taken for a sweet-and-innocent younger cousin of Madonna." Her heliumated voice would often be compared to new waver Lene Lovich.)

Semon had none of Paul Oberman's concerns towards Eric Stefani's lyrics or whimsical tunes, describing 'Ache' as "offbeat"; 'Get On The Ball' as "a spirited love romp"; and 'Move On' as "a parable for the band's chemistry and one's individuality". While this was hardly *Rolling Stone* – that venerable rag would overlook No Doubt until they hit big with 'Just A Girl' – the band must have been chuffed by such a glowing review.

More coverage was to come: Less than a week after a mid-afternoon in-store record launch at Anaheim's Tower Records – "Finally, It's Here!" screamed the flyer doing the rounds of the band's home town – the *Los Angeles Times'* Mike Boehm gave the band their first serious national coverage.

In a wide-ranging piece, Boehm covered everything from the band's slow rise to the majors to their useful links with third wave ska and The Untouchables and Fishbone, and the suicide of John Spence. As for Stefani's "high, airy" voice, Boehm likened her to a "sometimes piercing combination of Madonna, Lene Lovich and Betty Boop", which was as good as any other assessment.

As for the band's debut album, Boehm wasn't quite as effusive as Semon from the *Sunday Telegram*, but he noted their theatricality and Gwen Stefani's "almost vaudevillian flair for acting out a song's story line". He dug quite deeply into Eric Stefani's lyrics – well, as deeply as you could – revealing that 'Ache' dealt with the removal of his wisdom teeth and how, during 'Sad For Me', Eric actually addressed his former girlfriend as 'Miss Fried'. ("Miss" Jennifer Fried, Eric's ex, was sufficiently impressed to write and congratulate the band on their album, a note that Stefani produced during the interview.) Boehm also noted that 'Let's Get Back' was Gwen Stefani's attempt at a reconciliation-by-song with Kanal, with whom she'd briefly fallen out.

Before the subject became a no-go zone for the press, Gwen Stefani told Boehm that she and Kanal "were trying to keep their relationship separate" from their roles in the band, but admitted, "it's bound to turn off and on" in its influence upon inner-band relations. They'd rarely be that straight up about their relationship as the band's star began to rise. (Paul Oberman sensed that Interscope determined how to handle the relationhip in interviews. He said, "They developed her so smartly – there was the whole Tony thing, the right video directors, a personal trainer, probably vocal lessons – the works.")

No Doubt was pleased with the attention from the *Los Angeles Times*. "The timing is good," Gween admitted. "If it had been earlier, it would have been too soon. Now we're all ready"

Soon after that first piece appeared, the band was back in the *Los Angeles Times*, talking up a gig at the Anaconda Theater in Isla Vista, with writer Bill Locey. This was the first No Doubt feature to mention the "curse" of the OC area code, even though this was something that the band would later wear like a badge of honour. "It's one big cement city," Locey wrote, "where only the cops in the different cities drive different colour cars."

Gwen Stefani, to her credit, refused to buy into the "LA exciting/OC dull" stereotype. "There's not really a division between Orange County and LA," she stated. "Orange County kids will go up there to see us, but LA kids usually won't come down [to Orange County]. We turn down a lot of gigs because we need room for our fans to slam and dance. Most of our gigs are in LA." Stefani reflected upon their recent successful album launch at the Whisky, where Orange County's finest self-promoters (aka the band and their friends) spread the word by handing out No Doubt stickers and kazoos. (In fact, Gwen told Locey, "Today, I'm doing this interview and mailing back some defective kazoos," she told him.)

When not bemoaning their sad financial state – Gwen explained how the band's busy itinerary made it difficult to hold down day jobs; "What do you tell the boss: 'We're leaving for two weeks?'" – she made a point of keeping the band at arm's length from the ska purists. Even then you could sense that Gwen had one eye fixed on the mainstream. "The ska scene is really like a cult scene," she figured, accurately enough. "Ska music is really simple. There's definitely ska elements in our music, but that's not all we're into. We just add stuff to it – just everything thrown together into a big mix."

As eclectic as their music was, and despite the favourable media coverage, No Doubt just couldn't compete with the sonic beast that was emerging from the Pacific Northwest. And no-one – certainly not the band – could have predicted how Nirvana would completely reinvent both rock'n'roll and the mainstream, in pretty much the time it took to mumble, "Oh well, whatever, never mind". (And all this from a band who were described by their drummer, punk survivor Dave Grohl, as "three losers from Nowheresville".)

Tony Ferguson, however, was an astute observer of the cyclic nature of rock'n'roll, and while the rise of grunge inflicted a serious flesh wound on his new signing, he understood how this new, austere genre came into being. It was simply a reaction to all that had come before, especially hair metal. "After . . . Winger and Warrant . . . there was nowhere else to go," he said. "The [pretty] boys pretty much became a parody of themselves because the talent pool was completely drained dry, [so] they went the way of the dinosaur. That's why Nirvana and Pearl Jam came up with this much more direct, real, organic, in-your-face kind of street, dirty sound. It was a breath of fresh air."

But, still – Nirvana? The band's core, guitarist / screamer Kurt Cobain and bassman Chris Novoselic, had lost enough drummers to fill a football team by the time they spied Dave Grohl, a spindly punk with an ass-length mane, drumming for never-weres Scream in 1989. After the gig, Novoselic turned to Cobain and uttered the famous words: "I wish he was in our band." Nirvana's commercial worth rose considerably when Grohl joined in 1990. Always a live favourite, their crowds got progressively bigger, while Geffen/DGC bought out their contract with revered Seattle indie Sub Pop for a handy $287,000 US. By the time they connected with producer Butch Vig, whose star was also in the ascendance, you could almost smell the teen spirit in the air.

Nirvana had been out of step pretty much since forming in remote Aberdeen, Washinton, in 1987, but were now the right band with the right sound in the right place. A glance at the Top 50 songs spun in 1991 by rock radio KROQ showed how the musical mood was changing: R.E.M. from Athens, Georgia, a group that had always represented the acceptable edge of the unacceptable, were at the top with 'Losing My Religion', a deeply melodic mid-tempo tune that didn't undermine the outright oddness of singer and lyricist Michael Stipe. (Their pop pastiche, 'Shiny Happy People', sat in eighth position on the chart.) Nirvana's anthemic 'Smells Like Teen Spirit' – its chorus propulsive enough to stop a tank – was at number two, having exploded in the latter half of 1991. Amidst the usual Anglo-pop fare from The Cure and The Smiths – was 'Give It Away', a slap-bass-happy fusion of punk and funk from No Doubt's mentors, The Red Hot Chili Peppers.

Such other hard-rock contenders as L7 ('Pretend That We're Dead'), Temple of the Dog ('Hunger Strike') and England's Catherine Wheel ('Black Metallic') dominated the charts, along with New York art-rock veterans Sonic Youth ('100 percent') and Jesus and Mary Chain ('Far Gone and Out') – and, with the exception of the perennially bed-haired Robert

Smith of The Cure, there wasn't a haircut band in sight. It was clearly understood that a revolution had occurred when a band as uncompromising as Social Distortion, or as unrelenting as Nine Inch Nails, were amongst the year's most popular acts.

Even though there was still the expected fluff hanging around the business end of the more mainstream *Billboard* 200 chart, it was still very much a red letter day for alt-rock on February 1, 1992, when Nirvana's unstoppable *Nevermind* lassoed *Ropin' The Wind*, the latest bland offering from cowboy Garth Brooks, and planted its flag at the top of the chart.

Soon after, Metallica, Megadeth, the Beastie Boys and the aforementioned Red Hot Chili Peppers and Temple Of The Dog would be battling for chart placings with Billy Ray Cyrus, Mariah Carey and under-age rappers Kris Kross. It was the best of times, it was the weirdest of times, and it became increasingly hard to imagine how No Doubt and their odes to masturbation and unattainable supermodels could find their place in this new musical order. Famously, when Interscope tried out some of the tracks from *No Doubt* on the programmers at KROQ, they replied: "It would take an act of God for this band to get on the radio."

But No Doubt weren't the only ska-loving outfit cast to the wilderness by the *sturm und drang* of Seattle. Fellow third wave hopefuls The Mighty Mighty Bosstones — described by the *Los Angeles Times* as "a bizarre sort of cross between The English Beat and Megadeth" – released *More Noise And Other Disturbances*, which was simply overwhelmed by *Nevermind* and Pearl Jam's *Ten*. Even *Madstock*, the live return of Eric Stefani's idols Madness, failed to make an impression on the charts and the airwaves. No Doubt's peers and mentors, LA fusionists Fishbone, were bogged down in a power struggle with their label Columbia. Even with the help of agitator-cum-filmmaker Spike Lee, who directed the clip for 'Sunless Saturday', the lead single from their LP *The Reality Of My Surroundings*, it clearly wasn't happening for Fishbone. (The relationship between Fishbone and No Doubt might have become strained, too, when their keyboardist Chris Dowd made a move on Gwen Stefani.)

The legendary volatility of Fishbone leader Angelo Moore probably didn't help their situation. According to various reports, he physically attacked his wife, his mother, a friend and record producer David Kahne, which eventually led to the band being kicked off the label. "Angelo's a bad drunk," said Gerald Lokstadt, who knew Moore from No Doubt's early days. "When he gets loaded he's really aggro. I had him MC some of my shows but he'd drag on in between bands. He just wanted to be there. He was the funniest guy, though." Despite this, Gwen Stefani still looked up to the guy as a role model. "Angelo Moore . . . was a huge influence on me," she said in 2002. "He just had a sparkle to him. And that was always my goal, to give off that kind of energy." Kanal was another huge fan, especially of Fishbone's 1988 album *Truth And Soul*. "Fishbone are probably the band that influenced us the most," he said. "I can still remember hearing them do the [*Truth And Soul*] songs at sound check."

The only ska-influenced band to be embraced by generation grunge was Sublime, another outfit who'd play their part in the No Doubt story. And even then it took a couple of years, and a very unlikely radio hit – 'Date Rape' – before anyone started to pay attention to their 1992 album, *40 Oz. To Freedom*. The roots of the Long Beach trio – singer/guitarist Bradley Nowell, bassist Eric Wilson and drummer Floyd Gaugh (but you can call him Bud) – were as humble as No Doubt's.

Nowell, once described by the *Los Angeles Times* as "a man of many dimpled grins but few words", starting thrashing out punk songs with Wilson in the mid Eighties, when they were teenagers growing up in the Long Beach suburb of Belmont Shore. Nowell's first music lessons came from his home-builder father, who sometimes strummed a guitar at parties, and his piano-teacher mother. But whereas 2-Tone gave Eric Stefani a musical direction, it was Bob Marley and reggae that really filled a hole in Nowell's teenage soul. He pushed this new sound on a resistant Wilson, as well as trying to get his friend to learn UB40's cover of 'Cherry Oh Baby'. "We were horrible," Nowell told the *Los Angeles Times*' Mike Boehm. "[He] tried, but it just sounded like such garbage." After spending a few years studying – Nowell was a finance major – he headed back to Long Beach in 1988 and formed Sublime after enticing Gaugh to join the band. (He'd been taught to keep time by Wilson's father, a drummer.)

Sublime's path crossed with No Doubt's as they started playing the usual assortment of backyard parties and beer-bashes. "I remember getting a demo of theirs," Tony Kanal recalled, "and me and Gwen wore it out in the car. They played at my 22nd birthday party – Sublime in our suburban Orange County home, singing about licking pussy. You never knew what you were going to get with them." Some of Sublime's early shows were far tougher than the Kanal celebration. As Nowell told Boehm. "Gangster kids would show up at the parties and there would be trouble. Someone got stabbed one time."

Sublime's A&R industry liaison-guy-turned-manager, Jon Phillips acknowledged that these very different bands, shared a mutual respect. "They'd played tons of shows together coming up," he said in late 2006. "Brad and Gwen were friends; it was actually quite natural to tell the truth.

The bands, although sharing the same music scene, had totally different lifestyles: Sublime was more of a drug-and-alcohol induced keg party where you might end up in a fight, while No Doubt was more of a cookies-and-milk scene – but you got to eat 'em with Gwen. They were good kids. To Gwen he was just 'Bradley', you know? Those two shared a real affinity; they recognised each other's talent.

"There was this sort of all-ages thing going on," Phillips added. "This wasn't Hollywood, where all the clubs were, so down in the OC and Long Beach there were a lot of parties. Long Beach is distinctly different from Anaheim, which is more white, more suburban. But they shared a lot of audiences, kids that were growing up at that time, hanging at the beach, that sort of culture. I'm sure there were times when the guys from No Doubt went, 'These dudes are fucked up', but they had fun together." (Sublime, famously, would attend meetings at major labels with their dogs in tow – a Sublime hellhound even shat on the carpet of a label boss. It's hard to imagine the same situation taking place with Gwen Stefani's, a Lhasa Apso, Maggen.)

'Date Rape' was one song that Sublime wrote and premiered at these parties. When they finally recorded it, on a virtually non-existent production budget for their own tiny label, Skunk Records, Nowell sang the song's uncomfortable lyric in a goofy voice, while Gaugh and Wilson surged and thrashed behind him. When asked about the song's touchy subject matter, Nowell downplayed any social message. He said it was written "probably just 'cause a certain word rhymed with another. And from there, the song just took its course. There is no great message. Sorry, I'm just not a very deep guy." Bruce Springsteen clearly had nothing to fear.

Sublime's real interests lay elsewhere, mainly in getting very high, trying to avoid the 9-to-5 grind and staying as true as they could to their punk roots – the opening line of their debut album, *40 Oz. To Freedom* ("punk rock changed our lives") was actually the voice of the late D Boon, underground hero and leader of The Minutemen. Nowell also devoted a lot of time and energy to the upkeep of Lou Dog, his Dalmatian, who would travel with the band and often wander onstage during shows. Lou Dog also had a tendency to snap; he once took a chunk out of Gwen Stefani's ass and her red plastic dress – as seen on the *Tragic Kingdom* cover and bought for all of $14 at Contempo Casuals – when No Doubt played at the annual KROQ Weenie Roast. The dress, fang marks and all, was displayed in the Hard Rock Café and then the Fullerton Museum, where it was stolen. (The dog of Sublime bassist Eric Wilson also had an appetite for destruction; at the same Weenie Roast he bit Rob Kahane, the co-owner of Trauma

Records, and nipped at his daughter. Damage control was handled by Jon Phillips, who wrote an apologetic letter to KROQ. "You play clean-up when you're managing a band like Sublime," he shrugged.) But just like No Doubt, who shared a few bills with Sublime during this period, it would take a couple of years before the band emerged from the underground; in their case, it took the championing of 'Date Rape' by Tazy Phillipyz, of the KUCI program *The Ska Parade*, to finally get the provocative track noticed by KROQ (and raise the hackles of the Feminists Majority's Rock For Choice organisation, but that came with the territory).

In 1992, meanwhile, No Doubt may have already progressed to the majors, but they felt that Interscope weren't giving them all the support – read dollars – that they needed to make their debut LP anything more than a small-scale, parochial success. According to Alex Henderson, who was still enjoying his sideman role in the brass section, "The record company didn't push the record at all, and we ended up with these crappy support slots." But they did keep playing; once the album dropped, they played shows in Colorado, New Mexico, Canada, Seattle, San Francisco, Santa Barbara, Las Vegas, Tucson, Arizona and elsewhere, before settling in for a run of "home-town" shows at the Hollywood Palladium, and an in-store in Irvine, California, at Peer Records on June 5.

Three weeks later they were back at the Whisky, for the album's belated official launch. This time around, Tony Kanal sported a furry beanie, which he sensibly whipped off by the end of the instrumental intro – the Whisky's lights were bright enough to burn your skin – to reveal that he'd shaved his head into a neat Mohawk. As it turned out, Young, Eric Stefani and a goa-teed Dumont had also cropped their hair down to their skulls, possibly as an act of solidarity with their bassman. As for the horn section, they were now decked out in matching boaters and red and white pinstripe jackets; frankly, they looked ridiculous, like some kind of ska-pop barbershop trio. ("Most of the outfits, if matching, were goofy, we realised that," said saxman Eric Carpenter. "But at a time when hair bands ruled the Sunset Strip, we didn't mind the oddball factor of wearing bow ties or overalls. Though I preferred the loose overalls versus trying to breathe while wearing a button-down shirt and tie.")

But this was not their stage, anyway. After a perfunctory, "Ladies and gen-tlemen, please welcome, No Doubt", Stefani again got her own introduc-tion, and she strutted on stage like a lioness before launching the band into 'Get On The Ball'. Her energetic high kicks revealed a sensible pair of bloomers beneath her thigh-high skirt, which meant that any over-eager stage invaders – and there were plenty – wouldn't see *too* much of their ska-pop princess. Balloons emblazoned with the No Doubt logo floated in the air, just above the heads of the stage-divers, although sometimes they got sucked into the moshpit melee. There was no doubt that No Doubt were learning a thing or two about self-promotion.

Yet as the Whisky set continued, it seemed as though the proximity between crowd and singer was maybe a little too close; whenever a stage diver actually made it onto the stage, Stefani would take a few nervous steps backwards in the direction of Young's drum riser, just in case (although ever-present security gave these stage invaders short shrift, flinging them back into the melee within seconds). Even during such slower songs as 'Sometimes', their Whisky gig was all action, all the time, exactly the kind of frantic crowd behaviour that got Interscope's Tony Ferguson interested in the band.

This band was super-tight to begin with. A song such as 'Let's Get Back' proved just how slick a machine No Doubt had become. Kanal slapped his bass to within an inch of its life, while Young kept a tidy beat behind him, and Tom Dumont, as solid as ever, stepped forward for another blazing solo. (And he threw a skanking guitar rhythm into 'Ache', which gave the fairly rudimentary ska-pop novelty song extra muscle live.) Eric Stefani adroitly handled the fills – and, uncharacteristically, jumped up from his chair to "conduct" the horn section during an instrumental break in 'Let's Get Back'.

The energy on stage was palpable; everyone threw themselves into each song while somehow still keeping on track musically. And Gwen Stefani, while not quite the lithe, buffed superstar we know today, bounced around the stage like a juggernaut. The moshpit, frankly, went nuts – on occasions, the action in the pit looked more like the free-for-alls you'd see at hard rock shows, as bodies (and No Doubt balloons), flew in all directions.

The crowd's zeal actually got the better of them during the sort-of-ballad 'Sad For Me', when their well-intentioned attempts to clap in time basically fucked up the band's timing. But 'Total Hate 95' typified their herky-jerky on-stage energy; the band blazed through the song as if the Stefani's 11 p.m. curfew were still in place, while even more bodies flew here, there and everywhere (but mainly in the direction of the stage, hands outstretched towards Stefani). Despite the frenzy, No Doubt never came off the rails.

The love-in continued when a bouquet of flowers somehow emerged from the moshpit throng and onto the stage during a new song, 'Hide And Seek', another fairly rudimentary ska-pop number, featuring a faux-Madness, hurdy-gurdy keyboard break from Stefani. As uninspired as the song clearly was, the band still shone brightly, never missing a change in tempo or groove. Then a surprise: a bib-and-brace-wearing Alan Meade is called out on stage and works the crowd up into a lather during a skanking slow-dance with Stefani. He and Stefani even pull off some of the synchronised high-kicks they'd worked out during their brief time together as co-leaders of the band.

As it turned out, Meade had vague plans of trying to get back into No Doubt, but when that came to nought, he had to be content with this cameo. "Unfortunately, when I moved away I got buried in the married life," Meade said. "By the time I came back, I was still busy working and going to school; I could not have re-joined like I wanted to. I made an appearance [at the Whisky] and hung out once in a blue moon when I could, or when they were in town. Of course we are all still friends, we have history."

Above and beyond everything else, No Doubt clearly knew how to keep the crowd keen. There was very little in the way of between-song babble; as soon as one song ended and the surge subsided in the pit, the band unleashed another live favourite, be it 'Big City Train', 'Trapped In A Box' or 'Paulina', where Kanal acted as MC, introducing each member of the badly-dressed brass section as they stepped forward for their solos.

Despite the clearly disparate elements at work here – Kanal's nod to the Chili Peppers and Fishbone, Dumont's frantic hard-rock solos, Eric Stefani's love of 2-Tone, Gwen's occasionally over-cooked vocals – it all seemed to make a strange kind of musical sense, especially during the upbeat, people-together set closer, 'Brand New Day'. These wouldn't be the songs that would make No Doubt stars, but they worked really well live. By the time the house lights came on, the Whisky dripped sweat. But as well received as shows such as this were, there were no obvious signs that the band was making any impact at radio: that act of God seemed a long way off just yet.

They decided to pool $5,000 US of their own money to contribute towards a video for 'Trapped In A Box', thinking, reasonably enough, that if they didn't fit on KROQ, maybe MTV would go for a band with a thing for 2-Tone led by a comely frontwoman with an idiosyncratic sense of style. While it was never likely to bring home an armload of MTV awards, the video for 'Trapped In A Box' was a hallucinatory take on the song's theme of claustrophobia, mind control and paranoia. As it began, the band (sans horn section) were found squeezed into a suburban bedroom (one that just so happened to have No Doubt posters all over the walls), with the woozy camerawork of director Myke Zykoff, who'd go on to direct clips for the Smashing Pumpkins, R.E.M. and Alanis Morissette, heightening the song's sense of entrapment. It's only when Stefani flashed her polka dot boxers at the camera that the mood lightened.

During the next set-up, No Doubt were on a sound stage, Stefani resplendent in pearls and a green tutu, Kanal in braces, Dumont in powder blue jacket, bow tie and shorts and Young shirtless, as usual. (The men of brass are wearing their striped barbershop outfits.) Then the band exploded into life on an Anaheim rooftop, as Dumont, this time wearing pyjamas, tore off a high-quality solo, while Kanal head-banged (and brushed his teeth) and Stefani, in ridiculously over-sized sunglasses, writhed orgasmically like some kind of ska-pop Lolita. Then they returned, variously, to the bedroom, the sound stage (Dumont plucked at a banjo while Kanal wrapped himself around a double bass) and a darkened room, where Gwen Stefani was roughly passed around by a moshpit of No Doubt lovers, while the band played on. The video was like one of those animated Japanese freakshows that can induce convulsions in kids; the pace was relentless.

Even though she did her best to downplay her natural good looks − variously wearing a back-to-front baseball cap, a functional, rather than flattering tunic, and a scowl − it was obvious that Zykoff's camera loved Gwen Stefani, as it tracked her every move and virtually caressed her pearl-white skin. While the clip was met with the same commercial indifference that greeted the single and the *No Doubt* album, and, according to Dito Godwin, director Zykoff was "skinned alive by Interscope" on the shoot budget, the label must have realised that they had a star on their hands. All they needed to work out was the best way to sell her.

Yet even though Interscope, at least publicly, stated that they were pleased with the sales of the album − it was a hometown hit, which was all they expected − the relationship between band and label began to sour. "It was really frustrating," said Kanal, looking back on the period that would produce their "official bootleg", the *Beacon Street Collection* album, "and it was due to a lack of focus, because the label was expanding. The people that signed us moved onto other projects, so there wasn't focus on [us]. We were screaming for [support], but it wasn't happening. Some of us went back to school, some of us got jobs. During that time, we did whatever we could to keep the name alive." Also recently signed to Interscope − who were heading into their fractious agreement with the home of gangsta rap, Death Row Records − was the grunge era's own Phil Spector, Trent Reznor (aka Nine Inch Nails), who'd deliver his masterwork, *The Downward Spiral*, in 1994; fusionists Primus (who released *Sailing the Seas of Cheese* in 1991 and *Pork Soda* in 1993); Texan alt-rockers the Toadies, and hirsute teen rockers Bad4Good, whose 1992 LP, *Refugee*, was a flop to rank with the first No Doubt LP.

Some of the band, of course, already had escape plans, if (and most likely when) No Doubt fell by the wayside. Carpenter was studying journalism, Gwen Stefani had enrolled as an art major at Cal State Fullerton – while still dreaming of a husband and kids, of course – Kanal had started to study psychology, and Alex Henderson was already considering an offer from jazz legend Pancho Sanchez. "Pancho's thing," he told me, "was more about jazz and less about a show", and this suited Henderson just fine.

But the one member of No Doubt who most strongly felt the fallout from the "failure" of their first album, and the standoff with Interscope, was Eric Stefani. He was never a fan of touring, and, according to many band insiders, was the most emotionally vulnerable member of the group, even more so than his singing sister. More than one person I spoke with likened his situation to that of Beach Boy Brian Wilson, who, quite famously, unravelled emotionally and mentally under the pressure of pumping out hits while also seeking out new directions for his band. One colleague of No Doubt, who preferred not to be named, confirmed this. "Eric's central role to the foundation of the band and its sound is similar to Brian Wilson's role with the Beach Boys," I was told.

Gerald Lokstadt agreed with this. "He had a sort of breakdown, yeah," he told me. "It was just like Brian Wilson." It's a massive stretch to compare the two as songwriters – 'Trapped In A Box' was hardly 'God Only Knows' or 'In My Room', let alone 'Good Vibrations' – but their emotional dilemma was similar, as was their reaction to the situation. Both Wilson and Stefani became withdrawn.

On the one road trip in support of *No Doubt* that was financed by Interscope, Alex Henderson could sense that Eric Stefani was starting to pull away from the rest of the band. "Eric was always the creative leader," he said, "but on that first tour, people just weren't taking to the music. Tom and Tony wanted to change [musical] direction, too, and Eric didn't like that." An early acoustic version of 'Don't Speak', the band's breakout hit of 1996, was being tried out by Kanal and Dumont at this point, but mainly in hotel rooms and their new rehearsal space-cum-band house in Anaheim, which was owned by the Stefanis' grandparents, and was now occupied by Eric Stefani, Dumont and Young. Even in its skeletal form, 'Don't Speak' was a million miles away from 'Trapped In A Box' or 'Paulina', and Eric Stefani clearly knew that, as did Eric Carpenter.

"Yeah, 'Don't Speak' was our ballad on that tour," Carpenter recalled. "It was still called 'Don't Speak' but the lyrics were considerably different, although the song structure was substantially the same. We wouldn't play it every night because it was often perceived – by the first-time listener – as the lull in the set. That's why I was so surprised years later to see that song move up the charts so fast."

Eric Stefani was, of course, maintaining parallel careers while playing with and writing for No Doubt. He got lucky when some friends of his, who were working as "gofers" for Ralph Bakshi, the creator of Fritz the Cat, passed Stefani's CV along to the master animator. To Stefani's surprise, he got a call from Bakshi, who offered the very raw animator US$350 a week to work on his latest project, *The New Adventures Of Mighty Mouse*. Within a week, however, Stefani (and Bakshi) realised that he was way out of his depth and the offer was withdrawn, although Stefani did convince Bakshi to allow him to hang about the studio and learn the craft of animation. Soon after he had a new mentor, John Kricflausi, who'd go on to create *Ren & Stimpy*, but was at the time a director on *Mighty Mouse*. By 1989, with Kricflausi's support, Stefani had landed a plum job working on *The Simpsons* (although he did take a year off to study at Cal Arts), which was soon to become the most successful animated show in the history of the tube. So as No Doubt's relationship with Interscope became more strained – and the likelihood of them being anything other than local heroes seemed more unlikely – Stefani, wisely enough, established himself as a permanent fixture on the Matt Groening hit show. "He was a crackerjack illustrator," according to Paul Oberman.

Back on the road, Eric Carpenter, just like the rest of the band, had mixed feelings about their current situation. "We were so excited to be touring the country with that album," he admitted. "Still, there were times when fans would come up to us and say, "That's great. Where can we get your album?" And we'd find out there were none in the local stores. That was very frustrating; we wanted more consistent support [from the label]."

Alex Henderson, his fellow man of brass, he was more frustrated by some woefully mismatched bills, organised by Darren Murphy, their contact at the William Morris Agency. The worst of these was a slot with hip-hop icons Public Enemy, of all people, on October 11, 1992 at New Orleans. Admittedly, No Doubt had to take whatever gigs they were offered, but the notion of matching a 2-Tone-loving ska-pop combo from Orange County with the fiercely political groundbreakers from New York clearly didn't work. "[We were] booed off the stage," Henderson recalled. "Our quirky, upbeat, happy stuff didn't go over too well. That was the worst reception we got. But we also played in [other] weird places," he added. Sometimes we genuinely feared for our safety." Once No Doubt got the hell out of New Orleans, Henderson started to seriously re-consider his future with the band.

Eric Carpenter, however, has a different take on both that PE support and the entire tour. 'That show speaks to a couple of things,' he said. 'Firstly, it speaks to Tony Kanal''s ability to make things happen. He was a fan of the Chili Peppers and next thing we knew, we were opening a show at California State University, Long Beach, for them. He idolised Flea and somehow got Flea to produce the band's first real demo tape. His ability to get things done also accounted for us playing with Public Enemy that night. Tony was a fan and, through his connections at the William Morris Agency, got us on the gig. That whole fall 1992 tour was a guessing game. 'How big a venue would we play that night? How many people would show up?' "

Carpenter recalled how the band was especially looking forward to that PE show, having just played "a string of small towns and smaller venues". The gig was held in the State Palace Theater in New Orleans. "We'd hoped to meet Chuck D. and crew, but I think the best we were able to do was hand one of our CDs to the band's crew. No real interaction. And when we took to the stage, it appeared to be a hardcore hip-hop audience that wasn't really in the mood for our energy. Songs would end and there was a smattering of applause, but mostly it was PE fans with their arms crossed waiting for the main attraction. Very intimidating. But you never know."

The next night, when they again opened for PE, the reception was much improved. "We played with them in a smaller club atmosphere in Baton Rouge, Louisiana," Carpenter continued. "It was near Louisiana State University, a much younger college crowd. And that was a fantastic experience. Even though they were clearly there to see PE, they gave us a chance and we won them over." This, according to Carpenter, was one of several occasions when the band rose to the challenge of playing on a seemingly mismatched bill. "Sometimes we won, sometimes we lost. We also played with Dave Matthews Band in their hometown of Charlottesville, Virginia, on that tour. Great show. Great fans. We'd never heard of them before. But as soon as they took the stage, they blew us away. We struck up a quick friendship and they invited us the next night up to Richmond, Virginia, to play with them on what was a scheduled day off for us. That whole tour was a true rollercoaster ride. One night in front of 1000 people. A couple nights later [we'd be] in a sports bar opening for a Pearl Jam cover band, whose singer got off stage and struck up a conversation with Gwen, to give her advice on how she could be a better "frontman" – how to be a rock star. Night's like that, we'd try to laugh it off. We'd challenge ourselves to keep the energy up and make the best of it, whatever the circumstance. It really helped us grow as a family, as a band."

The PE show and the entire Fall 1992 tour might have been the beginning of the end for Alex Henderson, but Don Hammerstedt, however, had done more than just think about his future. He left No Doubt during 1992 and was replaced by trumpeter Phil Jordan, who'd stick it out with the band until 1995. Jordan, like Henderson before him, didn't know much of No Doubt until he caught them at the Palace in Hollywood in late 1990. "I was so turned on to their music," he told *Tragic Kingdom* fanzine, "I told my buddy there with me that I'd love to play in a band like that." His chance came when Rich Mrozek (now known as Rich Labbate), a good friend of his, heard that Hammerstedt had left the band; soon after Jordan found himself cramped into a backstage area at the Belly Up Tavern in California's Solana Beach, being talked through the horn part for the song 'Squeal' by Adrian Young. "I was pretty nervous," he admitted.

Jordan, however, adapted quickly to the No Doubt life, even though his musical tastes ran more to such standards as The Beatles, Queen, Miles Davis, Elvis Costello and David Bowie. "Typical tour days," he recalled, "consisted of smoking cigarettes in the morning to help ease the squeeze – when you're sitting in a cramped van for hours you tend to get a little stopped up – afternoon sound check, then just hang around wherever we were until the show. [Then] we would hold hands, say a little prayer written by Eric Carpenter, and play the show."

When they returned to the safety of Beacon Street, the band decided that the only way to deal with Interscope's indifference was to build their own studio in the garage of their shared house, and record versions of the 50-odd songs they'd written since the sessions for *No Doubt*. In a move that hinted at the creative power struggle that was happening within the band – it was becoming clear that Dumont and Kanal wanted to steer No Doubt in a different, more mainstream direction than Eric Stefani – the band's guitarist and bassist were the key figures in setting up the studio that would simply be known as Beacon Street, along with drummer Young. The band was moving into possibly the most difficult period of a frequently soap-opera-worthy career: they were about to lose a key member and endure the end of the Kanal / Stefani romance (virtually at the same time, a massive double-whammy).

"The studio was literally a two-car garage," according to Eric Carpenter. "Tony and Tom were instrumental in making that happen, making it a reasonable set up. But it was very basic, with a lot of homemade soundproofing. We tried to be respectful of the neighbours, but I'm sure they could hear the noise coming from inside. The beautiful part of that was that three of the band members [Young, Dumont and Eric Stefani] lived there. And there was no real time pressure. So whenever inspiration hit, we had a place to put down some musical ideas on tape. That time period was crucial to helping the band grow as musicians and closer as friends." Recording sessions, which would inadvertently result in some of the tracks for that out-takes compilation, *Beacon Street Collection*, began there in the summer of 1993, during a five week break from touring that was bookended by shows at LA's Glam Slam on June 30 and a return to the Whisky on August 4.

A rough video of the Glam Slam show captured a band that was very clearly in transition, somewhere between the freewheeling, though flawed, *No Doubt*, the holding pattern of *Beacon Street Collection* and the poptastic *Tragic Kingdom*. And Gwen Stefani's star was clearly on the rise; even before the band took the stage, the faithful had started up a "we want Gwen" chant that was loud enough to wake the dead. To prolong their excitement just that little bit further, rather than burst onto the stage, the Orange County hopefuls had hired a huge screen and aired the video for 'Trapped In A Box', which suggested that maybe there was some life left in the record, a full 12 months after it had been released. (There wasn't.) The video was, of course, received like the second coming of Jesus Christ himself.

Then, another change: Rather than bounce on stage to the strains of 'BND' or 'Let's Get Back', Adrian Young held down a primal drum beat as the band gradually found their places in the darkness. It was a completely different opening approach, a world away from their regular jaunty instrumental warm-up. With Kanal – his locks, as flailed in the 'Trapped' video, now shaved clean off – bouncing all over the stage, and Gwen Stefani, in a demure black-and-white dress, doing likewise, they moved into a prototype version of 'Tragic Kingdom', a lengthy, complex nod to the Anaheim's own Disneyland, but hardly the type of song to open a set in front of the faithful. Yet, to their credit, they pulled it off. Once the final note of 'Kingdom' had sounded, though, they headed back into the more familiar territory of 'Let's Get Back', much to the relief of the diehards down front.

The rest of the rapturously received set was a mixture of the familiar (*No Doubt's* 'Sinking', 'Ache', 'Sad For Me', 'Paulina', 'Trapped In A Box', et al) and the future: apart from 'Tragic Kingdom' they also pulled off a passable take of the marathon moodpiece 'Snakes', a Kanal / Gwen Stefani co-write than would appear on *Beacon Street*, plus the tearaway 'Excuse Me Mr', a Gwen Stefani / Dumont track that would be a *Tragic Kingdom* standout, and another of their co-writes, 'By The Way', which also appeared on *Beacon Street*. (But even the converted were unsure what to make of the trio of sari-clad dancers that appeared mid-set and shimmied their way around Stefani during 'Snakes'.)

This Glam Slam set was pivotal. It captured a band shaking things up, no longer dependent on Eric Stefani for all their musical moves. And this shift in direction definitely hinted at their more mainstream future. It seemed as though Kanal and Dumont were winning the struggle as to where the band should head, and (maybe co-incidentally, maybe not) the Eric Stefani performance piece, 'The Matador', had been dropped from their set. Things were definitely changing at the creative core of the band. Even the flawed concept of the dancing women-in-saris showed that Gwen Stefani's input was increasing; this was another idea that she'd borrow from her exposure to the Indian Kanal family.

Interscope, to their credit, hadn't completely given up on the band, even though the charts, by the time they began their summer sessions at Beacon Street and elsewhere, were still unlikely to welcome No Doubt. Apart from Rod Stewart's dire *Unplugged . . . And Seated* comeback, the soundtracks to summer, in no special order, were *Pocket Full Of Kryptonite*, from lucky pub rockers Spin Doctors; Janet Jackson's *Janet*; Aerosmith's *Get A Grip*; *The Chronic*, from Death Row maestro Dr Dre; *The Bodyguard* soundtrack; Stone Temple Pilots' excellent *Core* and Anthrax's *Sound Of White Noise*. With the heat finally reduced to a simmer on Nirvana's *Nevermind*, the charts were a curious mix of the predictable and the totally unexpected. But Interscope's next move, which appeared to be done with the best possible intentions, only alienated No Doubt that little bit further.

The label felt No Doubt needed was the input of a music industry veteran, someone who could show the band how hits were written, recorded and produced. And, admittedly, their choice was interesting: they hooked them up with Albhy Galuten, for two bouts of rehearsals-cum-pre-production in January and April/May 1993, followed by recording sessions in June. A native New Yorker, Galuten had played in some up-and-coming pop / rock bands early on, yet was a jazz lover deep inside. "But," as he told *Berklee Today*, "it was clear that I was never going to be Oscar Peterson. I found it impossible to play jazz but easy to play blues and rock-'n'roll." After serving the draft in the late Sixties, he enrolled at Berklee College of Music in Boston, on the advice of an army buddy who was also a gifted musician. Two years later, after studying composition and arranging, he headed south to Miami, to play keyboards on various sessions for Atlantic Records.

Like *No Doubt* engineer Michael Carnevale, served time as assistant to studio legend Tom Dowd. He, too, was hugely impressed by the man. "Tommy is incredible, a real innovator," he said. When asked to describe a period where he played keyboards and occasionally arranged tracks on sessions by the Allman Brothers, Derek and the Dominoes, Aretha Franklin and Carmen McRae, all Dowd productions, Galuten summed it up simply. "[It was like] being at the feet of a master."

But Galuten delivered his true money shot in 1976 when he was offered the chance to work with The Bee Gees. The brothers Gibb were going through some big changes: they'd shifted labels, and were moving away from Beatles-esque pop and morphing into their shirt-open-to-the-navel, white-soul-harmoniser phase. They also needed a producer. Engineer Karl Richardson suggested that Galuten would be the ideal studio cat to help them out. The resulting album, *Children Of The World*, was a moderate hit, but it set in action the studio relationship between Galuten, Richardson and Barry Gibb. The next year, while working in France, Galuten got the call to work with the Gibbs on four tracks for the *Saturday Night Fever* soundtrack – given that the tracks they cut included 'Stayin' Alive', 'Night Fever' and 'More Than A Woman', Galuten, like the Gibb brothers, was on his way to superstardom.

In the wake of *Saturday Night Fever's* runaway success, Galuten worked on sessions for such hit machines as the Eagles (*One Of These Nights, On The Border*), solo Eagle Don Henley, Barbra Streisand ('Guilty'), Kenny Loggins, Diana Ross (*Greatest Hits: The RCA Years*), Sammy Hagar, Dionne Warwick ('Heartbreaker') and Kenny Rogers. By the time he sat down with No Doubt in Total Access Studio in Redondo Beach, Galuten had worked his magic on 18 number one hit singles, helped shift more than 100 million records, and was even credited with creating the first drum loop (while cutting the Bee Gees' 'Stayin' Alive'). So it was a strange move: Galuten was either slumming it working with these kids from Orange County, or maybe Interscope truly had big plans for the band, and felt that Galuten was the guy to untap their inner pop band. Whatever the reason, some of the band were uncomfortable with Interscope's approach.

As Eric Carpenter recalled, "We felt the [label's] inconsistent support the most during what became *Beacon Street* [essentially an album of *Tragic Kingdom* cast-offs]. We had so many songs, and the message from Interscope was always, "Not bad. Keep writing." I was surprised the band was ever allowed to release *Beacon Street*, but in retrospect, I'm happy some of those songs got out. I think it's the only way they ever had a chance of seeing the light of day. And it's a good record of that long period of time between the debut album and *Tragic Kingdom*."

As for working with Galuten, Carpenter wasn't so thrilled. "I got the impression Interscope looked at us like a band that needed direction, that they sensed No Doubt could be big, but the timing wasn't right and they didn't want to risk us releasing another album that could bomb. On one

Stefani at the Nassau Coliseum, 1996. As *Tragic Kingdom* kept on selling, Stefani look-alikes, "Gwenabees", started appearing in numbers. Indian bindis, a look that bowerbird Stefani "borrowed" from Kanal's grandmother, were mandatory. (PATTI OUDERKIRK/WIREIMAGE)

Dumont on-stage at the Convention Hall in Ashbury Park, New Jersey, December 1996. Aged 13, Dumont got his first electric guitar, a black Les Paul copy, selected primarily because it was just like the guitar wielded by his hero, Ace Frehley of Kiss. (FRANK WHITE PHOTOGRAPHY)

Stefani, the anti-Courtney Love, at the same New Jersey gig. By the time of *Tragic Kingdom*'s release, her brother had left the band and she'd split with Kanal. "We went through some really bad times," she admitted, "and our whole way of dealing with that is humour." (FRANK WHITE PHOTOGRAPHY)

Stefani with her parents Dennis and Patti. When asked if his daughter was a sex symbol, her father seemed rattled. "That's a little troublesome. I think she's hit on a trend in society where blatant sexuality is really not what's happening." (RON WOLFSON/LFI)

Young, Stefani, Dumont and Kanal, March 1997 (from left). A few months earlier, the men of No Doubt had been digitally deleted from a *Spin* cover. "It's not like Gwen Stefani and the background loser boys," Stefani snapped. "I would feel naked without them." (**DEREK RIDGERS/LFI**)

Kanal, Dumont, Stefani and Young (from left) at the 1997 Grammys. Despite two nominations, the band went home without any silverware. "I used to watch the Grammys with my parents and make fun of them," said an unfazed Stefani. "Now we get to play at one. Isn't that cool?" (KEVIN MAZUR/LFI)

Stefani in London, September 1997. By this time she'd been involved with Bush's Gavin Rossdale for nearly a year and had begun to spend almost as much time at his Primrose Hill home as she did at her LA spread. (ANGELA LUBRANO/LIVE)

Stefani with Rossdale at the premiere of *Scream 2*, Hollywood, December 15, 1997. "I didn't want to break up with Tony [Kanal]," she admitted, although "it was the best thing to happen to me." Kanal, however, had some problems with his ex's new romance.

(DAVE LEWIS/REX FEATURES)

The Stefani siblings reunited, backstage at a Rolling Stones show, February 1998. They both went into therapy after Eric quit the band. "When I first heard 'Just A Girl' on the radio," Eric told the *Los Angeles Times*, "I had tears rolling down my face." **(JIM SMEAL/WIREIMAGE)**

Stefani fighting the power with Lenny Kravitz, MTV Awards, 1998. No Doubt spent part of that year cashing in on their success, recording with Elvis Costello and sharing a bill with Madness, their ska-pop heroes. **(CPS/LFI)**

A braces-wearing Stefani with Rossdale, during the *Return of Saturn* era. Stefani premiered her flamingo pink hair in the clip for the single 'New', a song produced by former Talking Head Jerry Harrison and featured in the clubbers' flick *Go*. **(KEVIN MAZUR/LFI)**

A rare shot of Adrian Young at least partly clothed while behind his kit, June 2000. "He's the only [golfer] with a Mohawk who plays in the nude," said friend Jon Phillips. "Adrian's mellow." **(KRISTIN CALLAHAN/LFI)**

Stefani at the 2000 Teen Choice Awards, Santa Monica, California. Inspired by a John Galliano creation, Stefani designed her mock wedding dress with video director Sophie Muller. She also sported it in the 'Simple Kind Of Life' video. **(RON WOLFSON/LFI)**

Stefani with guru of groove, Moby, December 2000. Their jam on his track 'South Side' was a massive hit. "I expected some really self-involved rock star," the elfin Moby admitted, "but she's lovely and down to earth." **(JEN LOWERY/LFI)**

Bling's the thing: Throughout their *Rock Steady* phase, Gwen Stefani embraced the over-sized, super-chunky stylings of hip-hop. The album connected, too – *Spin* declared that "suddenly [No Doubt] matter again." **(CPS/LFI)**

Stefani and hip-hopper Eve in 2001, soon after recording 'Let Me Blow Ya Mind'. "It was such an awesome experience," Stefani gushed, "this whole kind of cultural collision." Stefani soon started signing her emails "G-Loc". **(JEN LOWERY/LFI)**

With yet another MTV Award, New York, September 2002, days before her wedding(s) to Gavin Rossdale. "We didn't want to impose on anyone, so we decided to do it in both places," she said of their ceremonies in London and LA. (DENNIS VAN TINE/LFI)

Stefani and Rossdale snog at their London wedding. Rossdale started the big day with a trip to his local, while Stefani did time with designer John Galliano. "It was very punk rock," Stefani said of her dress, "which you couldn't really tell from the pictures." (THOMAS RABSCH/WIREIMAGE)

Finally, a Grammy for Young, Dumont, Stefani and Kanal (from left), New York February 2003. At the after-party, tunesmith Linda Perry got Stefani in a headlock and told her: "Call me about your solo album." She eventually obliged. (DENNIS VAN TINE/LFI)

On stage at the 2003 Grammys. (KEVIN MAZUR/WIREIMAGE)

hand, there was excitement about Albhy working with the band, because he had proven success. And he had strong ideas, which was good and bad.

"And I sensed that Eric Stefani didn't like the idea of somebody coming in and messing with the band's arrangements," Carpenter continued. "This was a project Eric had started out of high school with his sister. He liked the idea of success, of course, but not at the cost of losing creative control over the songwriting process, I think. You could sense his growing discontent working with outside producers. He didn't have the kind of childlike joy he used to at rehearsals. And when his energy was low, it dragged us all down."

Carpenter was especially incensed with the idea of hiring freelance horn players. This compounded the existing problem that the horn section was considered an "auxiliary" part of the group, according to their deal with Interscope. "And, frankly, that was frustrating," he said. "I'd been afforded a lot of great opportunities [the band had recently opened for The Special Beat, a re-formed mix of members of The English Beat and The Specials], but those of us in the horn section felt second class. The band had been approached by producers who had worked with other horn players and suggested them to record on a couple of tracks [Carpenter would blow on two tracks of *Beacon Street Collection*, with most of the horn work covered by new recruits Phil Jordan and Gabe McNair]. The rest of the band came to us and asked if it would be all right to use a hired horn section just on a couple of tracks. The way I saw it was that if we weren't official band members, we should at least be able to record all the horn arrangements. I was disappointed that they would even ask. But that's when it became clear to me that No Doubt had reached another level. And my part in it wasn't clear any more." Carpenter, just like his bandmate Henderson, was about to jump the good ship No Doubt.

As Henderson saw it, the situation with such Interscope people as Galuten damaged, rather than improved, inner-band harmony. "Interscope gave the band some gear and sent in Albhy G to "help" with the record, which didn't sit well with the band," he told me, "especially Eric Stefani. It was not a good experience. He was constantly criticising the horn parts, for one thing. It just didn't feel right. Nobody seemed too happy. [So] the producer thing was a little weird."

Other band members were more enthused about working with Galuten; ultimately, though, Interscope money ran out and the veteran producer moved onto his next project.

Admittedly, the songs that the band did cut with Galuten in the summer of 1993 were a step forward from the flaccid ska-pop of their debut LP. 'Blue In The Face' was a curious, samba-meets-rock-and-roll oddity, complete with punky, adrenalised guitars, drowsy, siesta-time horns and a highly theatrical vocal from Gwen Stefani. But, at a touch over four minutes, the track ran at least 90 seconds overtime. 'By The Way', a co-write from Dumont and Gwen Stefani, was another downbeat cut with Latin overtones, a sort of blueprint for 'Don't Speak', minus Dumont's rule-breaking Spanish guitar solo, of course. 'Snakes', a Bad Religion-inspired co-write between Kanal and Gwen, rocked harder, with one of Dumont's signature metallic riffs opening the song and Stefani wailing a Kanal lyric that took potshots at the music biz like some crazy drive-by shooter. ("[Those] lyrics were written at a time when we were actually very frustrated with the record industry," Kanal understated.) As for Stefani, she delivered Kanal's venom with the kind of throaty wail usually only heard coming from the mouths of so-called "divas". None of the tracks that the "gifted" Galuten (No Doubt's words) worked on were potential hits, but there were clear signs that they were freeing themselves of the ska-pop straitjacket. Yet what Gwen Stefani still needed to do was develop the confidence to write about what was going on in her life, especially her increasingly clandestine and always challenging relationship with Kanal.

The band, however, had never planned *Beacon Street Collection* as their second full-length album; the tracks for the LP were all recorded in tandem with the songs that ended up on *Tragic Kingdom*. "We [released] it because we were so frustrated with our situation," Gwen Stefani said in 1995. "We started by doing these vinyl singles in our garage. Our goal was to do a series of them and eventually put them on a CD; that was our dream."

Tony Kanal summed up the Beacon Street era pretty simply, when he said, "1993 through 1995 was a tough time for us." More than once the band members considered moving on with the rest of their lives.

At the same time, the ever unstable No Doubt line-up underwent a couple more changes. The band had a gig lined up at the Huntridge Theater in Las Vegas in January 1994, but without any financial support from Interscope, Henderson was advised that he and the rest of the brass section would have to share a hotel room floor. That was enough for the two-and-a-bit year veteran of the band. "When the Pancho [Sanchez] chance came up I took it," Henderson said. "It was an exciting opportunity." Henderson had been offered a spot on a two-year world tour with the renowned Sanchez; it had to be more fulfilling than another night on the floor with his No Doubt bandmates.

Yet, to the eternal credit of the band, they held Henderson's spot open in the band for some time, just in case he wanted to return. "They were very respectful," he recalled. But his replacement, trombonist Gabe McNair, was a much more natural fit. Younger than Henderson, and standing at an attention-grabbing six-feet-two inches, African American McNair was a West Covina, California, native, who'd been invited to his first No Doubt show by Phil Jordan in 1993. Like so many before him (including Henderson), McNair was an immediate convert. And, as Alex Henderson noted, as soon as McNair started playing with the band, the chemistry was obvious. "[No Doubt] ended up with the perfect people," he told me. "Gabe and [Phil Jordan's replacement] Stephen Bradley were the perfect guys. They could play, they could wear the spandex, pull off the dance moves, the whole thing."

One of seven children, McNair was a self-taught musician who started playing at nine years of age. He could easily move between the piano, the trombone, baritone and tuba, while holding his own on the guitar and bass. He was also strikingly good looking, something that wasn't lost on the many female members of the No Doubt audience. As for his musical tastes, they ran to such acts as John Spence's heroes, Bad Brains, as well as The Police, Bjork, Supergrass and Radiohead. But the one question he always asked himself, when faced with a key career decision, was this: What would Miles Davis do? "Miles Davis" autobiography is like a bible to me," he told *Tragic Kingdom* fanzine. "Miles is my biggest influence."

With yet another personnel change in place, the band resumed their regular live spots, but didn't stray outside of California: during May and June 1994 they played gigs at Santa Barbara, San Diego, Hollywood, Solana Beach, Palo Alto, Santa Cruz and as far north as San Francisco, but they simply couldn't afford to leave their West Coast comfort zone until December. Nonetheless, they took full advantage of their new clubhouse-cum-studio on Beacon Street, recording several tracks that would turn up on *Beacon Street Collection*, with Tom Dumont receiving the producer's credit.

None were obvious chart-busters. 'That's Just Me', a one-off co-write between Eric Stefani and band insider/historian Eric Keyes, was another Latin-tinged number, a la 'Blue In The Face', flavoured by stop-start rhythms and a tasty brass instrumental passage. Yet despite another full-throated Stefani vocal – her singing had improved noticeably by the time of *Beacon Street* – the song was little more than filler, that, like many of the album's 10 tracks, ran a good 60 seconds overtime. 'Squeal', one of three solo Eric Stefani tunes on the LP, was more ska-tinged padding, a song that seemed to be stitched together from several separate, unfinished pieces of music. Only a tasty Dumont solo and some punked-up time-keeping from Young gave the song any real juice, which would be notable mainly as the last No Doubt cut to feature the sax of Eric Carpenter. The final track recorded in the Beacon Street garage was 'Doghouse', more of the same pedestrian, mid-tempo ska-pop, a novelty piece in desperate need of a tune. It was also the first track recorded in the garage with hired help – in the form of sax-man Gerard Boisse, an old schoolfriend of Phil Jordan – a decision that forced Carpenter to take a long, hard look at his future with the band. (Admittedly, Boisse's unfettered solo is the best part of the song.)

By mid 1994, Carpenter knew his time was up. Throughout his tenure with the band – he was now the de-facto leader of the horn section – he'd been studying journalism at Cal State Fullerton (where Gwen Stefani, Kanal and Dumont were also enrolled) and, reasonably enough, figured that there was a more dependable future in the newspaper trade than there was in the fickle world of pop. And the lack of respect he'd felt from both Interscope and, to a lesser extent, the core of the band, was enough to force his hand. As he wrote in his sort-of-eulogy for his time in the band, published in the *Orange County Register* in January 1997, "After suffering more [recording] delays, an evaporating bank account and a producer's suggestion that a more "polished" horn section be used on a couple of [*Beacon Street*] tracks, not to mention my 24th birthday, I finally opted for the "smart thing" and returned to Cal State Fullerton in Spring 1994."

Carpenter soon learned that he had to develop a thick skin; when the band finally hit big in 1995, he was often referred to as the "Pete Best of No Doubt", a bitter nod to the man who was ejected from the Beatles just before the Liverpudlians took over the world.

"I still believe I left when I was meant to," Carpenter wrote. "Sure, I missed out on some fun and perhaps a decent chunk of change." Carpenter dug a little deeper when we spoke in 2006. "Personally, what I miss most is playing the small club shows with a group of musicians I love and feeding off that up-close energy from the fans," he said. "In all honesty, I came into the band thinking it'd be a fun side-project for a couple of years. I never dreamed No Doubt could reach the level of success it has. So I'm truly grateful that I got the opportunity to record, play with a great group of musicians and tour the country."

Like the band's many ex-members, Carpenter was treated with commendable respect by No Doubt. He bears no grudges whatsoever. "I honestly do root for them," he told me. "After I left the band, I remember hearing them on the radio the first time, during the day, and I was thrilled for them. A few weeks before *Tragic Kingdom* came out, I ran into Gwen's dad outside a bookstore. He was wearing a baseball cap with a cartoon image of Gwen on it and he was talking about how much he was rooting for the band to do well this time because, if *Tragic Kingdom* didn't sell, they'd likely have to go back to finish school and move on with their careers. I laugh at that moment now. Obviously neither he nor I could ever have envisioned the album soaring to the success it did.

"I've seen the band play in big arenas and there are times – say their homecoming gig at the Pond in Anaheim [on March 12, 1996] – when I thought about how much fun it would be to play on that stage. [But] I can't help but root for them," Carpenter added. "They travelled a long road that included overcoming tragedy, surviving personal turmoil and an amazing amount of hard work to get where they are. And they are genuinely thankful to the longtime friends and new fans that continue to support them."

No Doubt closed 1994 with their only interstate shows of the year, playing dates in Salt Lake City, as well as two shows for the ski bunnies in Colorado, before signing off with another gig at the Troubadour in LA on December 29. It had been an incredibly frustrating period for the group, with diminishing returns from their record company and no obvious plan in place to move them up the commercial ladder. And one key member of the band was also starting to seriously consider his future: Eric Stefani, just like Carpenter and various other ex-members of the group, had started to wonder whether his 2-Tone dream was turning into a nightmare.

CHAPTER SEVEN

Just A Girl

"Guys, I can't do it."
—Eric Stefani announces his departure, Christmas 1994

Before Eric Stefani confronted the decision that would irrevocably alter the direction of the band – some think for the better, others aren't so sure – the existing line-up finished the session that would complete their *Beacon Street Collection*. This time the band worked in North Hollywood's Clear Lake Audio studio, with engineer Colin Mitchell.

Four tracks were laid down over one weekend in February 1995. 'Open The Gate', a song written by all five core members of the band, was the first, a sure-fire live winner that was bound to light up the moshpit. Although still not a notch on some of the tracks that the band was also piecing together for *Tragic Kingdom*, 'Open The Gate' had the same sense of urgency – and a feisty Gwen Stefani vocal – that would become their trademark on such hits as 'Excuse Me Mr'. 'Stricken', meanwhile, a sweetly seductive mid-tempo, piano-powered pop tune was, as always, hampered by Eric Stefani's need to over-complicate almost everything he wrote. He knew his way around a heart-wrenching ballad – *No Doubt's* 'Sad For Me' proved that, beyond a doubt – but it seemed that every time 'Stricken' locked into a hummable, Madness-worthy groove, further accentuated by the horns of Phil Jordan and Gabe McNair, Stefani shifted the song elsewhere. Once more, it was his sister's heartfelt vocal that held

126

it together, even if she leaned a little too heavily on the button marked "melodrama".

'Greener Pastures' was notable mainly for the fact that it was a co-write between the band's lovers, Gwen Stefani and Kanal. A dirgy power ballad with sub-metallic riffing from the increasingly deft Tom Dumont, it was another prototype for the urgent blasts of pop / rock that would make *Tragic Kingdom* such an irresistible force of nature; such tracks as 'Spiderwebs' and 'Sunday Morning' were born out of this Gwen Stefani/Kanal creation. But the most entertaining slice of genre-jumping that would end up on *Beacon Street Collection* was the live standard 'Total Hate' – "an old school favourite from the Fender's Ballroom days", according to the band's album liner notes – now re-born as 'Total Hate '95'. It was a herky-jerky blending of ska, punk and abrupt, Chili Peppers-like shifts in tempo, with an elegantly wasted toast thrown in from Sublime's Bradley Nowell, who made it perfectly clear that he'd like to "rock this shit straight back to Anaheim". As disjointed as 'Total Hate '95' was, it remained the most attention-grabbing tune the band had so far committed to tape, certainly this side of 'Trapped In A Box'. "It's kind of funny because that's our best song," Dumont would admit, in his laconic style, well after the track was cut. "[And] the song was written in 1987 by some people who aren't in our band anymore. Interesting how that works."

Life had changed significantly for No Doubt's Long Beach buddies Sublime between the time in 1992 when they delivered their *40 Oz. To Freedom,* and early 1995 when they hooked up for 'Total Hate '95'. Much to the chagrin of such organisations as the Feminist Majority's Rock for Choice, Sublime's 'Date Rape' had become a major hit, thanks to the support of *The Ska Parade* and the all-powerful KROQ. For a song that dealt with such a potentially volatile subject – essentially, in its own off-handed way, the song told the story of a guy who raped his date and ended up in the big house, where he suffered a little karmic retribution of his own – it was hard not to be seduced by the song's catchiness, and it dominated both college radio and KROQ's playlist in the early months of 1995.

"I think we should ask why this song is on KROQ," said Du Vergne Gaines, coordinator of the Feminist Majority's Rock for Choice, as 'Date Rape' continued its unlikely climb up the charts. "What has caused it to come to the forefront? Because it's not exactly a great tune. I can't help but think it's because of its incredibly provocative nature, and somehow it's playing with our sentiments illegitimately. It's trying too hard to become something it never becomes. It's P.C. and not P.C. all in one, but unlike Nirvana's 'Rape Me', it cuts no new ground." Other naysayers included Karen Glauber, from the music trade magazine *Hits*. "It's a lame ska song to start with," Glauber told the *Los Angeles Times'* Mike Boehm. "But the main reason I don't like it is that while it's labelled an anti-date rape song, it says the only consequences of rape are that you'll go to jail and get [raped]. It's like you shouldn't rape a girl for no other reason than you will get [raped]. The basic moral to the story is that violence begets violence instead of, 'Respect women – don't do this because she is your equal, your peer.' It's not the best message out there for kids."

Sublime's reaction, as always, was to light up – or spike up, in the case of Nowell, who was developing a dangerous fondness for smack – and just let it be, dude. As Boehm wrote, "Hanging out with Sublime for a while does nothing to dispel the impression that this is a band that believes in the punk ethic of not making a great separation between life and art." But their fortunes were definitely on an upswing, unlike their buddies in No Doubt; when Sublime toured during the early months of 1995, it was the first time they'd been able to afford hotel rooms. With the focus back on *40 Oz. To Freedom*, and with a new album, *Robbin' The Hood* – which featured a payback Gwen Stefani cameo on the track 'Saw Red' – ready to roll, the band stitched up a distribution deal with Gasoline Alley, a subsidiary of MCA. Punters outside of the band's So-Cal comfort zone were finally able to get their hands on Sublime product (these were pre-MySpace days, don't forget). The band was swamped with 23,000 orders for both albums within weeks of the deal with MCA. By May 6, Sublime was headlining the Board In OC festival; No Doubt took the stage at 6:10 p.m., well down the bill, squeezed between old-school punks the Vandals and Face To Face.

As for the collaboration on 'Total Hate '95', it was undertaken in typical Sublime style. The session took place just before they were due to play a set at the Las Palmas Theater, so they stopped by the studio, their pet dogs in tow (including Gwen Stefani's nemesis, Nowell's beastly Dalmatian Lou Dog). "They drank most of the beer that was left, and smoked a lot of pot," Tom Dumont recalled. ("That'd be about right," laughed Jon Phillips, Sublime's manager, who drove the band to the session.) "And Brad was sitting there with Gwen trying to learn the song," Dumont continued, "and it seemed like he wasn't getting it. And all of a sudden . . . he did a dub reggae style rap in the middle that just came out perfect. The best thing we've ever done was written by other people [the song is credited to John Spence, Chris Leal and Gabe Gonzalez] and performed by another man."

With one last puff of smoke, Nowell and his Sublime buddies left the studio and the last track for *Beacon Street Collection* was done. Despite the lack of that one key song that might just change their luck at radio – the best cuts of their recent sessions were set aside for *Tragic Kingdom* – the 10-track collection was a large step forward from their eponymous debut. Gwen Stefani burned more brightly on the mic, Tom Dumont was beginning to really fire both on guitar and in the producer's seat, the band rocked harder and more regularly, and there was an urgency to the album's better tracks, such as 'Open the Gate', that showed they were paying more than lip service to such amped-up LA punks as Bad Religion. And Eric Stefani's novelty songs were kept at a minimum; no longer was he given the scope to write odes to his uncomfortable hour in the dentist's chair.

No Doubt had become accustomed to their unstable relationship with Interscope – as far back as 1992, one of the label's A&R reps had told them they'd best "focus" if they were ever to really move forward – and so, frustrated by the very rubbery deadline for *Tragic Kingdom*, decided to self-release *Beacon Street Collection*, on Sea Creature Records, a label set up by the band. (Interscope eventually agreed to distribute it.) This was the end play in a time that *Mean Street* magazine, reporting on the LP in June 1995, described as: "A flurry of exciting rumours involving covert albums, renegade musicians, label changes and hard feelings. But the sorry truth is that No Doubt is on the same damn label, and *Beacon Street Collection* is just your basic musical woodshedding."

The album was relatively hard to find, being available only at gigs, certain record stores and via mail order (for $11, via the Anaheim-based No Doubt Friend Club). Interviewed for the same *Mean Street* article, Kanal was his typically polite, if defiant self. "Since the record coming out is taking so long" – *Tragic Kingdom* was deep in production by this stage, an odyssey in itself – "they [Interscope] gave us permission to put out *Beacon Street Collection*. [It's] kind of like a B-sides collection . . . but we just couldn't wait any longer, so we did it ourselves." Kanal then explained the key motivation for the record's indie release. "The whole reason we put it out is for diehard people who are really waiting for new music," he explained. "It's kind of like a collector's thing. [It] has a couple of really old songs, like "Total Hate" from 1987 and the other stuff from the past two or three years. I'm really proud of it. I'm glad we did it."

When I asked the band, via their management, what the real story was regarding *Beacon Street*, they replied: "It was basically a collection of outtakes from *Tragic Kingdom* that the band decided to release themselves to bridge the widening gap between the first record and *Tragic Kingdom*. It sold well and Interscope eventually picked up distribution rights for the record." In the end, only seven months would separate these two releases, a nanosecond in music business time.

The band put in extra effort to make *Beacon Street* a sought-after item. Gwen Stefani, who was the art designer for the album's sleeve, sat down with layout artist Matt Wignall and leafed through hundreds of photos, many dating back to 1987, sent in by No Doubt true believers. The resulting four-page montage featured shots of the many faces (and hair colours) of Gwen Stefani, ranging from pink to blonde and brunette, along with images of band members past and present (including John Spence) and the group's committed fans. In its own low-rent way, it was No Doubt's homage to the Beatles' immortal *Sergeant Pepper's Lonely Hearts Club* sleeve, albeit one that featured a cover image of the Stefanis' paternal grandfather performing his favourite party trick, where he placed birdseed on his tongue and invited his golden-coloured budgie to peck away inside his mouth. As you do.

"Over the past few years," the band explained in the album's liner notes, dated March 1995, "we've written so many songs that we felt it was necessary to release some material between records. This collection of recordings spans a period of two years done over three separate sessions." Elsewhere, there were some interesting revelations on the album's sleeve: Interscope's Albhy Galuten, whose presence in the studio clearly wasn't embraced by all the members of No Doubt, is thanked for providing "musical guidance" on 'Snakes', 'Blue In The Face' and 'By The Way'. (On the one *Tragic Kingdom* track that he helped with, 'Different People', Galuten is credited, cryptically, as the 'Director of Paradigm'. This was done at his request, in an attempt to not impinge upon the producer credit for Matthew Wilder, who finished the track.) And Tony Kanal's dual roles in the band – three, if you include romantic partner to Stefani – are noted with the credit "business shit by Tony". Enough said.

As small-scale as the *Beacon Street* release was, it still received reasonable coverage in the *Los Angeles Times*, once again thanks to Mike Boehm, who gave the album two-and-a-half stars (out of a possible high score of five). From the get-go, Boehm made it clear that he agreed with the group; this was not a "proper" album. "It is an informal, interim release on the band's own label," he wrote, "intended for local fans who have grown impatient with the long delay between records. *Beacon Street* compiles 10 tracks that No Doubt cut between mid-1993 and early 1995 while trying to hone its style and its songwriting. Since the band and/or its label deemed them unsuitable for wider release, the collection should be taken as an inside look at musicians doing their woodshedding, rather than presenting the sum of their artistry to the world." Boehm went on to clarify that the album now known as *Tragic Kingdom* was slated for a likely July 1995 release on Interscope (he was close: it dropped in October 1995).

Accentuating the positive, Boehm gave due props to the band's solid playing throughout the record, as well as its eclectic outlook. "With the core of the band having played together since 1989, No Doubt's playing is sharp and cohesive even as the band roams stylistically through ska, Latin rhythms, funk and hard-edged guitar rock – with several contrasting currents typically emerging in each song." As for the individual tracks, he praised 'Open the Gate' for its "high-kicking funk-pop powered by bright, piercing horns", likening the track to up-and-comers the Dave Matthews Band. As for 'Stricken', Boehm noted how the track "nicely evokes love at its most extreme stage of starry-eyed bliss", while he namechecked David Bowie, the Stax studio band and even Bob Marley's 'No Woman, No Cry' as reference points for 'Greener Pastures'.

Boehm, however, also stated the bleeding obvious: the band's second album lacked the one killer tune that could make them something more than OC darlings. Given that the charts were currently under the spell of the mildly exotic pop of the Cranberries, Hootie & the Blowfish's saccharine soul, and the rootsy grooves of Sheryl Crow's *Tuesday Night Music Club*, it was unlikely that anything from *Beacon Street Collection* would find a place amidst such mainstream fodder. "What's largely missing," Boehm continued, "is a knack for the focused structures and strong melodic hooks that can give a song shape and staying power. The vocal melodies tend to be long, flowing vehicles for Gwen Stefani's thin-voiced, theatrical acting-out in scenarios of romantic splendour and woe; her delivery provides plenty of energy, but the parts she gets to play lack pop pith." In conclusion, he noted that the album was simply a stepping-off point along the road to the band's next "proper" release, and rightfully so. "*Beacon Street* chronicles a talented band trying to find its way to a mature style, but it's more like a series of quizzes than a final exam. The album yet to come will tell more about where No Doubt stands."

The album, however, was to become a fan's favourite, if its many on-line reviews are to be taken as gospel. "It is a perfect combination of ska and pop and is absolutely amazing," wrote one besotted fan at www.amazon.com. "This record is not short in the diversity area," wrote another, "making it a winner on all accounts." Many dedicated followers of No Doubt compared and contrasted *Beacon Street* with the *No Doubt* set. "I highly recommend this album," wrote a Dr Kay, "if you (1) are interested in hearing what No Doubt sounded like before *Tragic Kingdom;* (2) you really like Sublime; (3) you are just interested in high-quality albums that are generally avoided by the mass media. If you really like this one, be sure to check out the self-titled one." Even the reputable All-Music Guide joined the love-in, awarding the album four stars. "[*Beacon Street*] is their finest album," claimed reviewer John Bush. "The synth and new wave influences of the debut are pushed to the background and replaced by a raw sound inspired more by punk." But in spite of this high praise and some college radio interest, the album, just like its predecessor, sank like a stone, not even rating a mention on the Billboard album chart. As far as Interscope was concerned, the group had one more shot: and that was the set of songs that was now in the can, the record that would change all their lives irreversibly.

★ ★ ★

None of this really mattered a great deal to Matthew Wilder, who was hired to produce *Tragic Kingdom*. Just like the band, Wilder had plenty to prove – he had to shake off the legacy of being known as the archetypal one-hit wonder, whose brief moment in the sun occurred in January 1984, when his lightweight smash single 'Break My Stride' reached a US chart peak of No 4 (it subsequently reached the same chart high in the UK during February 1984, standing tall alongside Cyndi Lauper's 'Girls Just Want To Have Fun' and the Thompson Twins' 'Doctor Doctor'). But Wilder had served some hard time before his path intersected with No Doubt. Born in Manhattan in 1953, he was exposed to musical theatre very early on, as his father was a Broadway advertising agent. (Later on, his father introduced him to theatre impresario James Nederlander, who helped Wilder acquire the rights to the book *Cry To Heaven*, which he would help develop for the stage with Robert Stigwood, famous for his work with the Bee Gees and less famous for his dodgy screen adaptation of *Sergeant Pepper's Lonely Hearts Club Band*.)

Wilder started out as one half of the Greenwich Village-based folk duo Matthew & Peter, but when that fell apart he shifted base, first north to New England and then west to LA in 1978, where he sang on TV commercials and worked as a back-up vocalist for Rickie Lee Jones and Bette Midler. He finally scored a solo deal and released his debut, *I Don't Speak The Language*, in 1983. The runaway success of 'Break My Stride', a synth-pop throwaway that was catchier than most strains of flu, gained Wilder a profile, of sorts, and the album reached the top 50 of the Billboard album chart. But his subsequent LP, 1984's *Bouncin' Off The Walls*, sank like an overloaded Zeppelin. Clearly, his solo days were running out – "That ['Break My Stride'] was my five minutes in the sun," Wilder admitted – and he returned to studio work. "I was a new father [when *Bouncin' Off the Walls* flopped] and it was necessary to reinvent myself," Wilder said. "You have to eat. So I spent the late '80s and early '90s writing songs for others and picking up production jobs."

Accordingly, he added vocals to records from John Prine (*Aimless Love*),

Judy Collins (*Fires Of Eden*) and such compilations as Brenda Russell's *Greatest Hits*. Finally, when he hooked up with *Ally McBeal* regular Vonda Shepard, Wilder got the chance to prove his versatility – not only did he produce Shepard's 1992 Reprise album *Radical Light*, but he sang backing vocals, added bass and percussion and programmed parts for drums, synths and bass. Every inch the one-man band, Wilder also co-wrote the album's title track with Shepard. The LP was no masterpiece – one reviewer dismissed it as "pleasant but unremarkable" – but it was a chance for Wilder to prove his chops in the studio. He'd then help produce the soundtrack to the flick *Air Up There*, released in 1994, before becoming entangled in the soap opera that was *Tragic Kingdom*.

He was approached by Tony Ferguson in 1994, and jumped at the opportunity; frankly, it wasn't as though he was overwhelmed by offers. He could clearly identify something in No Doubt that he was struggling with himself. "It was a chance to prove I could do something besides 'Break My Stride'," Wilder figured. "They were young, struggling artists – some in school, some in jobs, hanging by a financial thread. It was a gruelling year and a half on that album . . . constantly redefining and redirecting – very painful labour. The band was so concerned about its audience and credibility. The point Tony Ferguson and I tried to drive home [to the band] is that there's a bigger world out there."

As the album progressed, track by painful track, Ferguson began to wonder about the wisdom in hiring the relatively green Wilder. "Matthew Wilder, God bless his heart," he said, "chewed off more than he could take because that was a hard record to make." (Wilder wasn't the first producer that Interscope had tried out for *Tragic Kingdom* – the album's liner notes contained more thank-yous than an Oscar-winner's speech, while the credits ran for a good two pages, even in microscopic type.) "We had tried various producers that didn't work," said Ferguson, "[and] we had to beg, borrow and steal studio time. We didn't really have enough in the budget to keep going in[to the studio]. We would have gone broke." *Tragic Kingdom's* mixer, Paul Palmer, who was also the co-president of Trauma Records, who were about to offer a lifeline to No Doubt, was more generous: "[Wilder] is just a very musical guy, not a one-trick pony in that he can do only one style." Band, producer and label compensated by working during the midnight shift, when studio rates were lower, while Wilder wore a groove in Highway 405, travelling every day from LA to the band's Orange County base.

The band weren't sure what to make of Wilder. Dumont's immediate response to the producer's tight, curled locks (and equally tight pants) was to ask out loud whether the band had signed up to work with hairy metal shouter Sammy Hagar. And Wilder didn't endear himself to the band when he presented them with one of his own songs, a tune called 'Walking On A Fine Line', which he thought they might want to record for the album. They hated the track, which was dropped like a steaming turd. "It was such an invasion, at first," Gwen Stefani admitted. Overall, Kanal likened the recording of *Tragic Kingdom* to a battleground. "It was the outcome of three years of struggle," he said.

More than a decade down the road, Wilder still feels uneasy talking on the record about his work on the album – despite its mammoth success – and his relationship with the band. After initially agreeing to speak for this book, he backed out, with the following explanation, sent via email: "My concern is two-fold . . . I don't wish my perspective to be farmed out to the No Doubt community for "response" . . . I know these people and am wary of the task ahead of you. I'm contemplating how candidly I wish to respond to your questions and this could influence the manner in which this "storytelling" unfolds. I've read numerous biographies about *my* heroes and have come to know that these types of books leave the reader with a definitive impression about history that is either hearsay or based on eyewitness. Having been an eyewitness and collaborator with these people at a very tumultuous time lends a perspective that could be considered controversial, depending on how much I wish to divulge. Honestly, I prefer to hang back . . . before I go on record and may even wish to see some of the transcript beforehand so I know what I'm getting myself into. I hope you understand." (Wilder, whose work on the 1998 *Mulan* soundtrack earned him an Oscar nomination, failed to reply to subsequent emails from the author.)

If nothing else, the seemingly never-ending sessions for *Tragic Kingdom*, which were conducted around the three key sessions for *Beacon Street Collection*, introduced No Doubt to some great studios with heavyweight histories. No less than 11 locations were used by the band and Wilder, as they laboriously pieced together the album's 14 tunes. They cut tracks at Total Access Studios in Redondo Beach, which would later be the chosen studio for the Long Beach All Stars, the band that formed in the wake of the OD death of Sublime's Brad Nowell in May 1996. No Doubt also used Clear Lake Audio in North Hollywood for *Tragic Kingdom*. If Clear Lake's baffled walls could speak, they'd spill some great stories, because the studio had previously been used by Crosby & Nash, Harry Nilsson and Ringo Starr, as well as The Dickies, one of Tony Ferguson's "other" bands at Interscope.

Also amongst the studios used for *Tragic Kingdom* was Rumbo Recorders, located in Canoga Park, California. This was a studio designed, built and owned for more than 20 years – at least until spring 2003, when it was sold – by Daryl Dragon, better known as the hat-wearing "Captain" half of wholesome pop twosome, the Captain & Tennille. They'd cut several of their high-carb pop hits there. Its other clients had included peerless janglers Tom Petty & the Heartbreakers, Cali punks Bad Religion, LA glam-slammers Guns N' Roses, pop princess Paula Abdul, plus Heart, Ronnie James Dio and – much to the delight of Tom Dumont, no doubt – facepainted rock'n'roll warriors, Kiss. Mars Recording in Santa Monica, another studio of choice for Wilder and the six different recording teams he used for *Tragic Kingdom*, had a more mixed past: Brian Wilson consort Van Dyke Parks had recorded his oddball *Orange Crate Art* LP there, which was no bad thing, but it had also been used by the second, failed album from Rob & Fab, the pop impostors formerly known as Milli Vanilli. Quality alt-rockers God Lives Underwater had also used Mars Recording.

As for Hollywood's Grandmaster Recorders, that was the preferred location for such alt-pop icons as Beck and Liz Phair, and it was also used by Fantomas, one of the many all-star combos formed by former Faith No More belter, Mike Patton. Beck had also cut tracks at NRG Studios in North Hollywood, as would a varied cast of stars, including Tracy Chapman, Motorhead, Slayer and Fiona Apple. But probably the most renowned studio that No Doubt used for *Tragic Kingdom* was The Record Plant in Hollywood. The first "proper" mix conduced in this revered studio had been the soundtrack to the film *Woodstock*, followed by the era-defining *Concert For Bangladesh*. Fleetwood Mac cut their squillion-selling LP *Rumours* at the Record Plant, while John Lennon used it for his high-quality covers album, *Rock & Roll*. Stevie Wonder recorded *Talking Book* there, while the Eagles' *Hotel California* was another Record Plant production.

As glamorous and sometimes inspiring as all this history clearly was for the band, they had more immediate concerns: not only was the record seemingly taking forever to complete, but this was an album that marked the end of founding member Eric Stefani's time with the band. It also documented the break-up of Kanal and Gwen Stefani in more detail than maybe either would have liked, with the benefit of hindsight. It was no *Blood On The Tracks*, but there were plenty of tears on the tapes of *Tragic Kingdom*.

★   ★   ★

Eric Stefani had endured some life-altering moments in the band: the death of his friend John Spence, the blossoming of his wallflower sister Gwen, the band's evolution from ska revivalists to something a little more accessible.

But as their third album slowly came together, he could sense that he was now losing creative control. First he had to deal with Interscope's "suggestions", now he watched as Dumont and Kanal – and his sister the lyricist – grew as songwriters. According to recent departee Eric Carpenter, "My recollection is that after four-plus years in the band, Tony and Tom played a more active role in the songwriting process. And because of their different musical backgrounds, the No Doubt sound started to change. I don't think they intentionally wanted to make it "more mainstream"; it just naturally blossomed into a different sound. Eric always had a very clear idea of what he wanted in his songs. And I think letting go of some of that creative control, whether to an outside producer, or to other bandmates, was a difficult transition."

Stefani had officially left the band way back in December 1994, several months before the release of either *Beacon Street* or *Tragic Kingdom*, but it simply didn't become an issue until the release of the former. The last, unrecorded song he offered to the band, in an act so thick with irony – albeit unintended – that you could just about carve it with a knife, was a valentine entitled 'Bye Bye Birdie'. It summed up his situation pretty damned precisely. When pressed about Stefani's departure by *Mean Street* magazine, Tony Kanal was diplomatic, if a little casual towards the big decision made by the band's co-founder. "He just decided he wanted to go more full-time into art work," the bassman said. "So now it's Gwen, Tom, Adrian and myself. Things haven't changed that much. We don't have live keyboards, but that may change soon." What Kanal omitted was the simple fact that among the many issues that were dragging Eric Stefani down was Kanal's relationship with Gwen (which was also drawing to a close). It couldn't have been easy for him to witness their unsteady romance up close. That, combined with the ongoing hassles with Interscope and the drudgery of touring, was too much for Stefani, whose creative role on *The Simpsons* was becoming more appealing with every passing day. "Eric never liked touring," Gwen said defensively, "and he's happy doing what he's doing with *The Simpsons*. So everybody's happy." Well, sort of.

Former manager Doug Fatone, who got to know Eric Stefani very well during his spell with the band, had a slightly different take on his motivation. "I've always thought that he didn't want to be famous," said Fatone. "He was never comfortable being upfront; I honestly don't think being in a band suited his personality. He liked it up the back, pulling the puppet strings. Maybe it just wasn't for him anymore."

Even during his time with the band, Eric Stefani rarely spoke on the record; he preferred to leave that onerous duty to his sister or Kanal. And since his departure he has mostly avoided talking about his troubles that led to his departure. (He does maintain a very interactive web site, www.ericstefani.com, but tends to dodge specific questions about his decision to leave the band.) What is known is that he broke his news on the eve of another round of touring, prior to dates in San Francisco, San Diego, Salt Lake City and elsewhere, just prior to Christmas 1994. He called the band together and, according to his sister, simply said, ' "Guys, I can't do it." He was going through a lot of personal problems," she added. "It was horrible to see someone so full of energy and creativity be so low. He was so down on himself when anyone would have traded places with him because he is so talented." The Stefani siblings would both go into therapy in the wake of Eric's departure from the band, on the suggestion of their parents, in an effort to maintain their relationship. Gwen admitted to feeling an almost overbearing sense of guilt because the band hadn't folded when Eric jumped ship. (She'd experience a similar bout of guilt, this time towards her bandmates, when she went solo several years later.)

As for Tom Dumont, his immediate reaction was to question, briefly, whether the band should keep on going. "We had put six or seven years of our life into this thing, and we just didn't want to give up. I think Eric would have been really bummed if we stopped. I think he felt like he had to get out of the way if he wanted us to move up. It was like he was a big tree in the forest and we were the little bushes in the shade. We weren't getting any sunlight." So No Doubt went out on tour regardless; Kanal stood in for Eric and handled the vocals on 'Paulina', while the band road-tested songs (and future singles) that they'd recently recorded, including 'Sunday Morning', 'Just A Girl' and 'Sixteen', and filled out their set with such older standards as 'Let's Get Back' and 'Trapped In A Box'. For a band that had already undergone its fair share of self-doubt and stalled momentum, this was a time of truly mixed feelings: Kanal and Dumont were now free to delve deeper into songwriting, with Gwen Stefani handling most of the lyrics, but all the time they knew that a key ex-member was now watching from the sidelines.

"That whole passage of my life is unclear," Eric Stefani admitted in a rare interview with the *Los Angeles Times*, some time after quitting No Doubt. "I was messed up inside. I was troubled. I didn't know what direction to go." In the same Q&A, Stefani denied that his loss of creative control forced him out of the band. Strangely echoing the words of his sister, who once described him as "in some ways the teacher, the Dad. He taught me everything I know", Stefani compared his departure to "like being the father of a kid, and it was time to let go," he said. "For the long run it worked out for the best for everyone, including myself . . . And all the musical juices were sucked out of me at that point." It didn't help Stefani's fragile emotional stability when curious fans would pull up out the front of his Anaheim home and ask him, "Hey, you're the guy who used to play with [No Doubt]. Why'd you quit?" "I wanted to go back to drawing," he'd tell them, before disappearing back inside his house. (A home smartly renovated, it should be noted, with his bounty of *Tragic Kingdom* royalties.)

In another interview, this time with *Rolling Stone*, Stefani tried to explain what motivated his decision, inferring that his loss of creative control *was* a key factor. "I was trying too hard," he said, "to put my personality, or my being, on this planet through the music. And I didn't know how to express myself any other way. So when that was compromised, I was lost. But I think I found myself more by losing that and having to act as a human."

Stefani found the perfect retreat; a characterless cubicle in a North Hollywood office building where 70-odd people laboured over illustrations of Marge, Bart, Homer, Lisa and Maggie Simpson, as well as the numerous other oddly-coloured, curiously-natured characters that made up the all-too-real cartoon world of *The Simpsons*. (Stefani's old school buddy, Eric Keyes, also worked on the show, as a layout artist.) One of Stefani's more notable contributions to *The Simpsons* was an action scene in a season six episode entitled "The Springfield Connection" (which first aired on May 7, 1995), in which Marge became a cop. He was required to illustrate a sequence where she took a tumble and then leapt up, gun in hand, ready to fire. In an attempt at verisimilitude, he asked several of his friends to imitate her actions on the front lawn of the No Doubt house on Beacon Street, and then sketched the results, while the neighbours scratched their heads and wondered what the hell was going on.

But Bart was his favourite character to draw, as he explained. "Bart was the whole reason I got involved [with the show]," he said in 1997. "I relate to him." Stefani also took some joy in inserting references to his former band into the show. A ND T-shirt cropped up in an episode entitled 'Separate Vocations', which first ran in 1992, while yet another can be spotted in an episode entitled 'Germ Warfare'. During 'Lisa's Rival', which first aired on September 11, 1994, another kid can be spotted wearing a No Doubt T-shirt. All this product placement, of course, was a shameless act of self-promotion, as it featured the logo that Eric had designed. And Stefani actually drew his sister Gwen, plus the rest of the band, for the episode Homerpalooza, which ran on May 19, 1996. She can be found in the crowd, sunglasses firmly in place. Eric Stefani appeared to hold no grudge towards his former band, if all of this was any guide.

If there was one simple yet overwhelmingly poignant metaphor that summed up Eric Stefani's state of mind at the time of his departure, it was writ large all over the sleeve of the *Tragic Kingdom* album, which was shot by photographer Daniel Arsenault and designed by Sean Alattore of Morbido / Bizzario. Like many of those who worked with No Doubt early on, Arsenault knew nothing of the band, as he told me. He'd made some inroads shooting such rappers as NWA's Easy E and Ice Cube, and was only tipped off to the No Doubt job by a friend who knew Interscope's Tony Ferguson. "I never knew No Doubt, I hadn't heard the tunes," Arsenault said, "but my bud had been told, 'Here's this band No Doubt, just shoot 'em quick, here's a little cash to do it.' The record company's attitude, I feel, was, 'Hey, another band, just shoot it and get it done.' No-one knew it was going to be huge."

In each of the band portraits, Eric Stefani is positioned at a slight distance from the rest of the group; in some shots he's actually staring off into the middle distance – it's as if he's either wondering whether he'd made the right decision to quit, or he's counting down the minutes until the shoot ends and he can move on. Although the published images strongly hint at Stefani's distance from the band, Arsenault doesn't remember the shoot that way (in the process dispelling a long-held belief about the metaphoric worth of the album's sleeve). "We had fun at the shoot; there were no difficulties," he said. "I felt he just wanted to move on, and that's OK. As far as Eric looking off and being isolated, well, we were trying to make a good composure in the shot and get everyone in there and get the tree in there. We had to get one of them to kneel down, to make it work. If I remember, we shot a lotta versions, and put different people in front and the back, and that's why Eric ended in the back for that reason [it was the best shot]. Although we did shoot the main group without Eric and with him."

The cold truth was that Eric had only been invited back for the album shoot on the insistence of his sister. Unlike Arsenault, she had less-then-fond memories of the long days spent on various streets in and around Orange and at some of the San Fernando Valley's most fecund orange groves, where the shoot took place. "It was very weird," she said. "It was horrible." However, after speaking with Arsenault, you'd swear that they were talking about different events. "There were no difficult circumstances at all, we all had a good time," he insisted. "I never felt there was anything wrong. It was a good shoot; all the band members were good to work with – we had a good flow and lots of laughs. I wish there were more like them. And they were up for anything – we were changing clothes in and out of the van, in alleys and wherever we felt like going. All of them were way cool," he continued. "Gwen was just great; very polite; the drummer was very cool – we had a lot of laughs. And I felt as if they were one; no-one was above or below each other." One of the locations chosen by the band and Arsenault was the drive-in theatre that appears on the back cover of the CD. This was a shot that almost didn't happen. "We drove in and got chased out," Arsenault recalled. Eventually they resorted to some guerilla-styled photography, racing back into the drive-in, taking the shot quickly and then heading for the exit. This time they were too quick to be evicted.

Eric Stefani's state of mind notwithstanding, it should be said that the sleeve for *Tragic Kingdom* is one of the more edgy and witty designs of the 1990s, even rating with Nirvana's *Nevermind* and its poisonous comment on greed. On the cover, Gwen – wearing that red vinyl dress that Brad Nowell's dog took such a shine to – strikes a pose, an orange held proudly aloft, like some kind of spokesmodel for Californian produce. But on closer inspection, the orange is full of holes and the copy near her right ankle reads "bought and sold out in the USA". The barren tree in the background of the shot was also significant, according to Arsenault who, along with designer Alatorre, had discussed the sleeve's themes, before the shoot, with the band at the No Doubt HQ on Beacon Street. "The dying orange tree was supposed to be tragic," Arsenault said. "If I remember correctly, the dead tree was important." But just like the drive-in shot, the image of the dead tree almost wasn't taken. "I remember getting lost on the freeway trying to find that damn tree," Arsenault said. "It was far away in the north country. There was a lot of yelling, but we got there finally."

And there's an overwhelming sense of despair, crossed with a deadpan humour, throughout the sleeve. The lyrics for the album's title track – an Eric Stefani composition – are quoted inside, running alongside Arsenault's portraits of the band that seem oddly stretched out of shape. (Gwen Stefani looks more like some lanky basketball hopeful than a pop star.) The lyrics read: "Once was a magical place / over time it was lost / They pay homage to a king / whose dreams are buried in their minds / disillusioned as they enter / they're unaware what's behind castle walls / welcome to the Tragic Kingdom / cornfields of popcorn are yet to spring open." Despite the Dungeons & Dragons overtones, Stefani's lyrics were not only a bittersweet valentine to his part of the world, but they might have read as a final farewell to his No Doubt bandmates.

The sleeve was definitely a farewell to Daniel Arsenault, who despite earning more kudos than cash from his work on *Tragic Kingdom*, never crossed paths with the band again. "My bud and I were just tossed aside like we weren't there and were never asked to do a video or shoot stills again with the band," he admitted. "It's just politics, and I have no problem with

No Doubt. They could have forced the record company to use me and my designer friend Sean again, but, wham, you're on a roll and that's it. Once I had backstage passes from them and I went back after the show, looking for them, and the bouncer tossed me out. It was such a lame-ass thing to do. From there it was so long and goodbye. My designer friend and I did that gig for virtually no money and we lived off promises. I'm not complaining, that's just the nature of the business."

Interestingly, during the long nights making the album, Sammy Hagar-lookalike Matthew Wilder was perceptive enough to note that Stefani was poised to leave the band, even while the sessions were taking place. While cutting 'Don't Speak', Stefani had planned on including an organ part that was, apparently, inspired by the Supertramp hit 'Breakfast In America'. But Wilder quietly suggested to Tom Dumont that the part be adapted for guitar, which would make it easier to re-create live. Wilder sensed that Eric wasn't going to stick around long enough to play the part in concert. Dumont confirmed this in an interview with *The Hub*. "I think Matthew Wilder foresaw that Eric was going to be leaving the band and maybe decided we should use a guitar, since we weren't going to have a keyboard player." Despite the unsteady relationship between band and producer, Wilder definitely read this situation correctly.

Eric Stefani, of course, wasn't the only casualty of *Tragic Kingdom*. The romance between No Doubt's singer and bassist ended at roughly the same time Stefani handed in his notice. Their romance had lasted almost eight years – a shock, really, given that after their first meeting, Stefani naively thought Kanal was Chinese – and had endured some incredibly tough times, but it simply wasn't built to last, at least to Kanal. The decision to split was his, and he would have to live with the flak that was hurled in his direction by disgruntled fans and friends who felt he'd done Gwen, and the band, a disservice. And Stefani was badly hurt by his decision; she'd frequently refer to Kanal as the "love of her life" and described their romance as "intense", at least until she came face-to-face with grunge pin-up Gavin Rossdale.

Stefani often admitted that she would have preferred to stay in a relationship with Kanal, no matter what impact it had on life in the band. She was the one who initiated the relationship – Stefani confessed how she "forced Tony to make out with me . . . he didn't even like me and I made him kiss me. Then I forced him to go out with me" – and she obviously would have preferred to be the one deciding their future. The plain truth was that she was still in love with him but somewhere along the line he'd fallen out of love with her. Upon his announcement, Stefani took to her room and, like a lovelorn teenager, tearily sang along to Elvis Costello's 'Almost Blue', over and over again. (She did, however, in the months after their split, convince Kanal to make out with her on demand, which must have felt like a small victory for the heart-broken singer.)

As recently as 2003, she stated: "I didn't want to break up with Tony", although she did add that "it was the best thing to happen to me." And to her credit, although she would draw upon their messy split for much of the subject matter on *Tragic Kingdom*, Stefani would continue to defend Kanal down the years. "I write about what happens to me and that was a major thing," she said. "It would be stupid to not talk about it. [But] then it got crazy because people were reading the lyrics and going, "That Tony is such a jerk, how could he do that to Gwen?" It's not fair to him because it's only my side of the story. He didn't write songs about Gwen being a jerk." Of course, there's a certain double standard at play here – Stefani must have known she'd be setting up Kanal by analysing their split in such tracks as 'Don't Speak', 'Happy Now', 'Sunday Morning' and 'Hey You' (where she as good as admits that she'd marry him if he asked), so her defence was most likely inspired by guilt, her frequent Achilles heel, as much as anything else.

Kanal has always been tight-lipped about his break-up with Stefani and the subsequent fall out. Typically, Stefani was left to explain why he chose to end things. "I think he started feeling really claustrophobic," she figured, "and he'd never had any kind of experience, as far as seeing other girls, since he was 16 years old. Of course", she added, with admirable cheek, "he was going out with the raddest girl in the planet." When pressed, Kanal offered a more blunt response. "I don't expect anyone to understand exactly what happened," he said, "and I really have no desire to justify or clarify. It's in the past and that's it." It's been suggested that Kanal grew uncomfortable when Stefani started talking about marriage, although neither has confirmed this. (Kanal, however, like many No Doubt insiders, did have some trouble adjusting to Stefani's subsequent relationship with Gavin Rossdale. Former No Doubt trombonist Alex Henderson, who, like so many ex members, maintained a very civil relationship with the band after his departure, recalled receiving a postcard from Kanal while No Doubt was on the road with Bush and the Goo Goo Dolls in 1996. Kanal told Henderson how tough it was looking on as the Rossdale / Stefani relationship bloomed. "Tony told me that it was hard for him to be around that," Henderson said.)

But while Kanal and Stefani may have dealt with their bust-up in their own ways, what Eric Stefani's departure meant was that No Doubt needed a new lyricist. When Gwen Stefani stepped forward, the band's creative evolution was complete: Kanal and Dumont were now the key songwriters, while Gwen took care of most of the words. And whereas her brother preferred a slightly surreal approach, as he moaned about his aching teeth and his burning desires, Gwen quickly realised that she now had some weightier subject to pick apart: her fucked-up love life. But what she didn't know was that she would soon be embraced as a role model for disaffected suburban girls, annoyed at their parents or their boyfriends' lack of commitment. Thanks to her loyal fans – the "Gwenabees" – Gwen Stefani was about to become Disneyland's answer to Hole shock-rocker Courtney Love.

★ ★ ★

In the Interscope bio that accompanied *Tragic Kingdom* on its release on October 10, 1995, Gwen Stefani neatly understated the turmoil, both personal and professional, that she and the band had lived through to get to this point. (Only just lived through, admittedly, because she'd had second thoughts about continuing when Eric left, an issue they dealt with in their shared therapy. She also contemplated her future with the band when Kanal ended their romance; how the hell could she keep it together if and when the many women in their audience made a play for her ex?) Apart from all the usual major label propaganda, Stefani explained the cutting wit that underscored such album standouts as 'Just A Girl'. "As people, we're angry," she said. "We went through some really bad times in the past couple of years – personally and bandwise – and our whole way of dealing with that is humour and I think that's really apparent in our record. Even though things have been bad, and some of the songs are sad if you really listen to them, there's still an element of humour to it all."

And from the opening drum roll that kicks *Tragic Kingdom* into life, you get the sense that this is not so much a new album, but an entirely new band. There's none of the lack of confidence or relentless genre-hopping that marked both their previous LPs. And as the lead track 'Spiderwebs' proves, they'd definitely left the lesser songs for *Beacon Street Collection* and saved the best for *Tragic Kingdom*. The song itself is a revved-up blast of punk-pop, with some lazy horns thrown into the mix to keep the third wave punters keen. Tom Dumont's guitars snapped and snarled like a pissed-off mongrel dog, the engine room of Kanal and Young kept the energy level on extreme, while Stefani's breathless vocal displayed an unexpected surliness. OK, so the song is about little more than using your answering machine as a barrier against someone's unwelcome advances, but Stefani growled her clever lyric – "communication, telephone invasion / I'm planning my escape" – as if she'd gotten inside her former partner's head. (Interestingly, this is one of four *Tragic Kingdom* songs featuring a Stefani /

Kanal songwriting credit; it was also one of five singles lifted from the album.)

'Excuse Me Mr', a Stefani / Tom Dumont co-write, was another out-pouring of pure pop-punk energy, again powered by red-hot riffing from Dumont, rock-steady rhythms from Kanal and Young and a supercharged vocal from Stefani. This truly sounded like a band playing for their musical lives (which, of course, they were). Gwen Stefani has often said that at the time of *Tragic Kingdom* she'd become a graduate of the "Eric Stefani School of Songwriting" and that becomes obvious during 'Mr', where a Dixieland shuffle echoes the outro of 'Trapped In A Box'. But like the best moments of the album, 'Excuse Me Mr' was more about capturing the band's raw energy on tape and less about copying Eric's irritating "cleverness". As the song closed, with a crash of drums and a screech of guitar, you'd swear that Wilder had simply instructed the band to plug in and play and let him know when they were finished. There's a rawness here that hadn't been heard from No Doubt this side of Fender's Ballroom.

The Orange County four then somehow managed to crank it up another notch with 'Just A Girl', the defining track on the album and its lead single, co-written by Dumont and Stefani. Again, it was a song that gave new meaning to the term "high energy", as Dumont's new wave-inspired licks rubbed up against Stefani's Lena-Lovich-on-helium vocals and her cynical lyrical put-down. The song, which would be embraced as an anthem for disaffected teens everywhere – a sort of G-rated take on Alanis Morrissette's muddleheaded angst, or 'Riot Grrrl for Dummies', according to one wag – was actually Stefani's reaction to her father's unhappiness with her noctur-nal rendezvous with Kanal. "I got the idea [for the song] when my dad would yell at me for going to Tony's house and coming home real late," Stefani said in the album's official press release. "I really don't think a lot of guys know what a burden it is to be a girl sometimes."

And, like the two tracks that preceded it, 'Just A Girl' came crashing to a halt as if the band had been recorded while playing yet another hot gig in front of their Orange County faithfuls. Wilder may not have connected per-sonally with the group, but he certainly found a way of transferring the band's unstoppable live energy into the studio. Dumont and Kanal did their best to explain this in the album's official press release. "It's not just this energy where it's a loud, fast beat and you can slam around," Dumont explained, "there's a real emotion thing that comes from the songs because they're so melodic. When Gwen sings she's just incredibly gripping and fas-cinating to watch. There's something magical about her." "Live, something happens that really transcends all the music," Kanal added. "What's cool is that because we have a female singing, Gwen gets the girls into it, lets them participate. With a lot of other bands, it's just a testosterone thing. Everyone feels like they're part of it, nobody gets left out." Few pop/rock albums of the 1990s opened with a more emphatic hat trick of knockout blows than *Tragic Kingdom*.

'Happy Now', yet another high-impact Stefani / Dumont / Kanal co-write (and another stroppy kiss-off to Kanal), swiftly followed. By now it was clear that this was a totally reinvented Gwen Stefani; whereas in the past she'd simply been the singer in the band, mouthing her brother's lyrics and providing appealing eye-candy on stage (and forcing her bandmates into occasionally ill-advised costumes), she was now a woman in charge. With an excess of humility, Stefani summed up her new role in the band for the album's official press release. "Before I just didn't have the experience to get too involved in the songwriting," she said. "But with this record I got really involved in the writing of songs and expressing myself, putting my personality into things. I think that's what makes this record so meaningful; it's really personal."

Finally, with the horn-heavy shuffle of 'Different People', one of Eric Stefani's five co writes on the album (he also took sole credit on two other tracks), the album takes a breather. Built around a righteously funky bass line from Kanal and some well-recorded horns, 'Different People', while still upbeat, chilled things out just slightly, which was just as well after such a blistering opening salvo.

'Hey You', the next Stefani / Kanal cut, was one of the album's lesser tracks, a fairly pedestrian pop/rock stomper – with added sitar, no less – but it did contain some of Stefani's most self-effacing lyrics, as she compared herself to her 'Ken and Barbie dolls', wistfully dreaming of a happily ever after that might never come her way. "Hey you with the wedding dress on," she snaps, as if she was waking from a dream, "Hey you with the dreams in your head." The droll repartee of legendary '70s husband-and-wife team Sonny & Cher had nothing on the Stefani and Kanal double act: at least as far as No Doubt's vocalist was concerned, everything and everyone was fair game in matters of lyrical content. And finally had something weighty to sing about.

The following track, Eric Stefani's seven-minute opus 'The Climb', may have been well intentioned and ambitious, with its layered vocals, atmospheric keyboards and me-against-the-world lyric, but this overly long and relentlessly austere moodpiece was like a heavy weight slung around the album's neck. *Tragic Kingdom* was built upon the simple catchiness, mad energy and lyrical accessibility of its many standout tracks – 'Excuse Me

Mr', 'Just A Girl', 'Sunday Morning' – and there was really no place for this plodding prog-rock epic. It wasn't a surprise that it was buried away at the album's mid-point, a time when most listeners stop to catch their breath (or top up their fluids). 'The Climb' would also become a buzz-killer in the band's upcoming live set – it signalled time for a toilet break and/or drinks run for the increasingly large crowds that the band would pull over the next two years.

Fortunately, No Doubt got back on track with the tearaway Kanal / Stefani track 'Sixteen', with its high-octane mix of Dumont's neo-metal riffing, and some subtle ska-pop rhythms, which are interspersed with the thunderclap drumming of Adrian Young (his playing, just like that of Kanal and Dumont, is one of *Tragic Kingdom's* many revelations). 'Sixteen' was a curious mix: part hard rock, part ska, part girlpower punk, but once again Wilder caught on tape a truly dynamic performance from a group that had discovered their musical mojo at a time when they were all chewing over their post-No Doubt futures. Lyrically speaking, Gwen Stefani again delivered: what teen-heavy audience couldn't connect with a song about youthful alienation punctuated by a chant of "you're only 16"? With 'Sunday Morning', another *Tragic Kingdom* standout, Stefani again turned inwards: "Sappy pathetic little me," she whined, "That was the girl I used to be." Then she shook off her negativity and turned the tasers on Kanal: "You sure have changed since yesterday," Stefani snaps. "I thought I knew you . . . well." (She even calls him a "parasite".) 'Sunday Morning' typified Stefani's remarkable reinvention throughout *Tragic Kingdom*; once "Just A Girl" in ska-punk clothing, she was now a lover scorned – and she wasn't going to let her ex off lightly. The fact that the song came complete with a kicking ska-pop melody rounded it off perfectly.

But if there was one track on the album that provided the last word on the Stefani / Kanal relationship, it was, of course, the bittersweet valentine 'Don't Speak'. It was the LP's obligatory power ballad – and the song that would make them stars. It's easy to see why it succeeded: from Dumont's "tasteful" acoustic solo to Stefani's beseeching dumped-and-dejected vocal and the subtle undertow of strings, 'Don't Speak' has last-dance-at-the-high-school-formal written all over it. But by comparison with the furious energy of much of what came before on the album, it's actually one of *Tragic Kingdom's* lesser musical moments. It's catchy as hell, sure, and more sentimental than Christmas, but there's a saccharine aftertaste that lingers long after Stefani has whispered "hush, hush darling / don't tell me 'cause it hurts".

By this point of the album, however, No Doubt and *Tragic Kingdom* had just about run out of steam. 'You Can Do It', punctuated by oddly discofied strings and cheesy wah-wah guitar from Dumont – and an even cheesier keyboard solo – sounds like some discard from their self-titled debut (or a porno soundtrack cast-off). The gentler 'World Go 'Round', the most "ska'd-up" cut on the LP, followed. It's little more than filler, despite another winning vocal from Stefani – her vocal melodies throughout the album simply dripped hummability – plus the seductive tug of Dumont's skanking guitar and the breezy horns of Phil Jordan and new recruit Gabe McNair. (If *Tragic Kingdom* had one major flaw, it was its length: at 14 tracks and an hour in length, it ran at least two tracks and 10 minutes overtime, and was "backended" with some weak tracks.) Although inoffensive, the midtempo 'End It On This' simply sounded like a prototype for the album's key songs – i.e. the five tracks that were lifted as singles. And while it may have been necessary as the album's central "statement", the Eric Stefani-penned title track, complete with its sonic sample lifted from both the Splash Mountain and Matterhorn rides at Disneyland – "remain seated please!", a stern voice implores – and a lyric that ponders whether the American dream (as typified by Disneyland) might actually be a nightmare, it's as ponderous as 'The Climb'.

The seven tracks that Eric Stefani contributed to the album would set him up for life, but very few of the 15 million punters that bought *Tragic Kingdom* would do so for his social commentary. In the main, people snapped up the LP for its unbeatable collection of pop-rock anthems, Gwen Stefani's astute take on life as "just a girl" in white, suburban, middle-class America, and her very upfront observations on how it felt to be jilted. Like the best pop, *Tragic Kingdom* worked because at least half the album – its best tracks, naturally – was simple, direct and irresistibly catchy, while the group's hot-wired playing pinned back your ears. And with the increasingly photogenic Gwen Stefani leading the way, they also looked great, a factor that would (finally) make them an easy sell at MTV. All the pieces, so it seemed, had fallen into place, at a time when the band seemed ready to reach for the white flag and surrender themselves to more "normal" lives away from music. Desperation, as the album proved, can be one of the best motivators you can find.

Quoted in the album press bio, Tony Kanal summed up No Doubt circa 1995. "We've been playing, recording, and touring for eight years as a band and with *Tragic Kingdom* the album has really found its own sound," he said, with admirable bravado and just a hint of desperation. "Now we're just really ready to tour and take it to the rest of the world." What Kanal didn't know was just how ready the rest of the world was for No Doubt.

CHAPTER EIGHT

The Climb

"We hate it when our friends become successful / And if they're No Doubt, that makes it even worse."

—Reel Big Fish song lyric

The American musical landscape had changed considerably between the release of No Doubt's debut album and *Tragic Kingdom*. Generation grunge, led by the razor-sharp melodies and anguished howls of Nirvana's Kurt Cobain, and further driven home by the king-sized riffs of Pearl Jam and Soundgarden, had crashed and burned not long after Cobain, a prisoner to both smack and superstardom, blew his head off in his Seattle garage on April 5, 1994. Sure, there was a legacy: Pearl Jam would morph into grunge's very own Grateful Dead, cutting consistently solid studio albums but finding more of a platform on stage, and Soundgarden's Hollywood-handsome Chris Cornell became a hard-rock poster boy. But by the mid 1990s, the charts were way more accommodating for this little band from Orange County and their an unapologetically catchy, and lyrically frank, third album. And the major-label cheque-wavers had picked the bones of Seattle clean; there was hardly a worthy band left in the American north-west that hadn't been snapped up by an eager label hoping to catch a little of *Nevermind's* slipstream. Like so many musical movements that preceded it, from punk to disco, grunge had run out of steam at almost the same moment that it was recognised as a commercial force.

148

A lot was now working in No Doubt's favour. For one thing, women were all over the charts by the mid 1990s. When *Tragic Kingdom* dropped on October 10, 1995, Alanis Morissette, a former child star in Canada and now a lanky, surly 21-year-old with a lot of emotional baggage to unload, was four months into a monumental 80-plus week run on the Billboard charts with her *Jagged Little Pill* LP. In early 1994, after two indifferent earlier albums, Morissette connected with producer Glen Ballard, who'd written the Michael Jackson hit 'Man in the Mirror', produced the hit Wilson-Philips album, and – for reasons best known to Ballard – had recorded with surfside soapie star David Hasselhoff. (Ballard, incidentally, was a man soon to enter No Doubt's orbit.) Together, Morissette and Ballard crafted *Jagged Little Pill*, and on the strength of the deeply melodic and lyrically potent singles 'You Oughta Know' and 'Hands In My Pocket', *Pill* became the 1995 summer soundtrack, selling so relentlessly that the record was eventually awarded Diamond status, denoting sales of 10 million copies. It's pop's answer to an Olympic gold medal. (Interestingly, tastemakers such as *Rolling Stone* completely missed Morissette's zeitgeist moment: they didn't even review *Jagged Little Pill* when it was released on June 13, 1995. Just like *Tragic Kingdom*, it was a record that snuck in under the cool-school radar and took some time to peak, reaching No 1 on October 7, 1995.)

Morissette was a far more complicated and tormented character than Gwen Stefani – definitely John Lennon to Stefani's Paul McCartney – but there wasn't an enormous gulf separating *Pill* from *Tragic Kingdom*. During their best moments, both records were peppered with enormously accessible pop/rock anthems about growing up, getting dumped and fighting back. And despite their sometimes weighty subject matter, neither album carried the same sense of darkness and foreboding as Nirvana's *Nevermind* or Pearl Jam's *Ten*: these were smart, accessible pop records designed for mainstream radio airplay, not existential cries of pain fuelled by heroin and smoking Marshall stacks. Grunge was also a very male-dominated musical world, while both *Jagged Little Pill* and *Tragic Kingdom*, not surprisingly, spoke far more loudly to women. According to Interscope's Tony Ferguson, the shift represented another of pop's cyclical periods. "Music is the same merry-go-round. Trends go round and round and round, but every time they come back around – whether it's metal, or rock, or pop, or disco, or dance music or whatever – there is always a new twist. You've got Alanis Morissette, who is the epitome of the angry woman, and here we had Gwen Stefani, who is a little bit more of the antithesis of that and is just enjoying herself."

Morissette wasn't the only woman making waves in the summer of '95.

TLC, a slick, sexy R&B trio out of Atlanta, Georgia, comprising Tionne "T-Boz" Watkins, Lisa "Left Eye" Lopes, and Rozonda "Chilli" Thomas, were also in the midst of a commercial hot streak. Their second album, *CrazySexyCool*, had spent almost a year in the *Billboard* 200 chart when *Tragic Kingdom* appeared, selling mainly on the strength of such irresistible hip-hop-pop singles as "Creep" and "Waterfalls". It also didn't hurt their momentum when a drunk Lopes was arrested, just before the album appeared, and charged with burning down the mansion of her NFL star boyfriend Andre Lison. A little tabloid controversy never hurt record sales, as everyone from Elvis Presley to Marilyn Manson could attest.

There were other women on the rise, too. Canadian crossover queen Shania Twain, a big-haired belter fond of songs with exclamation marks, and with a sound that bridged the gap between the slick country of CMT and mainstream pop, was also a hot chart property. Her second LP, *The Woman In Me* – smartly produced by her husband Robert John "Mutt" Lange, who'd previously worked with AC/DC and Def Leppard – was in the process of shifting nine million copies in the USA alone. (Her next album, the unstoppable *Come On Over*, sold an outrageous 36 million units worldwide.) Elsewhere, Garbage, a supergroup of esteemed studio cats – including *Nevermind's* producer, Butch Vig – and led by rock vixen Shirley Manson, were about to break out with their self-titled debut and such powerful statements as 'Stupid Girl' and 'Only Happy When It Rains'. By the time of *Tragic Kingdom*, she-rocker Liz Phair had also scored heavily with her 1993 LP *Exile In Guyville* and its sequel, 1994's *Whip-Smart*. In short, it wasn't a bad time, both on MTV and at such tastemaking radio stations as KROQ, for a band like No Doubt, playing punchy pop songs and fronted by a self-assured woman who was easy on the eyes.

The influence of MTV and KROQ – commercially and critically – couldn't be overstated. Both were hugely important players throughout the 1980s and much of the 1990s (until MTV opted for reality TV over music, that is, and started producing such hit shows as *Jackass* and the *Real World*). Exposure, either by a high-rotation clip in MTV's Buzz Bin, or primetime airplay and a subsequent invite to KROQ's annual Weenie Roast, almost assured an act of healthy returns at the almighty cash register and recognition, if not necessarily critical kudos, at such tastemaking journals as *Spin* and *Rolling Stone*. In fact, some music trade journals have said that at least 70 percent of the acts awarded Buzz Bin status, since MTV introduced the concept in 1990, have gone on to gold sales (500,000 copies) or better. No Doubt was one of the fortunate ones in 1995, along with Trauma labelmates

Bush, as well as the Stone Temple Pilots, Dave Matthews Band, Radiohead and Blind Melon.

During its halcyon period in the 1980s – MTV first went to air on August 1, 1981 – the cable network helped transform Culture Club, the Eurythmics, Van Halen, the Cars, Bon Jovi, Weird Al Jankovic, plus many others, into very bankable stars. It also resurrected the career of former child star Michael Jackson. Just like No Doubt, these were acts that understood the potential impact of accessible music *and* a strong visual presence. It came as no great shock that in a 2006 poll to celebrate MTV's 25th anniversary, 'Don't Speak' was voted 1996's top video. No Doubt, at their peak, didn't just sound great, they looked fabulous, too. (Other winners included Prince, Missy Elliott, Eminem and Green Day, acts that were also masters at juggling sound and vision.) And it would be fair to say that without an MTV to air (and sometimes ban) her agit-pop videos, Madonna's commercial stocks would have been considerably lower. It was the video age, and MTV had the power – and the many million viewers, all around the globe – to make or break a band. Songs by The Red Hot Chili Peppers, Dire Straits and ska-punkers Reel Big Fish and Bowling for Soup even included lyrical references to MTV, which didn't hurt their chances of network airtime. (However, the same couldn't be said of Sublime's 'Don't Wanna Be No MTV Motherfucker' or Beck's 'MTV Makes Me Want To Smoke Crack'; neither made it to the Buzz Bin.) Generation X was sometimes referred to as the MTV Generation, which confirmed the network's broad influence, at least during its heyday. No Doubt had understood this ever since the days they sat around the TV in the band house on Beacon Street, figuring out ways to get their music heard, and seen.

Although it had lived through any number of formats – country, prog-rock, even religious music – since its inception in September 1972, LA's KROQ was another crucial cog in the commercial wheel. Via such taste-making DJs as Rodney Bingenheimer and Jed Gould (aka Jed the Fish), the station had been one of the few outlets for punk and new wave in the 1970s; in 1979 their anything-goes playlist was combined with a Top 40 format and KROQ, the 'Rock of the Eighties', was born. The station's value was recognised by its peers, too: in 1986, Infinity Broadcasting bought out the station for a cheeky US$45 million.

Just like MTV's Buzz Bin, the station hosted several exercises in self-promotion that also served as barometers of a band's "hipness". These included the KROQ Acoustic Christmas, which began in 1990; the KROQ Top 106.7 Countdown, which went to air every New Year's Eve since 1980, and the KROQ Weenie Roast, which made its debut in 1993. No Doubt, along with Alanis Morissette, Bush, Foo Fighters, Goo Goo Dolls and others, would make the invite list for 1995's Acoustic Christmas; and first rocked the Weenie Roast, in the company of Everclear, The Red Hot Chili Peppers, the Fugees and Tom Dumont's cartoon heroes Kiss, on June 15, 1996. 'Just A Girl' would rank #37 on the station's Top 106.7 songs of 1995 and would reach #13 on KROQ's Top 300 songs of the 1990s. *Tragic Kingdom* tracks 'Spiderwebs' (#35), 'Don't Speak' (#50), 'Happy Now?' (#225), 'Excuse Me Mr' (#244) and 'Sunday Morning' (#150) also made the same list, a clear indication of the album's bankability and the band's suitability for the KROQ format. (It didn't harm their KROQ rating that the band was accessible, either; No Doubt was never the kind of band to hide behind a fleet of publicists.) *Tragic Kingdom* also rated #11 on the station's list of Top 70 albums from 1980 to 2005, just ahead of their Long Beach pals and peers, Sublime. And on Memorial Day 2006, when KROQ compiled an epic list of "500 Most Requested Songs of All Time", 'Just A Girl' peaked at No 8, one of nine No Doubt tracks that made the hitlist. And this was the same station that declared that it would take "an act of God" to get the band played there. Things, clearly, had changed.

★ ★ ★

But as with so much of their pre-arena career, No Doubt still had some difficulty spreading the word of their *Tragic Kingdom*, at least initially. As Eric Carpenter had explained earlier, Interscope's support for the band was "inconsistent" at best; throughout the recording of *Tragic Kingdom* their standard response to new tracks had been: "Not bad. Keep writing." Tony Kanal recalled that the entire *Tragic Kingdom* project typified the turbulent relationship between band and label. "All we got to do was record in spurts," he said, "one song here, a couple there [as the LP's lengthy credits attest]. There was time in between everything. It was really frustrating."

The upside of this, however, was that the band got to work with Paul Palmer, who mixed *Tragic Kingdom* at Hollywood's Cactus Studios. Along with Rob Kahane, Palmer was the co-owner of indie label Trauma Records, who'd just struck gold with English Nirvana clones, Bush. Their debut album, *Sixteen Stone*, which was produced by Englishmen Clive Langer and Alan Winstanley, better known for their smart pop records, was a huge hit Stateside, despite being little more than Nirvana-lite. On the strength of the six-million-selling album, Ferguson and Interscope had agreed to distribute Trauma's other releases. Not only was this a key moment in the history of No Doubt (Gwen Stefani would eventually bed, and wed, Bush's lead singer Gavin Rossdale), but the Platinum-plus success of *Sixteen Stone* also helped shape Interscope, as Ferguson stated. "We started to get more involved with pop stuff through our amalgamation with Trauma Records, and Rob Kahane and Paul Palmer especially," he said. "We got their band out of Hollywood Records called Bush, and that became a big seller. All of a sudden we were in the pop game as well, which broadened Interscope into a full-service company. It was no longer this little independent upstart that was being controversial – we now had this broad spectrum. That was a very pivotal move which happened around the end of 1995 and early 1996."

Unlike Interscope, Palmer sensed the commercial possibilities of No Doubt, and Trauma approached Interscope with the idea of having the band switch from their mother label to his indie-on-the-rise. Interscope agreed and the deal was done; *Tragic Kingdom* would (finally) appear on Trauma Records, with distribution to be handled by Interscope. (No Doubt management confirmed this via email in late 2006.) "We were doing a deal with Bush which came through Trauma," Ferguson explained. "[So we agreed on] a deal where No Doubt comes from Interscope, and Trauma will help us develop the act. And it went great. It just fucking took off. We were in the right place at the right time. A lot of people worked their asses off on that record big time. But still, there was a shitload of luck. It was just at the right place at the right time."

While the members of No Doubt had never held back when it came to giving Interscope an earful, they were uncharacteristically tight-lipped when the Trauma deal was done. "To make a long story short," Kanal said in late 1995, "we switched over to Trauma and it's really great for us." The way Kanal saw it, the band now had the "focus and attention" of an indie, yet at the same time would benefit from Interscope's "distribution and money". For a group that had at times been treated little better than lepers by their own label, this was the sweetest deal of all. Kanal, for one, agreed, "We have the best of both worlds," he said. But even then, Tom Dumont spoke for the band when he summed up their expectations for *Tragic Kingdom*. "We thought it would be like our other albums: big underground following, no mainstream interest whatsoever."

Initially, at least, Dumont wasn't far from the truth. With 'Just A Girl' quietly released as the first single, the band did what came naturally and got back on the road. After an in-store at Fullerton's Bionic Records on the day before the album emerged, they headed off for dates in Hawaii, plus West Coast shows in Santa Barbara, Costa Mesa and San Diego, before heading to Dallas, Austin, Atlanta, Philadelphia, New York, Boston and Chicago for more dates, heading back home via St Louis, Kansas City, Salt Lake City,

Seattle, Vancouver and Portland (many of these shows were as part of the annual Vans Warped skate-punk roadshow). On November 19, 1995, the night before a gig at the Great American Music Hall in San Francisco, and just as the band made the cover of *BAM* magazine, MTV debuted the video for 'Just A Girl' on their *120 Minutes* program. (The video was shot on October 31 and November 1.)

Directed by Mark Kohr, who'd shot videos for Alanis Morissette's 'Hand In My Pocket', Interscope act Primus, as well as Green Day and Everclear, 'Just A Girl' made a very clear statement: this was a live band, best sampled in a sweaty dive (not unlike the actual toilet that featured in the clip, which served as the band room). Kanal and Young had shaved their skulls, while Dumont – who wielded a Flying V guitar with dangerous intent – was resplendent in a Mohawk. But Stefani was the star of the video; Kohr's camera loved her almost as much as she loved it. Sporting what would become a trademark bindi between her eyes (the "holy dot", traditionally worn by Hindu women, was another nod to Kanal's Indian heritage), and wearing a tank-top proudly emblazoned with the word "Anaheim", Stefani offered everything you could possibly need in a late 20th century pop hero: she was young, athletic, good-looking and proud of who she was and where she came from. And the clip's all-in party sequence, where the crowd bounced as one while the band played on, was even more emphatic than 'Trapped In A Box'. While it didn't have the hefty budget and production values of their later clips, 'Just A Girl' was the perfect "introduction" to the band, some eight years after they first started playing together. Yet even with the clip in the can, Stefani voiced the band's uncertainty, when asked whether MTV would give it airtime. "I think the chances are really slim. They get over 100 videos a month, and they pick, like, three. But it was still really fun making it."

The 'Just A Girl' clip was also the first video to feature musical all-rounder Stephen Bradley, who replaced trumpeter Phil Jordan. (Jordan had recently become a parent – his daughter's name is Megan – and was unwilling to continue travelling with the band. "I love her more than anything in life," he said. "No trip . . . could ever keep me away from that, man.") The only northern Californian in the band – Bradley was born in Richmond, California – his recruitment constituted the last piece of the No Doubt puzzle. He'd actually played in a band that supported No Doubt in 1991, named Private Culture, and was impressed by the headliners. "They were big in the underground scene," he said of the time. At that gig, Bradley had worn suspenders, and that's what the band remembered the most when he met with them in 1995 – he reminded them of Fishbone's Angelo Moore.

The go-between was Kerry James, a friend of Bradley's who'd gotten a call from Kanal looking for a stand-in for the upcoming San Francisco gig on July 26. But the connection almost didn't happen: In a mix-up that nearly cost Bradley his spot in the band, the CD that Kanal sent to him, in order to familiarise himself with the songs, had ended up with Bradley's next-door neighbour. A replacement arrived the night before the San Fran show. "I sat up all night, transcribing," Bradley recalled. He may have been under-prepared, but Bradley was a natural fit with No Doubt. Just like recent recruit Gabe McNair, Bradley – who had been playing trumpet since his days in the high school band – was a good-looking African / American with a livewire on-stage manner (in the 'Girl' clip, he and McNair pogo madly in unison, as if they've both been hit with a cattle prod). On stage, McNair was now freed up to move between brass and keyboards, while he and Bradley mapped out some simple but effectively choreographed stage moves, which drew more female punters to the front of the stage, and eased the performance load on Stefani. As former No Doubt-er Alex Henderson said earlier, McNair and Bradley weren't just dependable musicians, but they both "looked good in spandex". Phil Jordan saw that, too. "The guy they got now," he said, referring to Bradley, "is one hell of a performer. There's no way I could top his show." In what must have been a good omen for the band, the San Francisco gig, Bradley's debut, was a sell-out, even if the venue was only a 500-seater.

By late 1995, No Doubt were both a musically solid and a visually striking outfit, and these were just the qualities that they needed to make their mark at MTV. And 'Just A Girl' was the right clip at the right time, too. Just as crucially, KROQ were now very interested in No Doubt. The first time that 'Just A Girl' was played by KROQ – squeezed between tracks from U2 and the Offspring – left an indelible impression on many No Doubt insiders. Tony Kanal may have been the band's strongest advocate, a real true believer, but even he was stunned. "It was like, 'What's going on here?'," he said after hearing the single's on-air debut. "We couldn't even believe it. Then we started doing shows with other bands we love, and that was just too much." Eric Carpenter also has a vivid recollection of that fateful day in the band's rise. "I remember hearing them on the radio the first time, during the day. I was thrilled for them." (As documented elsewhere, this was the same time that Carpenter bumped into Dennis Stefani in Anaheim, who was wearing a cap featuring Gwen's cartoon image.)

Also tuned in was recent departee Eric Stefani. "When I first heard "Just A Girl" on the radio," he told the *Los Angeles Times'* Mike Boehm, "I had tears rolling down my face. After eight years, it was such a rush just to see we were making some impact on the world." Boehm was sensitive enough not to push, but these were clearly tears of both joy and frustration; Stefani had quit the band just as the world started to listen.

Airplay at MTV and KROQ was crucial for the band's forward momentum, but it also significantly helped their cause when 'Just A Girl' was added to the soundtrack for the flick *Clueless*, a smart-yet-dumb vehicle for then-very-hot starlet Alicia Silverstone. No Doubt were now rubbing shoulders with such KROQ favourites as Counting Crows, Beastie Boys, Radiohead and the Mighty Mighty Bosstones, all of whom contributed to the soundtrack. By mid-summer, the fish-out-of-water comedy had grossed US$50 million, and its success may have well been a forecast of what was to come for No Doubt.

Between its release and the end of 1995, reviews started to trickle in for *Tragic Kingdom*. While not even Nostradamus could have predicted just how big the album would become, there was definitely more media interest in the band this time around. Writing in the *Los Angeles Times*, long-time observer Mike Boehm figured that the LP represented a "mission accomplished" for No Doubt. "The talented Anaheim band has found a way to weave its diverse stylistic strands into catchy, adventurously but cohesively structured songs that improve markedly upon the diffuse, rambling songwriting of its two previous CDs," he figured, before noting that the band's musical reach was far greater than on their earlier, ska-pop heavy efforts. "No Doubt [is] confidently meshing reggae and ska with edgy New Wave guitar rock and throwing in touches of metal, Motown funk, a handful of Beatles references and even a bit of neo-Dixieland. The band is bright, hard-hitting and kinetic, as sharp production captures the core, four-man instrumental team and adjunct horn section at their best." While uncertain as to how the band would fare without Eric Stefani, Boehm did note that 'Don't Speak' was a hit-in-waiting, even if he wasn't its biggest fan. He dismissed the song as "a conventional take on the heartbroken pop ballad form that sounds like something a more serious-minded Mariah Carey might attempt", which was hardly high praise.

Boehm was more impressed by 'Just A Girl' and its punked-up take on girl power. "The subject is the subjugation of women through violence and fear," Boehm wrote, "but Stefani's irony and indirection make this a more artful and resonant salvo than if she had rendered it as an openly wrathful indictment." Although he didn't say it out loud, Boehm might well have been pointing out that Stefani was a more palatable role model than tormented grunge widow Courtney Love, who was making inroads with her band Hole, or the current queen of pain, Alanis Morissette. A wholesome, honest suburban 20-something had to be an improvement on the drug-fucked Love or the man-loathing Morissette.

Writing in the *San Francisco Chronicle*, Aidin Vaziri was impressed by the album's sheer diversity. "Musically, the Orange County residents cram as much as possible into each song," he wrote, "matching funky bass lines, heavy-metal riffs, reggae beats and new wave synth lines with a rowdy punk shuffle. But it's singer Gwen Stefani's striking purr that pulls the hodge-podge of sound together." He heaped praise on the tracks 'Spiderwebs' and 'Just A Girl', seeing them as moments where "Stefani uses her seductive, whimsical voice to hold No Doubt's boisterous, uprooted funk together". And, just as crucially, Vaziri noted, the band definitely sounded like they were having a hell of a good time, unlike many of their stony-faced peers. "No Doubt rarely gets too serious," he said in conclusion. "It's too busy frolicking in its own irrelevance." It's unlikely that Tony Kanal, for one, would have appreciated the final line, but this was a distinct improvement on reviews of their previous two albums, which were barely noticed outside of their So-Cal HQ.

Not everyone was a convert. *Rolling Stone* magazine took some time to get on board the No Doubt bandwagon, although even this venerable institution, with its roots in the "hippie" era of the 1960s, couldn't ignore the momentum that the band gathered during the early months of 1996. (They'd finally become cover stars on May 1, 1997.) In his review of *Tragic Kingdom*, long-time Stone staffer David Fricke cut straight to the chase: Gwen Stefani, she of the bared midriff and Indian bindi, was the main reason that the band was moving on up. "A platinum blond peach of a female singer, Stefani . . . breaks up the asexual baggy-shorts-and-balloon-pants monotony of alt-nation guy rock," Fricke wrote, with his usual precision. "No Doubt have a spry, white-suburban take on ska and Blondie-esque pop," he added, before dumping on 'Don't Speak'. It was "irritating swill", just like all power ballads, according to Fricke.

The All Music Guide was more generous with their praise of the band's third LP: "Led by the infectious, pseudo-new wave single "Just A Girl", No Doubt's major-label debut [sic] *Tragic Kingdom* straddles the line between '90s punk, third wave ska, and pop sensibility," the site reported. *All-Music* also praised the No Doubt / Wilder combination, which they viewed as "a clever mainstream co-opting of new wave quirkiness, and, as such, an ideal pairing . . . Wilder [keeps] his production lean and accessible, accentuating No Doubt's appealing mix of new wave melodicism, post-grunge rock, and West Coast sunshine."

Thanks to the cumulative impact of radio and video airplay, by Christmas

1995 No Doubt was a band in demand. They played the X-Mas Fest, hosted by radio station KCXX at the Orange Pavilion in San Bernadino. No Doubt topped the nine-act, five-and-a-bit-hour bill above Alaskan pop poetess Jewel, singer/strummers Jill Sobule and Matthew Sweet, and Bang!, the new outfit fronted by former English Beat guy David Wakeling. Suddenly the OC five weren't just sharing bills with such heroes as Wakeling, they were actually headlining. No Doubt, who took the stage just before midnight, as the crowd began to thin, weren't exactly in their milieu: when Stefani asked how many "old-schoolers" were in the house, she was met with a deafening silence. Nonetheless, the band, especially Stefani, made a strong showing, according to a reporter from the *Press-Enterprise* who covered the bash.

"A cross between a '40s pinup queen and a Marine sergeant, she's become a bit of a heroine – cute and strong aren't mutually exclusive, and being a girl doesn't mean you're not a person," read the review. "The music is pop with roots in reggae and ska, but the band's attitude is definitely punk. A pair of horn players added the perfect bit of brassy ska. The band thrashed up its current hit, 'Just A Girl', and the reggae-flavoured 'Spiderwebs' sounded like a sure follow-up."

Soon after, No Doubt played the Sunday night of KROQ's Almost Acoustic Christmas, sharing the bill with both fellow up-and-comers – Tony Ferguson signing the Toadies, the Dave Grohl-led Foo Fighters, English moodists Radiohead – and more established acts like New Yorkers Sonic Youth. Also on the bill was current chart-toppers Bush, who were led by the handsome, brooding Cobain-clone Gavin Rossdale. Although she was still recovering from her bust-up with Kanal, Gwen Stefani was about to have a very close encounter with the love of her life.

★   ★   ★

They may have taken their name from their home of Shepherd's Bush in London, but Bush, whose members also included bassist Dave Parsons, drummer Robin Goodridge and guitarist Nigel Pulsford, always had their eyes on America: they signed a US deal while still label-less in the UK. And in the wake of Kurt Cobain's suicide, their timing couldn't have been better; Bush's watered-down take on Seattle grunge was a sonic placebo for devastated Nirvana-lovers. Gavin Rossdale's upbringing, however, was a world apart from Cobain's hardscrabble, drug-fucked existence: his father, Douglas, was a doctor, and when his parents split, the 11-year-old Rossdale lived a middle-class, tennis-playing life in London with his aunt. He rebelled, of course, and was almost expelled from boarding school; in his late teens he ran with a cross-dressing crowd. According to Boy George's 1995 memoir, *Take It Like A Man*, Rossdale had maintained a long-term gay relationship with drag-queen-cum-one-hit-wonder, Marilyn. (The Boy wrote that Rossdale – a "very flirtatious and ambitious" man – had attempted to talk him into cutting it from the book. Rossdale subsequently claimed he and Marilyn were "just good friends".)

Bush's debut album, *Sixteen Stone* (also mixed by Paul Palmer) was released in December 1994; propelled by the radio staples 'Everything Zen' (an MTV Buzz Bin pick), 'Little Things', 'Comedown' and 'Glycerine', it was one of the biggest albums of the post-*Nevermind* era, selling upwards of six million units, despite almost universally bad press. As the *Toronto Sun's* review of the album pointed out, "The trouble with the rapid rise of any genre is that said genre will invariably be codified, its essence reduced to a series of stylistic tics . . . all entirely beyond the point." An *NME* review of a London show was even more succinct: "Bush . . . look like a band whose moment hasn't just passed, but never really happened in the first place." Ouch. It's no coincidence that while the album's four singles charted highly on Billboard's Modern Rock and Mainstream Rock charts, only one – 'Comedown' – even brushed the UK Top 20. Though hardly authentic in look, sound or style, Bush was a band with a plan: America or bust. It obviously worked, because when Rossdale met Stefani, he owned a five-storey Primrose Hill townhouse, valued at a rather useful US$2.3 million.

The Stefani / Rossdale KROQ encounter had just a whiff of Mills & Boon about it. After being introduced by a staffer from Trauma, Rossdale took one look at Stefani and told her, point blank: "You're gorgeous." Although flattered, she wasn't sure that she wanted to get tangled up with another musician, even a movie-star-handsome middle-class Englishman, as she confessed in an interview with *YM* magazine. "I wasn't looking to go out with a boy in a band," Stefani said, "especially one who's that good-looking. I'm usually attracted to guys with personalities, ones that make me laugh. That's what I think is sexy – not some dude with flowing curls who's tall and gorgeous." While Stefani's words may have offered a flicker of hope for ordinary guys everywhere, it wasn't long before she contradicted her own no-band-guys policy, and started dating Rossdale. Stefani admitted that there was something "familiar" about him that she recognised in that first meeting. "[It was] in his eyes; there was something about him. I said something like, "You've got gorgeous eyes" and I never say stuff like that. It was really cheesy, but it just came out. That night he told me I was gorgeous; I thought that was pretty great."

While Bush's *Sixteen Stone* stubbornly refused to leave the charts, No

Doubt's 'Just A Girl' also started to rise. The *Billboard* charts, just like American radio formats, were only decipherable to those who sweated on their weekly rankings, which explains why 'Girl' started to rate on four separate charts: the Hot 100, where it debuted at No 84 on December 16 (peaking at No 23 in April '96); Modern Rock Tracks (debuting at 33 in mid-November and reaching No 10 on January 27); Hot 100 Singles Airplay (No 66 debut, No 32 peak) and an oddity called 'The Rock Big Picture', where it would reach a high of No 19 in mid-February. Meanwhile, its parent album, *Tragic Kingdom*, also started to make inroads on various LP charts, the most crucial being The Billboard 200, where it began its slow march to the top on January 20, 1996, with a modest chart ranking of No 175. Over time, of course, that would improve.

Trauma recognised the potential pay-off in bringing together its two red-hot bands, and a joint tour, with No Doubt opening the show, was swiftly arranged. A drunken Tom Dumont, however, almost derailed the campaign before it began. When Dumont drank, he morphed into a character known as The Douche, and it was he who burst into the Bush dressing room at the KROQ gig, advising Fender-guitar-user Nigel Pulsford that "Fenders suck", before being shown the door. One threatening phone call from Trauma staff later, and Dumont's alter ego was locked away, at least for the time being.

At the same time, there was also a very rare spotting of a drunken Gwen Stefani. She turned up at a show by The Skeletones, with whom No Doubt had shared some bills in the days before *Tragic Kingdom*. As Skeletone Paul Hampton told me, "I've only seen Gwen drunk once, at the Showcase Theater. I was there with my girlfriend, who's now my wife. We were backstage and Gwen was pretty lit up. It might have been during the Tony [break-up] thing. You know what girls can be like when they're drunk, really flirtatious, and she's hanging all over me going, 'Hey, what's going on?' My wife's like, 'Who the hell's this?' We had to go on stage, so I'm thinking that someone better take care of this girl, she's pretty fucked up. That was the last I saw of her, leaving her in a precarious situation, but she had a lot of girlfriends there. She was a real free spirit." (Stefani has only admitted to being loaded once, downing tequila shots when *Tragic Kingdom* hit number one. She described the experience as "self torture".)

Hampton had actually been one of the first people outside the band to hear tracks from *Tragic Kingdom* before it was released; he sensed almost immediately that things had improved for No Doubt, and that they'd outgrown their third wave peers. "Adrian sent me a copy of a couple of *Tragic Kingdom* songs," he told me, "and called me up and said, 'Hey, check them out, what do you think?' When I first heard 'Just A Girl', the keyboard bridge was really loud in the mix. I told him that everything was cool except for this keyboard part. I figured if it was going to be a huge success it'd need a mix job. But I figured everything [else] was sounding great. It was better than the last album and better than everything on the "red" album, the first album. One thing about No Doubt," he continued, "is that from day one they've always mixed pop with ska. Fishbone were the band that mixed funk with ska. We were the band that tried to mix new wave with ska and rock. You had other bands that were doing silly ska. They always mixed it up. They've never changed, they just got better."

Another thing that kept improving was the band's commercial worth; on January 30, 1996, while in New York, they made their debut on *Late Night With Conan O'Brien*, tearing through 'Just A Girl' as if they had a limo waiting outside with its engine running. It was a great few moments of live TV: Stefani, in what was by now her trademark bindi-and-bared-midriff look – complete with a top that simply read "Gwen" – prowled the stage, batting her heavily mascara-d eyelashes coyly at the camera while riffing on her lyrics ("I'm just your typical prototype", she chuckled, acting out the dumb blonde role while simultaneously doing her bit for girl power). Kanal, now with centre parting and wearing another of his favourite warm-up track-suits, pulled off some slick breakdancing moves, while Dumont – whose T-shirt declared 'Sell Out' – riffed powerfully and Young powered away on a kit that proudly bore the Eric Stefani-designed band logo. To his side, McNair attacked his keyboards while Bradley blew his lungs dry, even though his trumpet was barely audible amidst the bottom-heavy mix. In the end, it mattered little: No Doubt looked, and sounded, like a powerhouse rock'n'roll machine. Even the unflappable O'Brien seemed impressed, leaving his desk to shake the band's hands as he threw to a commercial break. They couldn't have made a more emphatic mainstream TV debut.

A few weeks later they were back in the *Los Angeles Times*, only this time featuring in a much larger, more broad-ranging piece than ever before. Speaking candidly with writer Steve Appleford, Stefani confessed to a weakness for new wave, an obvious influence on 'Just A Girl', but at the same time she may have been explaining away her band's recent success. "Those were great songs," she said of the 1980s. "It's so happy and fresh sounding, compared to a lot of the grunge and dark stuff that's been coming out lately." In the same interview, which precisely captured a band in transition from honest toilers to platinum-plated stars, Stefani also took the time to play down 'Girl' as any kind of hard-line feminist anthem. "A lot of people have taken it even further than I've wanted it, like some big . . .

statement, which it really isn't," she said. "It's just random daily burdens of being a girl. It's awesome though, I can't believe it would have that kind of response."

No Doubt's next stop was a history-making event, not only for the band but also for music in Orange County. Opening up for Bush and the Goo Goo Dolls, No Doubt played the Pond in Anaheim on March 12, in the process becoming the first OC band to do so. Tastemakers called this triple-header "the hottest alternative rock bill of the season", which was fair enough, too, given that *Sixteen Stone's* sales were now being measured in the millions, the Goo Goo Dolls' *A Boy Named Goo* album, mainly on the strength of the power ballad 'Name', had gone Platinum, and *Tragic Kingdom* had just tipped the 200,000 sales mark, selling at a healthy rate of 25,000 per week.

Up until then, the members of No Doubt had only seen The Pond from a passing car, or, at best, looking on from the cheap seats somewhere deep in the 18,000-capacity venue's darkness. But on the day of the gig – dubbed "The Longest [Day] on Earth" by their over-heated publicist – they were virtual hostages of this cavernous Anaheim concrete bunker, spending the best part of 12 hours holed up doing interviews, smiling for a photo shoot with teen mag *Sassy* – but only after Stefani had raced home to track down her forgotten make-up bag – and conferring with potential managers and agents. Although running way behind schedule (Stefani actually arrived with her hair still in curlers, covered by a kerchief), the band's lead singer was nothing less than radiant, according to the *Los Angeles Times'* Mike Boehm. "She looked wonderfully camera-ready in her bangs, halter top and snug turquoise sequined pants," he reported, "like a cross between Jessica Lange and a naughty cheerleader."

He was equally impressed by her almost Olympian physicality and unde-niable charisma when the band finally hit the stage for their seven-song, 35-minute set. "Stefani, a marvel of aerobic fitness who passes slow days on the road roller-blading around empty arenas, bounded and sauntered tirelessly," Boehm reported. "She played the hometown card, mimicking Judy Garland as Dorothy ("there's no place like home") and cajoling the crowd to sing along so she could impress her watching grandparents." Also looking on backstage were members of Adrian Young's family, Tony Kanal's cousin, Naveen Kanal, and his father, Gulab. When asked what was next for the band, Kanal Sr put things in perspective. "They have a lot of hard work ahead of them, and success doesn't come without hard work," he said. "If they wanted to have an easy life, they'd get real jobs." Getting a "real job" was the furthest thing from their minds when the band returned to New York on

March 28 for its debut appearance on David Letterman, again cranking out 'Just A Girl'. Just like Conan O'Brien before him, Letterman – smug host of the most watched and most influential late show on US TV – was smitten by the OC five, tapping along to yet another furious version of 'Girl'.

With the Bush tour in overdrive, and Stefani's love life on the improve the more time she spent with Rossdale, Trauma delivered 'Spiderwebs', another high-energy slice of *Tragic Kingdom*, as the band's next single. Although not a runaway smash – that honour was reserved for 'Don't Speak', still several months off in the future – 'Spiderwebs' made its mark on almost as many Billboard charts as 'Just A Girl', reaching a healthy No 11 peak in the Top 40 Mainstream list. In fact, the only bum note in the hottest few months of the band's life to date happened in early May, when Stefani over-extended herself during their opening spot and broke her foot. Yet even then the show limped on; the band knew that if they ever wanted to become something more than the best little act in Orange County, their time was now.

Up next was a sort of homecoming; a two-night stand at the Palladium in the LA, this time sans Bush. After several months of playing what were effectively 35 minute musical infomercials, No Doubt finally had the chance to stretch out for an hour-and-a-half (even if stretching was a physical impossibility for Stefani). And for a change they could actually see all the faces in the venue, not just those of the Rossdale groupies in the first few rows. Though not totally sold on the band, one reviewer accepted that right now No Doubt could do no wrong, especially in front of an excitable hometown crowd. "Stefani strutted and mugged, leading her capering bandmates through a . . . set that kept the packed crowd boppin' and moshin' to the tune of such hits as 'Just A Girl' and 'Spiderwebs'," noted Sandy Masuo. "The music, constructed as it is from big, friendly, easy-to-read elements, even defied the Palladium's notoriously bad acoustics."

★　★　★

The breakout success of *Tragic Kingdom*, which was now racing towards its first million units sold and settling in for a remarkable 90 weeks in The Billboard 200 chart, finally gave record label A&R scouts a new hotspot to plunder. A few years earlier, exploring what lurked behind the "Orange Curtain" was a notion that didn't even register on the radar of major labels. But now it was seen as a breeding ground for musical talent, in just the same way that virtually every garage in Seattle had been scoured in the wake of Nirvana's *Nevermind* (as documented, with all due cynicism, on the excellent rockumentary *Hype!*).

The *Orange County Register* first mentioned the invasion in May, 1996, with a piece that asked: "Is ska Orange County's next big thing? More importantly, is Orange County ska the next big thing?" Many OC acts were now benefiting from the success of No Doubt and Sublime, including ska-punkers Reel Big Fish and Goldfinger (who'd already produced a hit single, 'Here In My Bedroom'). Both bands signed deals with Santa Monica-based Mojo Records. Meanwhile, such up-and-comers as Pocket Lent, My Superhero, the Aquabats – voted the one band "who deserve to have their own Saturday morning cartoon" – and the much-fancied Save Ferris, were, as reporter Steven Lynch wrote, "looking like truffles waiting to be unearthed" by eager record company A&R guys, chequebooks in hand. The charts may have been a confusing place, with Bush, No Doubt and Alanis Morissette jostling for position with the likes of George Strait, Hootie & the Blowfish and Celine Dion, but for Orange County it was the best of times.

Even though he'd dropped out of the music scene upon leaving No Doubt, horn man Eric Carpenter sensed the change in the industry's attitude towards So-Cal. "As a resident of Orange County, I did suddenly hear bands that reminded me a lot of our sound getting airplay," he said. "So it was clear that the record companies were doing here what they had done in Seattle and other places – one band hits and suddenly there are a lot of prospectors mining for more gold in the same mine. It was funny to watch, considering that just a couple of years before our sound was considered unmarketable. I couldn't help but think about how many record industry "showcase" shows we'd played where nobody from the industry showed up. I think No Doubt helped solidify Orange County as a legitimate breeding ground for talent."

Sublime manager Jon Phillips witnessed this first-hand when he and the Long Beach Dub All Stars, the band that emerged from the ashes of Sublime, were sniffed out by A&R heavyweight Michael Goldstone, who'd helped sign Pearl Jam and Rage Against the Machine. They were invited to the estate of music biz mogul David Geffen, "complete with butlers, maids, circular courtyards for gardening vehicles and walls [full] of Jackson Pollack, Keith Haring, etcetera," said Phillips. "His staff made a formal lunch for us – fish, and it wasn't that good, either – and assembled us in front of a team of industry vets that made every attempt to convince us not to sign to Epitaph Records. They said Brett [Gurewitz, founder of the label and member of Bad Religion] was a drug addict. Pretty classic stuff, really. I thought Geffen was a little impersonal, stuck up, and pretty much a prick, although they had the money to make an offer that we couldn't refuse at the time with eight mouths to feed in the band." (A footnote to this is the tale of Slightly Stoopid, another band managed by Phillips and once signed to Brad Nowell's Skunk Records. In 1998, barely three years after *Tragic Kingdom*, they recorded what Phillips considered an "awesome album", called *The Longest Barrel Ride*, and "couldn't get arrested – not a single label wanted to touch them. Not surprising," Phillips shrugged, "no-one in Hollywood wanted to touch Sublime, either.")

Twenty-year-old Monique Powell, the lead singer of Save Ferris, was seen as the woman-most-likely to succeed Gwen Stefani. In the band's official bio, Powell was described as a 'rock goddess ... sexy, intelligent, strong, capable, extremely lovable and immensely talented' – all terms used to describe Stefani. In a curious, though probably unrelated coincidence, Save Ferris were first noticed when they covered Dexy's Midnight Runners' 'Come On Eileen', a song whose original video had inspired Gwen Stefani to dress No Doubt's brass section in less-than-flattering dungarees. And Powell later developed the fashion lines Msquared and August, harbingers of Gwen Stefani's own LAMB label, and she also dabbled in acting, a la Stefani. Who made the first move in each instance is anyone's guess. When asked what made their take on ska so consumer-friendly, Powell replied that their upbeat musical mélange, which mixed ska with pop and swing, was simply more life-affirming than grunge. Fun was definitely the new black. "It's about time we rose above all this depression," she said. "We went through this suicide phase, and now there's us."

Aaron Barrett, the leader of Reel Big Fish, told me that there was definitely an increase in the number of bands coming out of OC once Sublime and No Doubt went large. "You started to see more ska bands pop up," he said. "There were shows all over. [But] we really didn't feel there was any rivalry between ska bands; we were all just happy to discover that there were other bands doing what we did." Before *Tragic Kingdom*, at a time when third wave ska was pretty much the domain of a few well-informed "rudies" with *NME* subscriptions, Reel Big Fish had endured a phase where their original lead singer Ben Guzman "suddenly wanted to turn us into R.E.M.," according to Barrett. That was short-lived. Soon after, Barrett heard such tracks as the Mighty Mighty Bosstones' 'Someday I Suppose' and Rancid's 'Timebomb' played on local radio, and was hooked. "All sorts of ska-punk type bands started springing up [in OC]," he said. "The Aquabats, Save Ferris, My Superhero – we also loved Hepcat, Dance Hall Crashers and Skankin' Pickle; they were a big inspiration to the mid-'90s ska-punk bands." Another key inspiration for Barrett, and many other OC bands hoping to seize a little of No Doubt's momentum, was the *California Ska Quake* compilation. "That was a great CD," he gushed. "It had No Doubt, Let's Go Bowling, Skeletones – all the greats are on that one."

Reel Big Fish, however – just like No Doubt – was a band on the outer with ska purists, in part because of Barrett's tendency to take the piss in his lyrics. "[We were] mocking the seriousness of the "rudies" and their exclusivity," he told me. "We newer bands got a lot of shit for not being 'true' ska. No Doubt and Sublime didn't really fit in the ska scene [either] and kind of formed their own cult followings. We started to see more bastardised versions of ska and reggae, and we knew that was for us." High amongst the list of heretics were the outfits Suburban Rhythm and the Nuckle Brothers, "the arch nemesis of the 2-Tone scene," said Barrett. This new wave of ska-punks also turned up their noses at the standard 2-Tone uniform of pork-pie hat, Fred Perrys and braces. "We were more into bright colours and crazy clashing patterns. I wore a lot of Hawaiian shirts back then," Barrett added.

Barrett was in no doubt (pun intended) how Reel Big Fish became one of the many OC bands to score a deal. "No Doubt and Sublime were everywhere," he said, "and so was the word ska. We all started getting record deals. As soon as the word ska kept turning up, the record labels jumped on the opportunity and pushed us as hard as they could. Suddenly we were on the radio with a hit song [appropriately called "Sellout"], too." Barrett and his band weren't huge fans of *Tragic Kingdom* – "we loved their old stuff" – but were chuffed that their peers No Doubt and Sublime had gotten out of the So-Cal ska-punk ghetto. "We never really could relate to No Doubt's song lyrics," he admitted, "they were kind of weird and vague. But we loved the music – and we loved Gwen." (Both Save Ferris and Reel Big Fish would score Gold records, before the spotlight moved away from Orange County ska-pop.)

Despite this sense of brotherhood, it didn't stop Barrett from taking a potshot at No Doubt with their reworking of the Morrissey track, 'We Hate It When Our Friends Become Successful', where they altered the lyrics to read: "We hate it when our friends become successful / And if they're No Doubt, that makes it even worse." Although Barrett admits that Stefani and co "were quite upset about it," this didn't stop him stirring the pot – after all, this was the man behind such cheeky downers as 'Don't Start A Band', 'Turn The Radio Off' and 'One Hit Wonderful'. "Being as mean-spirited as we are," Barrett laughed, "we have kept on poking fun at them through the years. [But] No Doubt has always been a big inspiration for this band."

As reassuring as all this praise was, No Doubt was about to suffer another major body blow: Sublime's Brad Nowell, both a peer and pal of the band,

OD'd and died of a heroin overdose in a San Francisco hotel room on May 25, 1996, just one day before the *Orange County Register* feature that acknowledged their role in the seemingly unstoppable rise of third wave ska. His death was hard to comprehend: The band's third album was done and dusted, while the 28-year-old Nowell had recently become a first-time father and had married his partner Troy Dendekker just a week before his sordid death. As journalist Jerry Crowe noted in his eulogy for the singer / guitarist, "in his exit last weekend, Brad Nowell became the embodiment of sad showbiz cliches", he wrote. "[However] it's worth remembering the honest, emotionally unstinting and stylistically varied way in which much of his music grapples with what was in his own consciousness," he added, "fundamental questions of escape versus responsibility and despair versus hope." "Brad was a natural to self-destruct," said Jon Phillips, when I asked him about Nowell's death. "You can only do so much to control chaos, you know what I'm saying?"

No Doubt was in New York, on their seemingly endless tour pushing *Tragic Kingdom*, when the news of Nowell's death reached the band. Stefani, who'd twice recorded with Nowell, was devastated. "His voice [was] like candy to your ears," Stefani told the *Los Angeles Times'* Crowe from the tour bus. "Bradley definitely had a gift, and it sickens me that I'm not going to be able to enjoy his voice anymore. It's not sad for him – he's gone – but it's sad for everybody else. He had such a huge impact on so many people in the whole [local music] scene." Nowell's father Jim succinctly summed up the general feeling of loss and despair. "It's nice that his songs had so much effect on people. But I'd rather he was an accountant and still around. I feel like I gave my son to the music industry. And I didn't get anything back."

Former No Doubt-er Eric Carpenter recalled the first time that the bands" paths intersected. "Sublime and No Doubt did move in different circles early on," he said. "As I recall, the first we ever heard of Sublime was when a friend of theirs came up to Tony Kanal after a show and said, in essence, "You guys are great. You should open a show for my friend's band", and handed him a Sublime tape. Needless to say, that didn't really start things out on the right foot when he suggested we open for a band we'd never heard of." Carpenter and the band, however, were in for a shock when they got around to playing the tape: the songs turned out to be demos for Sublime's breakthrough album, *40 Oz. To Freedom*. "We all fell in love with it and that led to a friendship between bands," he continued. "During my time, I think we played about a half-dozen shows together. They were remarkably talented, but spotty live. Some shows were outstanding, others forgettable, I think mostly because of Brad's substance abuse. They were always good to us and, in Sublime we found friendship and a similar musical vibe — even if our sounds were quite different. They put a different spin on similar influences of Jamaican ska and Southern California beach culture."

No Doubt did their bit for Nowell's legacy, playing the Enuff Already fund-raiser, held at the Palladium in Hollywood, headlining a bill that also included Pennywise and Bad Brains' HR, while also marking the debut of the Long Beach Dub All Stars, the band that featured the remaining members of Sublime. "No Doubt were very supportive; they could relate, for sure," said Jon Phillips, casting his mind back to the death of John Spence. "And Brad [Nowell] was the man for a lot of these people. When people heard this last album, after he was gone, they were like, "Holy shit". That was the music that was hitting; it was different to any other person who died young — the Cobains, the Hendrixes, the Janises, they were already playing to hundreds of thousands of people. This guy was just peaking."

There was a curios footnote to the No Doubt / Sublime axis. At the time Gwen Stefani joined them in the studio to work on the track 'Saw Red', Sublime were still trying to sort out a label deal. Money for this session had been coughed up by Epitaph, the label owned by Bad Religion's Brett Gurewitz. Jon Phillips picked up the story. "Sublime was touring around, some people were taking notice. Epitaph gave them some studio time and they cut six cuts, for demos or whatever. One of them was "Saw Red". [Afterwards] I kept asking the Sublime guys why Epitaph hadn't signed them. I asked Brett, when Epitaph wanted to sign Long Beach Dubs, after Brad died. He said, "They were working with some girl and I just didn't get it." That was Gwen — and this was coming from the guru of punk rock. Two of the biggest stars of the decade right there and boom, they missed it. I thought that was interesting."

★ ★ ★

Despite their loss, No Doubt continued playing, barely stopping for breath. Between the time of Nowell's death and the release of *Tragic Kingdom's* next single, they played almost 70 shows, which took them away from North America for the first time, playing dates throughout Europe (including a Wembley Arena show on July 11), Australia and New Zealand, followed by a return appearance on Letterman. Just when it seemed that maybe the band and *Tragic Kingdom*, which had passed sales of two million, was finally running out of steam, No Doubt delivered the killer blow: their syrupy 'Don't Speak', another break-up song that seemed to be lifted directly from Stefani's diary. Their transition from band to brand was almost complete.

In its original form, 'Don't Speak' was one of the last songs that Eric Stefani wrote for No Doubt. As with much of his songwriting, the tune came to him in the middle of the night; he had quickly nailed the melody, and he also had a title and some cursory lyrics. The following day he played it to his sister, who transformed it into the lovelorn ballad that much of America could not avoid throughout the rest of 1996. (This, of course, happened well before the track was recorded; the band had been tinkering with it, on stage and in rehearsal, for several years.) In Gwen's hands, it became a very clear and concise – if turgid – farewell to Kanal, the "love of her life". Her lyric was nothing like her brother had originally intended for the song; apparently, he had it envisaged as a "decidedly unromantic self-indictment," according to writer Mike Boehm – but it was almost impossible to resist the finished version's melodramatic tug at the heartstrings.

'Don't Speak' also marked the first occasion that Sophie Muller directed a clip for the band. Muller has rarely gone on the record about her work – she passed on the chance to speak for this book – preferring to let her dayglo images do the talking, but she has admitted what drew her to No Doubt, after Tom Atencio, formerly of MCA and now with management firm Atencio & Associates, first connected band and video-maker. (Before working with No Doubt, Atencio's lengthy track record included breaking such acts as Tom Petty, Nils Lofgren, New Order and, erm, Men Without Hats in the USA; later on he'd represent Jane's Addiction and help establish Lollapalooza. Jennifer Herrema of the alt-rock band Royal Trux claims that if her band hadn't fired Atencio, just before he connected with Stefani and co, "No Doubt wouldn't have existed.")

"One of the reasons I wanted to work with No Doubt in the first place," Muller said in the notes for *Live In The Tragic Kingdom*, the concert DVD she directed, "is that I saw them play live. It seems only fair that the rest of the world be allowed this same honour. Plus," she added, "it was really fun." The love was reciprocal; Gwen Stefani, with whom Muller has become especially tight, admitted that she'd always admired Muller's videos, going so far as to label her "a genius". "I was a fan of Sophie's work before I even imagined working with her," Stefani said. "She has a very pronounced style and taste that drew me in. I think she has the gift of being able to bring out the artist's personality, emotion and style."

Just like Tony Kanal, Muller was born in London, but was raised on the Isle of Man, before returning to the mainland to study at the Central Saint Martins College of Art and Design, gaining a Foundation Diploma in Art. She attained her masters in Film and Television at the Royal College of Art. Muller's first paying gig was as a third assistant on the horror thriller

Company of Wolves, but she soon found her niche in video – and, with the rise of MTV, her timing couldn't have been better. Muller directed her first clip in 1987 (the Eurythmics' "Beethoven", one of 13 Eurythmics clips she has directed), and also worked with Sade, Sinead O'Connor, World Party, Shakespear's Sister, The Cure, Bjork and the Stefanis' old Loara High buddy, Jeff Buckley, before she hooked up with the little band from Orange County. It was the beginning of a beautiful working relationship; to date, Muller has directed seven No Doubt clips and two solo Stefani videos. 'Don't Speak' claimed the Best Group Video gong at the 1997 MTV Music Video Awards; it was there that Stefani got the chance to lavish praise on Muller, "one of my most talented friends".

Of all these No Doubt collabs, however, 'Don't Speak' was a pivotal moment in both the careers of the band and the director. And it's an undeniably potent clip, both a powerful comment on the growing friction within the band, as they rose to the top, and the song's original reason for being: the break-up of Stefani and Kanal. (At one point, Stefani all but shouts her pained lyrics into Kanal's face, who barely twitches, the insensitive bastard.) As the video began, Kanal, quite bizarrely, was dressed as a satyr-like character, running his eyes over a rotting orange, the key symbol for Eric Stefani's Tragic Kingdom. Then Muller's camera located the band in the garage of their Beacon Avenue HQ – Adrian Young proudly wore a Madness T-shirt, staying true to the band's 2-Tone roots – as they pounded their way through the track. (This "performance" was cut up with live footage of the band sweating it out on-stage at New York's Roseland Ballroom on August 21, 1996.) In the main this was a grim-faced No Doubt; their stony demeanours emphasising the internal problems they'd been experiencing: the more records they sold, they discovered, the higher Gwen Stefani was being hoisted up the ladder of fame, unintentionally leaving her bandmates eating her dust. This came to a head in the clip during a mock photo shoot, where the group mugged for the camera, only to learn that everyone bar golden girl Stefani had been cropped out of the final image.

This was a classic case of art imitating life. Around the same time as the shoot, the band had been photographed for the cover of *Spin's* November 1996 issue, as No Doubt mania continued to explode all over the world. When the mag hit the stands, Young, Kanal and Dumont found out that they had suffered death-by-Photoshop, leaving Stefani alone on the cover. Despite this, the article still declared: "No Doubt Is The Last American New Wave Group." (Images of Young, Kanal and Dumont were relegated to the table of contents.) Stefani was uncomfortable with the omission, while the men of No Doubt, although obviously disappointed, said little about the incident. When pushed, Kanal admitted to *Details* magazine that he'd come to learn that this was how the media operated. "It's not something that we've been dealing with for a long time," Kanal said, "but I think we've gotten used to it. [And] if you've seen Gwen perform, you can see that she deserves it." Stefani was not so guarded. "It's not like Gwen Stefani and the No Doubt background loser boys," she snapped. "I would feel naked without them." Dumont was just as angry. "Has it got to the point," he asked a writer from *Rolling Stone*, "if Gwen doesn't speak, we mean nothing?" The tension was palpable during the 'Don't Speak' video; the band admitted that, once again, the idea of splitting up was aired during its angst-filled shoot. But after almost 10 years of hand-to-mouth struggle, no-one was foolish enough to kill this platinum-plated baby, especially once 'Don't Speak' started to climb Billboard's many and varied charts.

The single, the third lifted from *Tragic Kingdom*, first charted in mid October, as the band readied itself for a series of increasingly high-profile dates, including a Madison Square Garden gig and a star spot on *Saturday Night Live*, that would take them through to the end of their remarkable year. Interestingly, 'Don't Speak' didn't chart on Billboard's key chart, the Hot 100, because it was a radio-only single (it wasn't sold in stores). Nonetheless, it reached the pole position on the Hot 100 Singles Airplay chart and stayed on that chart for 16 weeks, and also topped the Top 40 Mainstream chart. It scaled as high as number two on the Modern Rock Tracks list, No Doubt's key radio format at the time, and also peaked in fourth position on the Rock Big Picture chart.

But the success of 'Don't Speak' wasn't some localised phenomenon – it was a number one hit in the UK (for three weeks), Canada, Australia (for no less than eight weeks), Holland, France and Switzerland. It would also come in at number 81 on a *Rolling Stone* list of "100 Greatest Pop Songs". And, of course, it gave *Tragic Kingdom* further momentum at the cash register; the album may have briefly slipped out of the Top 10 for the first three weeks of October 1996, but then it returned on October 26 and began its unstoppable climb to the lofty number one position on December 21. And with the exception of the February 15, 1997 chart, when the *Gridlock'd* soundtrack briefly claimed number one, *Tragic Kingdom* would own the top spot until February 22, an amazing run of nine weeks at the head of the pop class (and 36 weeks in the top 10, all up). Not bad stats at all, considering that its competition included releases from certified chart-busters Celine Dion, Whitney Houston, the Spice Girls and Toni Braxton.

The *Tragic Kingdom* sales figures were astounding: by December 1996 it had sold almost five million copies (four times that of R.E.M.'s recent *New Adventures In Hi-Fi* or Pearl Jam's *No Code*). At the same time, 'Don't Speak', not coincidentally, was receiving 10,000-plus radio plays per week, a Beatles-like figure. (Both 'Don't Speak' and 'Spiderwebs' would win ASCAP Pop Music Awards for most-performed songs.) And during the week that *Tragic Kingdom* achieved the seemingly impossible and reached number one, in the process overhauling *Razorblade Suitcase*, the album from labelmates (and lover, in Stefani's case) Bush, the LP sold a mind-boggling 229,000 copies. The band was every bit as gobsmacked as the music biz's chart-watchers and money-counters, but they also understood the flipside. "We're just going to enjoy the moment while it's here," Stefani said, "because ... we could be like Milli Vanilli or Vanilla Ice. It happens whenever you get that big."

Even though they were clearly tiring – the band actually stopped for three weeks over Christmas and New Year and played only two dates in January 1997 – the No Doubt bandwagon managed to keep on rolling. If there was one show (well, two, actually) that summed up how far *Tragic Kingdom* had taken them, it was their two-night stand at the Pond in Anaheim, over the nights of May 31 and June 1, 1997. Sophie Muller and crew were there to capture all the action, both on- and off-stage, for the *Live In The Tragic Kingdom* DVD, while the Vandals and Eric Stefani were amongst the invitees there to help toast the band's unlikely climb to what The Beatles referred to as "the toppermost of the poppermost". (Speaking of whom, Eric Stefani was amongst the many welcome stage-invaders during the band's anarchic set closer, 'Ob-Li-Di Ob-La-Da'. He'd return once more in 2000 to play 'Trapped In A Box' during a filming of VH-1's *Storytellers*.)

The lead-up to their two nights at the Pond couldn't be better: the entire band made the cover of *Rolling Stone* in May, which helped erase some of the memories of the *Spin* incident of a few months earlier, while film-maker George Lucas (and his daughter) were among the well-wishers at a very full house of 20,000 punters at the Shoreline Ampitheater on May 30. This meant the world to the more sci-fi obsessed members of the band; not only was *Star Wars* and its sequels amongst their favourite movies, but they'd taken to using the movie's portentous theme – 'The Imperial March' – as outro music to their sold-out shows. Tony Kanal, perhaps the biggest Ewok-nut in the band, would even liken No Doubt's rise to the narrative arc of the *Star Wars* trilogy, not something a sci-fi geek would state casually. (A few years later, while the band was in London, Lucas repaid the favour and gave them a sneak preview of a light-saber fight sequence from *The Phantom Menace*.)

The band's outrageous fortune wasn't restricted to record sales; their live returns were also on a sharp incline. On November 2, 1995, they plugged in at the Middle East Club in Philadelphia and 20 people showed – "that was a terrible time and performance," Stefani recalled – but when they returned to Philly, a little over 12 months later, they filled the 3000-seat Electric Factory. A few nights later they packed out the 5000-seat International Ballroom in Atlanta, for a gross of $75,000; when you consider that most headliners pocket 20 percent of the net takings from gigs, it was a handy return for a one-night stand. In the shows leading up to their Anaheim homecoming, they netted $270,000 and some change from a show at the Rose Garden in Portland; $450,000 from the aforementioned Shoreline Ampitheater gig, and almost $400,000 from one show at the Gorge in Washington State. It's no surprise that the band stayed on the road with *Tragic Kingdom* for almost two years; the numbers, and the returns, were simply too tempting to resist, especially after so many hardscrabble years. Eric Carpenter's $905 income return must have seemed like some bizarre memory from a parallel universe.

The nights at the Pond also added some extra zeroes to the No Doubt retirement fund; with alt-rockers Weezer in support, the band pulled 26,197 punters over the two nights, collecting a tick over $500,000 at the door (also a handy payday for Paul Tollett and Goldenvoice, who were co-producers of the shows). But while the money was wonderful, it was the moment that meant more to the band; sure, they'd played the Pond back in March 1996, making some OC musical history in the process, but that night they were the opening the show, and now they were top of the bill. And, with all credit to the band, they made the effort to remind the rapturous audiences – once again bursting at the seams with Stefani look-alikes, the omnipresent Gwenabees – just where their roots lay. Early on in their set, sandwiched between a frenzied 'Happy Now?' and 'End It On This', was a faithful cover of Sublime's 'DJs', and they also tore through 'Total Hate', their jam with the late Nowell and co that was a standout of *Beacon Street Collection*. OC punks the Vandals, whose paths would often intersect with No Doubt over the next couple of years, were in the midst of the on-stage melee during the messy finale, their run through the Beatles' 'Ob-La-Di Ob-La-Da'. With No Doubt playing in front of an elaborate stage set based on the concept of the Tragic Kingdom – even though it actually resembled some kind of haunted forest straight out of the Brothers Grimm – it was quite the homecoming. Outside the venue, $20 tickets were scalped for up to $150.

These Pond shows also marked another turning point for the band. The audience was heavy on teens, even pre-teens – "I like Gwen's attitude; I like her personality," 11-year-old Ariana Tosatto of Sherman Oaks told the *Los Angeles Times* – but noticeably shy on long-time fans from the band's many nights at Fender's Ballroom in the late 1980s, who felt, with some justification, that their heroes had "gone mainstream". But, ultimately, this was a small price to pay. The two-night stand marked the pinnacle of *Tragic Kingdom*, even though the band still had some big moments ahead of them. These included their first visit to Kanal's homeland of India – where Kanal's family looked on from the front row as they played and Sophie Muller shot the *Band On The Run*-styled video for their skank-pop cover of the Vandals' 'Oi To The World' – plus a dalliance with some toxic space cakes during a night off in Amsterdam. There was also a sold-out show in Israel that, briefly, brought together Jews and Palestinians, followed by a group dip in the Dead Sea; a private audience and jam with Kanal's hero Prince, after a show in his hometown of Minneapolis, which led to later collaborations; and a personal tour of the White House, no less.

In the crowd at the Pond, looking on, was one Robert 'Big Sandy' Williams, a veteran of the well-regarded Anaheim roots outfit, Big Sandy & His Fly-Rite Boys, a band highly unlikely to ever fill this type of concrete bunker. "If you're a musician, this is what you dream for," he said, waving towards the stage. "If you say anything else, you're lying. To play in front of your hometown audience, and have them know every song." Williams was right, of course: who wouldn't be overcome by the impact of thousands of voices screaming your lyrics back in your face? But the question confronting No Doubt, now that they'd actually lived out their dream of pop success, was this: where to next?

CHAPTER NINE

A Simple Kind Of Life

"The person who wrote "Just A Girl" [wasn't] me anymore."

–Gwen Stefani

No Doubt weren't the first band to discover upon achieving their dream that fantastic sales, packed arenas and gushing fans didn't necessarily equate to personal satisfaction. The Beatles weren't messing around when they sang how money couldn't buy them love; in fact, if rock'n'roll history is any guide, it seems that the bigger an act becomes, the more likely it is that they'll start to scratch and claw at each other like wildcats. Admittedly, Gwen Stefani's relationship with Gavin Rossdale brought some joy to her life, despite the occasional bump in the road (such as the rumour he'd slept with Courtney Love after he and Stefani briefly fell out), but, at the end of the Tragic Kingdom era, after two years of living in the spotlight – and in her bandmates' pockets – she wasn't in the best mental shape. It was one weird trip: she's started the Tragic Kingdom ride in therapy with her brother Eric, dealing with the guilt she felt when he left the band, and now she was suffering from a massive comedown after two very high years.

So Stefani, instead of using her handsome royalties to grab a slice of Hollywood real estate – she'd do that later, first buying a Los Feliz mansion and then snapping up J Lo's 10,000 square foot Beverly Hills' spread in 2006 for a reported US$15 million – did what any troubled suburban girl would do: she went home. Admittedly, Stefani had never got around to actually

175

leaving home – she'd spent so much time on the road that she simply hadn't bothered finding her own place – but suburban Anaheim still seemed like the least likely hiding place for one of planet pop's newest and shiniest stars. She was now 27 years old, exhausted, and feeling, as she would later admit, "like an old, fat tennis shoe. I think I lost bits of myself while I was on tour." Stefani's closest confidante was her Lhasa Apso Maggen, who'd been her uncomplaining companion for the past 14 years.

Holed up in Anaheim, she did what any troubled superstar would do, and immersed herself in the tortured prose of Sylvia Plath's *Bell Jar* (not necessarily the best move for someone trying to get their head back together, as she found out) as well as searching out anything written about Plath. And she tuned in to the erudite, searching music of Joni Mitchell, looking for some kind of inspiration. She also started keeping a journal, which would prove handy as a source for future lyrics. "The person who wrote "Just A Girl" [wasn't] me anymore," said Stefani, when asked about her *Tragic Kingdom* hangover. Marriage and children were still high priorities for Stefani, but now she also had to consider the band's next move. It was quite the juggling act. "We were in our weird little world when we were on tour," Stefani said, upon reflection. "Coming home, at first I thought I was fine, but then I slipped into this weird depression. I felt like I was going through some transition or growing pains."

Stefani wasn't the only member of No Doubt trying hard to get back to the real world. Tony Kanal and Tom Dumont even toyed with the idea of returning to school and completing their respective degrees (both were one semester short of graduating). Dumont and Adrian Young – who, to their credit, managed to stick with their long-time girlfriends through the craziest two years of their lives – bought homes in Long Beach and Lakewood, respectively, and both, in their own way, attempted to come to grips with their new lives. While Young hung out with his partner, Nina (a former employee of the band) and worked on his golf swing and his magazine *Schwing* – "I take this game more seriously than I take anything in life," he only half-joked – Dumont develop a rep as the most level-headed (and tight-fisted) member of the band. Maybe the time he'd spent in go-nowhere metal bands had taught him some lessons about the fickle nature of fame. "I want to maintain my old lifestyle and not outspend my means," he said, "and not think I'm rich and have it all fall apart. Success has the potential to poison your mind with weird, crappy thoughts. It's a slimy business."

The "slimy" music business, however, had been more than willing to recognise the band's supernova rise. At the 1997 Grammys, *Tragic Kingdom* had been shortlisted for Best Rock Album, while the band was also nominated for Best New Artist (a gesture absolutely swimming in irony, given that they'd been around for a decade). Even though they failed to score on both counts, Stefani and Kanal, in particular, were chuffed by the recognition and the chance to play at the ceremony. "It's so weird," Stefani admitted, "because I used to watch the Grammys with my parents and make fun of them. Now we get to play at one. Isn't that cool?" They lost out again at the 1998 awards, despite being nominated for the Best Pop Performance and Song of the Year ('Don't Speak', naturally). The band were also nominated as Favourite Pop / Rock New Artist at the 1997 American Music Awards, yet lost out to neo-folkie Jewel. Finally they came out winners at the 1998 California Music Awards, when Stefani was crowned Outstanding Female Vocalist and the band declared Outstanding Group.

Early in 1998, an offer came along that the band simply couldn't refuse: a chance to play a pair of dates with Madness, the one band that influenced their very existence. Just prior to leaving for these two gigs in Hawaii, on May 1 and 2, they'd met up with another hero, recording a one-off with Elvis Costello, in late April. The band cut the song, 'I Throw My Toys Around' – which Costello wrote with his then-wife, Cait O'Riordan – in one afternoon at Hollywood's legendary Ocean Way Studios, with Costello manning the desk. The track was mixed the next day. 'I Throw My Toys Around' was a curious contrast in styles – it featured one of Dumont's trademark scratchy, raggedy riffs, which was set against a breathy and seductive vocal come-on from Stefani, with a nursery-rhyme like melody thrown in for good measure. And when Costello chimed in on the chorus, No Doubt suddenly sounded remarkably like his long-time backing band the Attractions. Though little more than a chance to work with one of their idols – something the band would now do at regular intervals – 'I Throw My Toys Around' was an oddity; it was a kid's song for adults.

"The experience was great for us," Tom Dumont reported. "The song turned out very, very, well." Costello agreed, joining in the lovefest. "Gwen did a great job singing it," he said, "and the band played great. And when we all played together, it sounded great." But this wasn't a song destined for their next album; instead it was earmarked for the soundtrack of the *Rugrats* movie, which was released in November. And there were other cameos, as the band cashed in on their newfound status: just prior to their Hawaiian adventure, Stefani recorded the track 'You're The Boss', with former Stray Cat Brian Setzer for his album *Dirty Boogie*. Then the man with the sneer, Billy Idol, fronted No Doubt for an afternoon, sharing the mic with Stefani for their cover of 'Hateful', which was recorded for a Clash tribute album that finally saw the light of a record store shelf in May 1999. And Stefani put in a cameo, on April 16, at the Stormy Weather benefit in LA, a fund-raiser set up by Eagle Don Henley for his Walden Pond Foundation. Proving that she could adopt a different persona with almost as much ease as Madonna, Stefani turned torch singer for the night, crooning the Andrews Sisters' 'I Can Dream, Can't I', and Elvis Costello's devastating 'Almost Blue', the ballad she'd turned to for comfort when she and Kanal split. (Also on the all-star bill were Joni Mitchell, Bjork, Stevie Nicks, Sheryl Crow and Paula Cole.)

As satisfying as these red-letter sessions with Costello, Setzer and Idol undoubtedly were, the dates with Madness were really the highlight of the early months of 1998. Ever since the day that Eric Stefani introduced his sister to Madness' 'Baggy Trousers', and Gwen admitted that "I have been in love with [Suggs] for so long", the band had been itching to share a stage with their ska-pop heroes. A week before flying to Honolulu for their first show, the starstruck group – plus Eric Stefani – met with Madness prior to their set at LA's Universal Ampitheater. Then the OC five pushed their way down front as they began to play, eyes glued on the stage. The show was a blast; as guitarist-turned-reporter Tom Dumont wrote, Young, for one, was sufficiently inspired to "display his finest skank moves".

As stages go, No Doubt picked some large-scale venues for their two Hawaiian gigs: the May 1 show was staged at the 5000-capacity Arts & Cultural Center in Maui, and the next night they filled Oahu's Richardson Field, headlining the Nomad Festival. Also along for the nostalgia trip were the Cherry Poppin' Daddies and So-Cal punks the Vandals, whose set Stefani watched eagerly from sidestage. It had been five months since No Doubt last plugged in, and given that they were free of the usual touring routine, the band took the chance to tinker with their setlist. They opened their first Hawaiian show with 'Different People', which fed straight into an emphatic 'Excuse Me Mr', then 'End It On This' and 'Sunday Morning'. They also tried out 'New', a fourth album song-under-development; when she introduced the track, Stefani suggested that all potential bootleggers "get their tape recorders out". They ended their first night with the usual all-in melee, although this time they laughed and stumbled through 'Oi To The World', with the Vandals and the Cherry Poppin' Daddies – but no Madness, sadly – throwing themselves around the stage like lemmings on a cliff top.

On the next night, Madness frontman Suggs reminded another full house of his peerless sartorial splendour, donning a splendid pink suit, seemingly immune to the intense tropical heat. And even as a volley of sneakers rained

178

down upon the English legends, they maintained their cool, working their way through a best-of set that featured such standards as 'Our House'. The barrage of shoes continued when No Doubt took the stage, and continued, seemingly without a break, until they tore through 'Spiderwebs' and exited, stage left. When they returned, this time for a riotous take on 'Ob-La-Di, Ob-La-Da', the men from Madness were in tow for the now-obligatory end-of-set carnage. It made for the perfect finale to No Doubt's working holiday; they wouldn't play live again for another turbulent 18 months.

★ ★ ★

Despite their Hawaiian high, No Doubt was about to make another wrong move. Only a few months into a period of post-*Tragic Kingdom* R&R, they chose to return to the studio in June 1998 with producer Matthew Wilder. The logic was understandable – the band knew that they needed to capitalise on the mammoth success of *Tragic Kingdom*, and the quicker the better – but the simple truth was that they weren't ready. Since February they'd been convening at their new "band house", a rented Hollywood Hills home on the panoramic, secluded Woodrow Wilson Drive. Eventually they came up with around 20 new songs. The band would work Monday through Friday, starting at 1pm and continuing "until we were exhausted", according to Stefani. However, lyrically speaking, she was completely dry; Stefani had absolutely nothing to say. And the fact that the squeeze was definitely on only made it harder for her to come up with any ideas. Clearly, she'd drained the emotional well with 'Don't Speak', et al: so where was she to turn next? "I just couldn't write words," she admitted. "It was one of the darkest phases of my life. And there was so much pressure, because everybody was waiting on me." She put in a call to her brother and together they wrote a song called 'Everything In Time', but that was the total output of their writing session. (The sadly beautiful ballad would be demoed, and rejected, for both *Return Of Saturn* and *Rock Steady*, and was eventually buried away on the No Doubt *Boom Box* compilation, in two different versions.)

Despite Stefani's dry spell, seven tracks were cut with Wilder during June and July, including the original versions of 'Magic's In The Makeup', 'Comforting Lie', 'Big Distraction' and an instrumental take on 'Too Late'. In early July 1998, Dumont, now the band's on-line diarist, reported on the results of their 12-hour-long days. "The recording process is going well so far," he wrote. "We've pretty much finished the first five songs. They sound both familiar and nothing like anything we've ever done before." Wilder and the band tried two distinctly different techniques: some songs were essentially cut live, while others were pieced together, jigsaw-style, after hours of over-dubs. And the band experimented with unfamiliar gear: Dumont wrapped himself around a 12-string Rickenbacker, a la John Lennon and Byrd Roger McGuinn; Stefani used an old Telefunken mic; McNair tapped away at a Jupiter 8 keyboard; Young, meanwhile, went over-dub crazy.

The sessions paused briefly for a shared Kanal / Young birthday party, where the guests included members of Weezer, 311, the Vandals and Sugar Ray, as well as the band's videographer Sophie Muller. Young, typically, par-tied harder than most, wrapping himself around a tree at 4am, vomiting on his shoes. (The birthday boy was just back from Europe, where he'd spent the early weeks of August on the road, drumming for the Vandals, occasion-ally teasing No Doubt-friendly audiences by thumping out the intro to 'Spiderwebs' between songs.) Once Young's hangover subsided, the band shifted recording venues, moving to what Dumont described as "an old-school cramped rehearsal studio in the hot, smoggy pit of LA". Even though he insisted that the "vibe is good", the band, clearly, was searching for some new inspiration.

Upon playback of the new tracks, No Doubt sensed that they'd made a mistake. "A lot of the stuff we were doing sounded like a caricature of our-selves," Stefani admitted. And, in a move that hinted at desperation, they turned on their producer, Matthew Wilder, and fired him, not long after their final session in July 1998. (In his on-line diary, Dumont would enig-matically refer to this as "the producer situation".)

When pushed about their decision, Stefani took the "it's not you, it's me" line, but this tack wasn't especially convincing. "It was like something was wrong," Stefani said, "and not with him, but with us. We just weren't ready to be in the studio; we just felt like we were too comfortable. We needed to be outside our comfort zone and pushed a little further." It was one of the few occasions in pop history that a record producer has been sacked for making a band feel "too comfortable". Wilder said little in response; as reported elsewhere, he backed out of an interview for this book, despite originally agreeing to do so. It's highly likely that the payout he would have received for these aborted sessions also contributed to his vow of silence. Only one track from the Wilder sessions, 'Big Distraction', would make the final cut for No Doubt's fourth album, and only then as a bonus cut on the Australian edition. (It's also on the *Boom Box* and *Everything In Time* collec-tions.)

This dismissal had been coming for some time, apparently. In March 1998, even before Wilder started working with the band, they'd met with producer Rick Rubin, the hirsute "fifth" member of The Red Hot Chili Peppers, and raised the possibility of working together. Michael Beinhorn (a New Yorker renowned for working with far heavier acts, including Soundgarden, Korn, Ozzy Osbourne and Hole), had also had discussions with No Doubt, in September 1998. Nothing came of these meetings, apart from more confusion in the No Doubt camp.

After another break, this time for a Halloween party hosted by Offspring's Dexter Holland – Stefani, in case you need to know, dressed as a vampire, Kanal came as a French fry, Young was a nun and Dumont was "something politically incorrect", which he thought best not to clarify – Dumont filed another report, on December 1: "We've pretty much finished the whole album," he wrote. While the tracks may have been complete, this was still an album without a producer to help pull it all together.

Unsure what to do next, band opted for another one-off session, this time with former Talking Head Jerry Harrison, in January 1999. Just like their *Rugrats* session with Elvis Costello, they cut this new track, 'Go', almost on the fly. This song would turn up on a soundtrack for the clubber's film *Go*, released in late March, and served as a useful indicator for the musical direction that the band intended on taking: they were tapping into their new wave past, a move that must have especially pleased Kanal, whose obsession with the '80s hadn't faded over the years.

The 'New' video introduced a new Gwen Stefani: part Ziggy Stardust, part China Doll, her hair now a blazing flamingo pink, which became her colour of choice during the *Return Of Saturn* period. In the full throttle clip, she was at the wheel and on the lam, with her accomplice Kanal in the back seat of the car. Young played her pursuer, tracking Stefani down to a warehouse rave, where she and Kanal blended with the clubbers. Dumont, meanwhile, put in a bit part as a clean-cut GI, turned away at the door (he then later appeared as a very convincing corpse on the club floor). As watchable as the Jake Scott-directed video was, the single introduced a different-sounding No Doubt. While Stefani's urgent vocal came straight from the template they'd forged with 'Excuse Me Mr', et al, Harrison added a harsh, syncopated rhythm track – it was if Young was banging on metal pipes rather than drums – while there was a coldness to the production that did No Doubt no favours. And, crucially, it was a chilly keyboard that carried the song's not-quite-hummable melody, rather than Dumont's crunching guitar.

Nonetheless, 'New' returned the band to the airwaves, delivering useful returns across several Billboard charts and hanging about No Doubt's second home, the Modern Rock Tracks list, for almost six months, peaking at number seven. *Tragic Kingdom*, meanwhile, was still lingering; it would remain in the charts well into the year 2000, an astounding run. With 'New' on high rotation, band and management – they were now handled by West Coast-based Rebel Waltz, heavy-hitters (and Clash fans, obviously) who oversaw the careers of Trent Reznor, the Offspring and Social Distortion – focused on sorting out the "producer situation", once and for all. (Silverback, the management firm who handled Sublime, had made a bid for No Doubt, but Jon Phillips knew that Rebel Waltz would win out, mainly because of their potential to break the band globally. "It was the phase that they were still underground but you knew they were going to be a big, big hit," he said. "We approached them and went and met everyone at Tony's house. I remember later on, Adrian saying, "Dude, everything you said was so fucking true, they're selling us out, I wish we'd worked with you guys." I think at that time they were dealing with that identity crisis: you know, "We're a band, we're not just Gwen." It was the same sort of thing with Sublime, except that we had a singer who died, which makes it even more enigmatic. I felt in my heart they liked us as truth speakers and people, but they went with someone that was a lot more established. I wasn't surprised.")

In many ways, producer Glen Ballard was the ideal guy for the tricky situation in which No Doubt found themselves. A man with a scruffy beard and an intense gaze, who could have passed for a cult leader, the charismatic Ballard didn't so much produce records as get each member of the band on the couch and coax songs out of their psyches. It also helped that he was currently very much in demand, having produced Alanis Morissette's record-busting *Jagged Little Pill*, a record that would tally up more than 30 million sales worldwide. He'd also claimed a Grammy in 1997, and had been nominated for a second (Record of the Year for Morissette's 'Ironic') and was crowned the 1997 Songwriter of the Year by the National Academy of Songwriters. He'd also won a similar award at the recent ASCAP Pop Music Awards. It couldn't hurt the commercial worth of No Doubt's "difficult" new album – or the band's profile – if it featured the credit of the industry's number-one hit-maker. Ballard was officially hired in February 1999, around the same time that Adrian Young hosted his *Schwing* mag charity golf day, where members of Smashmouth, the Cherry Poppin' Daddies and the Vandals proved that ugly trousers were not strictly the domain of pro golfers. (According to Jon Phillips, Young is no slouch on the links; he said that Young is probably among the five best celebrity golfers today. "And he's the only one with a Mohawk who plays in the nude," he added.)

Glen Ballard had learned from the best; he'd been a staff producer /

arranger for the legendary Quincy Jones, working on records from such heavy-hitters as the Pointer Sisters and Teddy Pendergrass. But it was writing songs for Jones' biggest star, Michael Jackson, that got Ballard bumped up to the A-list; after the success of 'Man In The Middle', he wrote tunes for Aretha Franklin ('Mercy'), Wilson Phillips ('You Won't See Me Crying'), Chaka Khan, Barbra Streisand, Sheena Easton, Aerosmith ('Pink', 'Falling In Love [Is Hard On The Knees]') and many others. The next logical step was a move into the producer's seat – he struck gold with Aerosmith's *Nine Lives* and the eponymous *Wilson Phillips* LP and also worked with the Corrs, Gregory Hines, Van Halen and John Hiatt, before meeting Morissette, the former child star turned angry-young-pop singer. Ballard was a hit machine, without doubt, and a safe bet for a band trying to work out how to match a record whose sales were currently nudging the 10 million mark.

Still, it was a strange situation, because Ballard was hired to work on tracks that were, in some cases, 12 months old. Adrian Young, for one, was unsure that Ballard was the right man for the job; the records that he'd made didn't register on the drummer's radar. "I'm sure for a lot of people," Young admitted, "they thought it's a weird thing for No Doubt to hire Glen Ballard. I mean, at first I was a bit apprehensive, too." But Young, and the rest of the band, settled into a rhythm with Ballard, almost as soon as he told them that he was keen to embrace the band's "quirkiness and weirdness". But it was a curious deal-sealer from Ballard, because the finished record had none of the wit and feistiness of *Tragic Kingdom*. Nonetheless, Kanal described the sessions as "my most comfortable record making experience." Young agreed. "He let us be us," the drummer said. "That made me real happy." Tom Dumont, however, was the lone dissenting voice; he found the prolonged sessions with Ballard "unpleasant and painful".

What Ballard did figure out pretty quickly was that the Jerry Harrison-produced 'New' was a sonic template for the rest of the album (whose working title was *Artificial Sweetener*). When asked about this, Ballard spoke like the guru that many thought he was. "The songs" DNA contained a profound knowledge of "80s pop," he stated, with due gravitas. "And I think there was an unconscious decision to key in on the sounds and textures that evoked what Gwen was writing about, in terms of a reflective look back." Psycho-babble aside, what Ballard was saying was this: the band was tapping into the type of music they loved as kids, prior to 2-Tone taking over their lives. "We love music from the '80s," Kanal said with way more precision than his producer, "even the cheesiness of it. That's what we grew up with."

Apart from his Yoda-worthy declarations, Ballard took on a number of roles during the re-making of the album. Ballard was, in the words of Kanal, "a referee of sorts", someone to bring a little objectivity to the situation. "He kind of helped us focus," Kanal said, "and finish the record up." "[I had] to perform triage on this huge body of material they'd collected," Ballard said, when asked to describe his role. He also helped to strip away a little of the sonic baggage that some of the almost-finished songs were carrying. "[He] put all the songs on diets," Stefani said, "and helped us to slim them down." Dietician and midwife, Ballard also loaned the band some of his gear, as the sessions continued – in a very *Tragic Kingdom* kind of way – in numerous studios, including Aerowave in Encino, Hollywood's A&M, Ocean Way, NRG and elsewhere. (It's an unintended irony that the band shot that would appear on the album's sleeve showed a stone-faced No Doubt hanging about in a studio control room. Studios were now their second home.)

But above and beyond his many and varied roles, Ballard needed to find a way to deal with Stefani's lyrical constipation. She insisted that she wasn't the same lyricist who snarled 'I'm just a girl', so Ballard suggested that Stefani write about what was currently happening in her life. "She had to figure out where she was emotionally," Ballard said, "and that's always a hard thing to do." So Stefani reverted to the winning, if somewhat indiscreet, method she used for the band's career-maker of an album, and started writing about her new life with Rossdale and the insecurities that she felt in their relationship, a feeling best summed up by the paranoid pop of 'Ex-Girlfriend'. When it was finally released in April 2000, the album would be cheekily christened The Gavin Report.

Among these tunes was 'Simple Kind Of Life', the song that would typify her slightly muddled mindset at the time – Stefani wished for a less complicated existence, where "all I needed was a simple man / so I could be a wife", but at the same time acknowledged that this was unlikely, given her newfound stardom. "Now all these simple things are simply too complicated for my life," she sighs. So what motivated this indisputably poignant snapshot of her life? Her menstrual cycle, as it turned out. "I had just gotten my period, so I was like, real emotional," she told *Spin's* Chris Norris in 2000. "And I went to play it for the guys and I was on the verge of tears, because it was so emotional." Both the band and Ballard gave the thumbs-up to what was originally a stark acoustic ballad that hinted at R.E.M.'s 'Losing My Religion'. (Ballard called it "amazing".) Stefani's cycle aside, 'Life' meant the world to her for another reason: it was the first song that she'd written from top to bottom. "I just started playing these chords," she said, "and I was like, 'Hey, I just wrote a song'."

'Simple Kind Of Life' was one of two songs cut for what the band

Kanal and Stefani at the 2004 Brit Awards. "They were clearly very in love [in the band's early days]," said a former No Doubt member. "But they also respected the band and knew that it wouldn't go over well that they were dating." (GEORGE CHIN/WIREIMAGE)

Dumont on stage at Jones Beach, New York, June 2004. He once shared a house with Eric Stefani and Young, which became the band's HQ. "That time period was crucial to helping the band grow as musicians and closer as friends," said Eric Carpenter. (KRISTIN CALLAHAN/LFI)

Dumont (left) and Kanal, with friends, at a 2004 Grammy after-party. While the boys in the band partied, Stefani was "devastated" by the news that Rossdale was actually the father of his teenage god-daughter, Daisy Lowe. (AMY GRAVES/WIREIMAGE)

The *Rock Steady* crew, 2001: Young, Stefani, Dumont and Kanal (from left). The idea for the album was born during the relentlessly upbeat vibe at their Return of Saturn shows the year before. (**ANTONIO PETRONZIO**)

Stefani with her new "besties", the Harajuku Girls, at the 2004 American Music Awards. She was so besotted with these Japanese fashionistas that she cut a song in their honour and named her publishing company Harajuku Lover Music. (JEN LOWERY/LFI)

Stefani working the red carpet with Leonardo Di Caprio, in a scene from *The Aviator*. Her on-screen roles and solo success led the *Los Angeles Times* to crown her "the biggest female rock star of the last decade". **(LFI)**

Flying solo, at the Brit Awards, February 2005. "She never said that she was leaving No Doubt; there was no talk of her being simply Gwen Stefani from now on. There'll be another No Doubt record, for sure," said friend and collaborator Linda Perry. **(DAVE FISHER/LFI)**

Mr and Mrs Rossdale, at the 2005 Oscars. When they first met, Stefani was unsure he was the one. "I'm usually attracted to guys with personalities, ones that make me laugh; not some dude with flowing curls who's tall and gorgeous." **(DAVE FISHER/LFI)**

The new queen of style, at the LAMB fashion show, New York, September 2005. Her LAMB range encompassed all of Stefani's looks, "from my punker pants to the present," she revealed. One T-shirt even featured an X-ray of Kanal's broken finger.

(DENNIS VAN TINE/LFI)

Stefani with style icon, Vivienne Westwood. Stefani wore one of Westwood's out-there designs, resplendent with polka dots, to the 2003 Grammy after-party. Westwood also designed the corset that Stefani squeezed into for the 'Spiderwebs' video. (KLEIN-HOUNSFIELD/ABACA/PA PHOTOS)

Tony Kanal (left) jams with Perry Farrell, as part of Satellite Party, Lollapalooza 2005. During No Doubt downtime, in between co-writes with Stefani for her solo albums, Kanal established his own label Kingsbury Studios. (ROB GRABOWSKI 2005/GRABOWSKIPHOTO.COM/RETNA)

Young keeping the beat with the reformed Bow Wow Wow, New Year's Eve 2005. With No Doubt on hold, Young also drummed for Cali punks The Vandals, and recorded with Kelis, Fishbone, Unwritten Law and Matt Costa. **(KELLY A. SWIFT/RETNA)**

Kanal and Dumont at the 2006 Grammys. "Obviously that much success is going to change you, but they're not like evil, you know?," said Jon Phillips. "They never got caught up in the drug scene, they've made a lot of money and enjoy life on their own terms." **(JEFFREY MAYER/WIREIMAGE)**

Bono greets Stefani's baby bump at the 2006 Grammys. Stefani had spent the final dates of her first solo tour coping with her pregnancy; the waistband on her cheerleader's outfit was let out after almost every performance. (BOB RIHA JR/WIREIMAGE)

Stefani arriving for another Letterman guest spot, December 2006, with baby Kingston James McGregor in tow. He was born by Caesarean section on May 25, 2006. "It's beautiful; it's a very sweet baby," said Dave Stewart. (DENNIS VAN TINE/LFI)

Dumont, Young, Stefani and Kanal (from left). Despite Stefani's solo rise and their own musical pursuits, band management insists there's more to come from No Doubt. "[They are] just starting to work on some new ideas — long term, though. Next chapter is still a way off." (NELA KONIG/RETNA)

Gwen Stefani, pop star, clothes designer, role model, mother, wife, friend: "I remember them as kids, seriously," said a friend. "And then in the blink of an eye she's got fashion lines and *Vogue* covers. It was only a matter of a few years ago when I saw Gwen at a club and she had braces." **(FRANK LOTHAR LANGE)**

thought were the final sessions for the album (the other was 'Bathwater'). Written on a Friday, 'Life' was recorded on the following Monday, at Royaltone Studios in North Hollywood. "It ended up being very spontaneous and true to the version that Gwen wrote on acoustic guitar," Dumont said. "Real strummy, without us going too crazy over it." It was arguably the best song – and certainly the finest ballad – that No Doubt had ever recorded and would become the second single lifted from their new album.

Few of the other tracks that would appear on *Return Of Saturn* emerged as naturally as 'Simple Kind Of Life' – apart from the swinging, New Orleans-flavoured production number 'Bathwater', another Stefani song about obsessive love, which Tom Dumont insisted was written in 10 minutes flat. And the band was thinly stretched; a Dumont report from July 16, 1999, a day he christened "triple threat Friday", typified this. This was a day in which mixer Jack Joseph Puig was "fixing" 'Too Late' (then known as 'Too Late Now') in one studio, Stefani was recording additional vocals in another, while Dumont, Kanal and Young were holed up across town in the home studio of engineer Alain Johannes, working on overdubs for the band's Prince collaboration, 'Waiting Room' (which wouldn't surface until their 2001 album *Rock Steady*). "Also at some point during the day," Dumont added, "I bet at least one of us will eat at the California Chicken Café."

'Ex Girlfriend' was one of many songs that went through a lengthy evolution, and it typified the band's key objective with *Return Of Saturn* (apart from getting the damned thing finished): they wanted to prove themselves to be "serious" musicians who could handle a variety of styles. Just like 'Simple Kind Of Life', Stefani had given birth to 'Ex Girlfriend' – she'd use the pregnancy / childbirth metaphor more than once while talking up the album, a neat counterpoint to Ballard's role as musical midwife – in her room, on an acoustic guitar. It was a slow, dirgey ballad, a sort of funereal 'Don't Speak', with a typically questioning Stefani lyric. Ballard liked the track, but felt that the last thing the album needed was another slo-mo moodpiece; the song needed some juice. So Stefani and Kanal hooked up with Dumont at his home in Long Beach, where he'd installed a ProTools kit; Stefani eventually found herself alone in the room, rapping her lyrics over a skeletal programmed drum track. (Young's drums were filtered through various guitar 'stomp boxes'.) It was the first time that the band experimented with "loops", the idea of recording one part and then repeating it endlessly. And in order to achieve a reggae-flavoured groove, Dumont and Stefani "borrowed" a sample from a Tricky CD that set the right mood.

They were sufficiently satisfied with the results to earmark 'Ex-Girlfriend' as the album's lead single. However, although the band has never admitted it, there's a strong rumour that 'Ex-Girlfriend' was only written after a "request" from the band's label to return to the studio and come up with a "surefire" radio hit. Once again, or so it seemed, band and label weren't sharing the love. If it was fact, it was a bizarre situation: what label would send a 15 million-album-selling band back into the studio – and what band with the kind of clout No Doubt had would cave to such a demand? 'Ex-Girlfriend' and 'Magic's In The Makeup' were the final *Saturn* tracks laid to rest; they were recorded in November 1999.

The genesis of numerous other tracks was equally complex: for 'Marry Me', yet another cut-the-crap outpouring from Stefani, Dumont's guitar part – played on a 1940s-era Harmony acoustic – was his attempt at capturing the feel of the Carlos Santana licks that can be heard on Lauryn Hill's 'To Zion'. Dumont wasn't at his best that day – he admitted that "it was one of those days I didn't feel like being there" – so he recorded some simple parts and then left to buy a sandwich, asking Ballard and his crew to "edit together whatever you like out of my part". By the time he returned, they'd created what Dumont described as "this great little loop for the song". Devo was a big influence on Dumont's guitar part for 'New' – hence its unmistakable new wave flavour – while the ages-old sound of Reverend Horton Heat, a big favourite of Dumont's at the time, had a major impact on the wicked tremolo guitar sound on 'Bathwater'. "I was trying to cop that attitude," he said. Dumont had also become a big fan of Cake's Greg Brown, another influence on his guitar playing throughout *Return Of Saturn*.

But above and beyond the many clever studio effects used by the band, Ballard and engineer Alain Johannes (a close friend of The Red Hot Chili Peppers and member of the band Eleven), and the influences they were drawing on, it was Stefani's lyrics that would receive the closest scrutiny. If *Tragic Kingdom* was a document of a 20-something dealing with life, love and loss in the OC suburbs, *Return Of Saturn* was the statement of a woman fast approaching her 30th birthday and struggling to get the life / career balance right. "I really did feel like I was going through a transitional phase in my life as I made the album," she said, and that sense of uncertainty was all over such tracks as 'Marry Me', 'Comforting Lie' and, especially, 'Simple Kind Of Life'. Upon reflection, Stefani admitted that writing the songs for the album helped her deal with her 30th, a milestone that she reached on October 3, 1999. "Gwen was going through a period where she was reassessing her life," said Dumont, who had an astute way of explaining his bandmate's state of mind. "The term "Saturn return" captured that theme," he added.

The album's astrologically-themed title referred to a period in your life when the planet Saturn returns to the position it was in at your birth, an occurrence that typically happens when you reach the age of 29. Saturn's return signals a new beginning in your life — in Stefani's case, a new album and her life with Rossdale – and a number of challenges that she had to overcome (ditto). "Being 28 sucked," Stefani admitted, "and being 29 was really hard for me. I don't know if this was just coming off the Tragic Kingdom tour, or if it was just that age. [But] there's so much to look forward to – I still need to get married, I still want to have a family, major things."

The band's more immediate concern, however, was getting *Return Of Saturn* released. In one of his many on-line reports, Dumont saw an upside to their endless recording sessions. "One positive thing about having written and recorded so much music is that we'll have more than one album's worth by the time we're done," he wrote, "and there'll be plenty of exclusive songs for B-sides as singles are released." (At least two dozens tracks were recorded for the LP; discards included 'Everything In Time', 'Leftovers', 'Full Circle', 'Cellophane Boy', amongst others, all which made the *Boom Box* collection.)

The album, bar 'Ex-Girlfriend', had been ready for mastering in the autumn of 1999, but the need for that extra track – possibly on the "request" of their label – held up a record that had already been in production for the best part of two years, a la *Tragic Kingdom*. So the band did what they'd always done when the studio started to feel like a prison, and hit the highway. And to their credit, rather than pocket the easy money and return to the arenas circuit, No Doubt, who made all their key decisions re touring, opted for an eight-date West Coast club hop, playing such venues as LA's cosy House of Blues. (The tour announcement had been held up for a few days while Stefani unsuccessfully auditioned for a part in the film *Chicago;* Mya got the role. Stefani has also auditioned for roles in the Pitt / Jolie vehicle *Mr & Mrs Smith*, plus *Fight Club* and *Girl, Interrupted*.) The tour was especially momentous for Adrian Young: towards the end of the band's set at The Fillmore in San Francisco on October 9, 1999, the drummer stopped the show, invited his partner Nina on stage, dropped to one knee, professed his undying love, and proposed to her. Fortunately, she accepted. The teary soon-to-be-newlyweds disappeared into the night, and the Vandals' Josh Freese filled in for Young for the rest of the show. (They were married on January 16, 2000, at Young's house, with family and friends from the Vandals and Sugar Ray looking on. Stefani was a bridesmaid and Kanal and Dumont did their bit as groomsmen.)

★   ★   ★

187

By January 2000, with the tour done, 'Ex-Girlfriend' in high rotation on KROQ, and a Hype Williams-directed video in the can, band and management took a deep breath and announced that *Return Of Saturn* would be in the stores on April 11. All it had taken was three producers, six studios, the best part of two years, a 19-hour photo shoot with David LaChapelle, many hundreds of thousands of dollars in studio time and at least two major landmarks – Young's marriage, Stefani's 30th – for the band to complete their follow-up to *Tragic Kingdom*. "I think we took the making of *Return Of Saturn* very seriously," Kanal understated. "[It] was a tough record to make; we expected it to take a year." (**78**) Young backed this up when he was asked about the pressure to come up with something as big as *Tragic Kingdom*. "If we had wanted to maintain as much success as possible," the drummer said, "we would have hired a team of songwriters to write us 10 new 'Don't Speaks'. We had no interest in that."

While making the album might have been hard, the media blitz for the band was almost as tough. The band played three weeks of dates leading up to the record's release, while MTV aired the 'Ex-Girlfriend' video with their now-standard extreme prejudice, and ran a 'Making The Video' for the clip. No Doubt also featured on MTV's hugely influential (if incredibly naff) *Total Request Live*, and played both the Conan O'Brien and Jay Leno tonight shows in this lead-up period. Oh, and they also made the cover of *Spin*, but this time around, all four members of the band were included, much to Stefani's relief. And they answered the same questions – "How much pressure was there to follow up *Tragic Kingdom*?" "Why is your hair pink?" – for hundreds of dailies, mags, rags, TV shows and websites.

And if these lively weeks leading up to the album's release weren't hectic enough, they also had to play down rumours that this was the end for the band. Much had been made of an offhand comment that they approached *Return Of Saturn* as if it were their final album. What began as a statement of intent – an admission that they made the record as if their lives depended on it – was distorted into an announcement of No Doubt's impending demise. "It's not true," Dumont wrote in a March 7th, 2000 posting. "We have had no discussions within the band about hanging it up after this album. We are excited about playing these new songs for everyone. See you soon." Case closed, apparently.

★ ★ ★

Even though 'Ex-Girlfriend', *Return Of Saturn's* opening track, has a similar urgency to *Tragic Kingdom's* best moments, it's immediately clear that this is a different band and a very different record. For starters, the production of

Ballard is cleaner and colder than Wilder's – while the latter was inclined to leave a little hair on *Kingdom's* rockier tracks, this is sleek, slick, late 20th century pop music, as pristine as anything else on FM radio during a time that was dominated by the diva-pop of Christina Aguilera and Faith Hill, boy band 'NSYNC and the 'Smooth' chart rebirth of Carlos Santana. (The year's top four songs were Santana's 'Maria Maria', Destiny Child's 'Independent Woman', 'Breathe' by Faith Hill and Madonna's 'Music', which made you wonder whether grunge had ever really happened.) The record's ultra-contemporary sound is driven home during the bridge of 'Ex-Girlfriend', where Stefani raps over a wavering synth line that could have been lifted from one of Dr Dre's peerless production jobs.

Thankfully, No Doubt then head straight into the album's highlight, 'Simple Kind Of Life', a rare moment from *Saturn* where Stefani's dead-earnest vocal and the song's haunting melody take precedence over the glossy production. Although way more downbeat than the pick of *Tragic Kingdom*, 'Simple Kind Of Life' is one of the few tracks from *Saturn* that would have sat comfortably on that massive-seller. And Stefani's fearlessly frank lyric, in which she does her best to get her head around the peculiar situation she found herself in – how did an uncomplicated girl from Orange County become a star, and was it tearing her away from what she really wanted? – was far and away the best of these new batch of songs. As conflicted as she sounds, Stefani insisted that she had no regrets. "I'm happy that I've gotten to experience all these things," she said, "[And] I look forward to all that [marriage and family] stuff. But it is complicated to try to understand: how did all those things I thought I'd be really good at get so far from me and how did I get so self-centred and so faithful to my freedom?"

Then the brassy, sassy 'Bathwater' kicked in, another standout moment from *Saturn*. A production piece to rival anything heard this side of Broadway, 'Bathwater' sounded like some hitherto-unheard relic from the golden age of the big bands: this song swings like a gate. Gabe McNair's horn-heavy arrangement was his finest few minutes on *Saturn*, and while Stefani delivered another paranoid lyric, this one came with a swing of her hips that could have taken out an eye. The new wave influence that the band talked up like a mantra really showed itself on 'Six Feet Under', a song that nailed the same herky-jerky rhythms and emotional edginess that characterised the Cars' best tracks (think 'Best Friend's Girl'). But as energetic as the track was, it simply lacked a killer melody, which was a worrying sign considering that the album was only four tracks deep.

The next tune, 'Magic's In The Makeup', was a step in a more interesting direction. A sonic and thematic companion piece to 'Simple Kind Of Life', this was another track where Stefani asked herself some hard questions: "Who am I?" "What do I really want from life?" "Does this shit really mean anything?" And the layered acoustic guitars of Dumont and a gentle reggae undertow, as supplied by a steady-handed Young, gave the track some real colour. The same couldn't be said for 'Artificial Sweetener', the track that referred to the trouble in Stefani's astrological chart; it stumbled from quiet contemplation to riff-heavy head-banging, but achieved little in the process. The addition of layers of burbling electronics did nothing but drag a mediocre track further into the mire. 'Marry Me', another slick piece of Ballard gloss that seemed to drift just a few feet above the ground, was interesting mainly for the fact that it was it was a Stefani / Kanal co-write. The idea of the two former lovers penning a song where Stefani asked, repeatedly, "Who will be the one to marry me?" did have a certain perverse attraction. Yet, musically speaking, even the band's well-chilled attempt at deep dub was a yawn. And by this point, Stefani's lyrical self-absorption had started to wear pretty thin.

The Jerry Harrison-produced 'New' followed, a song that returned a little verve to an album that was becoming bogged down in the type of navel contemplation rarely heard this side of the sensitive singer-songwriter school of the 1970s. 'New' didn't rate with 'Excuse Me Mr' or 'Just A Girl' – Stefani and the band had, for better or worse, clearly moved on as players and lyricists – but it did revive the flagging *Return Of Saturn*, albeit briefly. In parts, the next track, 'Too Late', appeared to be a curious experiment in down-tuned guitars and minor-key guitar-pop – sort of a Californian response to Pearl Jam's broodiness – but this was offset by the application of studio gloss, scrubbed acoustic guitars and a ridiculous, 'Penny Lane'-styled horn section. And, once again, Stefani laid on the "serious young artist" attitude with a trowel. Somewhere between the final notes of *Tragic Kingdom* and *Return Of Saturn*, Gwen Stefani had misplaced her smile, and if anything, that was the LP's major flaw. This girl simply didn't want to have any fun anymore. And as for the vibrant sound of ska, the musical style that had gotten them noticed in the first place, well that was now long gone, much like Eric Stefani or those wild nights at Fender's Ballroom.

By the time of the rockier, dirtier – at least by No Doubt standards – 'Comforting Lie', it became clear that there were some similarities between this album and its predecessor: both ran a few tracks overtime. And what had seemed like an interesting question at the beginning of the album – "I'm just a normal person / When did it change?" Stefani asks out loud – was now a serious drag. The daftly-titled 'Suspension Without Suspense', the album's other Stefani-only composition, didn't help her cause any; the woman who had batted her eyelashes and sarcastically snapped that she was "just a girl", was now moaning about the "pessimistic protection plan". Maybe she should have tried to persuade Kanal into a reunion; if the bulk of *Saturn's* lyrics were any gauge, the so called Gavin Report wasn't an especially promising take on their romance. As least her time with Kanal – and the ensuing split, which Stefani now jokingly referred to as "the amputation" – had resulted in some great tunes.

The feisty throwaway 'Staring Problem' was a long-overdue attempt at reclaiming a little of *Tragic Kingdom's* sonic territory, and Stefani did pull off the finest Lena Lovich impression of her career, complete with "ooh-hoo" harmonies lifted straight from 'Lucky Number'. But by the time the band reached 'Home Now', the album's penultimate track – if you exclude the muzak-y version of 'Too Late' that was tacked onto the end – most listeners had decided that the title was an omen. As she beat herself up over one of the many challenges in her trans-Atlantic love life, such as the tyranny of distance between LA and Rossdale's London HQ, this frustrated listener, for one, started considering a whip-around to buy her an air ticket and be done with it. Despite a sugary-sweet vocal harmony, the following cut 'Dark Blue' went nowhere, and not fast enough.

Even though it was their fourth long-player, *Return Of Saturn* felt more like the classic difficult second album; the band was torn between trying to replicate the monumental success of their breakthrough album and at the same time establish themselves as "serious" musicians and thinkers. (Despite their best efforts, they failed on both counts.) They had none of these pressures when they were recording their debut album or *Beacon Street Collection*; the band didn't know who, if anyone, was going to buy those records, so their expectations were virtually non-existent. But now they were fully aware that 15 million people had spent their hard-earned on *Tragic Kingdom* – and the commercial expectations of this album were every bit as high as *In Utero*, Nirvana's raw 1993 follow-up to *Nevermind*, or *Supposed Former Infatuation Junkie*, Alanis Morissette's flaccid sequel to *Jagged Little Pill*, which appeared in 1998. No Doubt knew only too well that both these records stiffed, at least by comparison to the career-making records that preceded them. And Ballard had produced Morissette's *Infatuation Junkie*, so while he may have had the golden touch, he was just as adept at producing flops.

According to Jim Kerr, from trade mag *Radio & Records*, the commercial possibilities of *Return Of Saturn* were just as strong as its predecessor. "It's not a bubblegum pop band that is going to go away in a year," he said at the time of the album's April 11, 2000 release. "They do so many things well.

No Doubt will get their shot at both pop and alternative radio, and where it goes from there is up to the audience." But first up the band had to pass the critical test, as reviews poured in for *Saturn*.

Rolling Stone gushed, giving the album a four star rating. "*Return Of Saturn* is a rare achievement," declared Barry Walters, "a superstar follow–up that not only betters its predecessor but also radically departs from it." In an interesting, if somewhat inaccurate, perspective, given the two album's very different characters, Walters insisted: "If you liked *Tragic Kingdom*, you should love *Return Of Saturn*." Justifiably singled out for praise was 'Simple Kind Of Life', a "symphonic rock ballad [at] once grand, fragile and very, very sad . . . a song that that can sit on the same shelf with the likes of Elliott Smith and Aimee Mann." (It was also likened to "peak–era R.E.M.".) 'Bathwater', shrewdly, was described as a commingling of "their beloved 2-Tone ska heroes with some Gilbert & Sullivan slap-shtick thrown in", while both Hole and Korn, respectively, were named as reference points for 'Artificial Sweetener' and 'Comforting Lie'. And the band's engine room of Kanal and Young was also given high praise; in *Rolling Stone's* view, they could now match "any rap-metal rhythm section's bluster".

As far as the mag was concerned, the two years "spent writing, recording, trashing and re-recording" the album was time well spent, even though the band would beg to differ. "*Return Of Saturn* is bittersweetly conflicted," Walters' review stated in conclusion. "No Doubt want to live up to their name and believe in themselves [yet] Stefani's inability to do just that enables her to finally transcend the band's cartoon persona. No longer just a girl, this skanking flirt has finally grown into a woman." The All-Music Guide was just as taken by the album. Stephen Thomas Erlewine wrote that Stefani was "tired of being another "ex-girlfriend" – she wants to fall in love, get married, and have a family. It's a subject that's surprisingly uncommon in pop music, which would alone make *Return Of Saturn* an interesting album. What makes it a successful one is that the band delivers an aural equivalent of Stefani's lyrical themes. No Doubt have made a terrific, layered record that exceeds any expectations set by *Tragic Kingdom*."

Leading English rag *NME* was not so impressed, surmising that "when it comes to love and songwriting, honesty is not necessarily the best policy . . . *Return Of Saturn* shows that they still haven't learned that basic lesson". The influential weekly scored a bullseye as they dissected Stefani's morose state of mind. They noted how "dull and repetitive" it would be to deal with the fallout "if your diary was published in a national newspaper two years after writing it" (which, in essence, was the period of her life that Stefani covered during *Saturn*). In the end, the *NME* felt that Stefani's obsessions were so overbearing that "it's easy to spend at least the first (and the best) half of this album pondering the state of Gwen and Gavin's relationship and entirely forget to listen to the songs themselves". And this, of course, was a crying shame: it reduced Gwen the Great of *Tragic Kingdom* to an ordinary woman overwhelmed by her partner. "Gwen is every bit the match for Gavin's po-faced stadium rock," they insisted, and rightfully so, "and yet here, tragically, she seems content to live in his shadow." And with that the mag summed up the key problem with the album: Stefani had lost her fighting spirit.

Other reviews trod a more conservative middle ground. Long-time supporters the *Los Angeles Times* commended the band's "playful maturity", and even praised Ballard's knack for "smoothing out the band's trademark blend of rock, new wave, punk and ska without making things overly slick". The "wistful, folk-pop" of 'Simple Kind Of Life', once again, scored top marks. "It's kind of sweet (and maybe not so surprising) that the defiant protagonist of "Just A Girl" dares to daydream about marriage and motherhood," the *Times* declared. "Thankfully, she stops short of Madonna-esque reverie." Even then, reviewer Natalie Nichols wasn't so sure that Stefani's admission that "sometimes I wish for a mistake" – i.e. an unplanned pregnancy, as she admits during 'Life' – was the best advice for this role model to hand out to her legion of bindi-wearing Gwenabees. As far as MTV.com was concerned, the album opened with its ace, 'Ex-Girlfriend', and despite the "broad palette of emotions, styles and sounds" on display, this lead single was "the most exciting and visceral thing here". Nonetheless, they ranked *Saturn* as one of 2000's better pop albums. "Let's hope Gwen Stefani stays single," they concluded. "How else can she keep turning misery into majesty?"

Generally, it was an indifferent response at best, but this didn't hurt the momentum of either 'Ex-Girlfriend' or its parent album in the US charts. Clearly, the runaway success of *Tragic Kingdom* gave the band a kick-start commercially, even though almost five years had passed between albums. The single scored heavily across four Billboard charts, reaching the penultimate spot in the Modern Rock Tracks list, where it lingered for 18 weeks. By April 29, a little over a fortnight on from its release, *Return Of Saturn* had sold its first million copies, peaking at number two in the Billboard Top 200 and reaching the same spot in the Canadian charts (although, notably, it didn't get beyond No 31 in the UK). *Tragic Kingdom*, by comparison, took almost a year to shift as many units. But *Return Of Saturn* was cursed from the start: no matter how many copies it sold, and a million-plus was hardly a failure, it would always be compared with *Tragic Kingdom's* Wall Street-worthy numbers.

The band reconnected with video-maker Sophie Muller for 'Simple Kind Of Life', the second single from the album. Here Stefani took the opportunity to live out her wedding fantasy (in slow-mo, of course), look-ing especially glam in a wedding gown that she and Muller designed, based on a John Galliano creation. (Galliano would get much closer to Stefani soon after, as her bent for clothes and design threatened to overrun her life in music.) Rejecting the adage that a woman should never be seen in the same outfit twice, Stefani also wore the dress when the band plugged in at the Teen Choice Awards soon after. And although 'Simple Kind Of Life' didn't pack the same commercial punch as 'Don't Speak', it was the album's most successful single, reaching number 38 on the Hot 100 singles chart and charting reasonably well around the globe, on its release in June 2000. 'Bathwater', which followed later in the year, didn't fare as well, although it did give the band the chance to play dress-up on Jay Leno's show, on August 4. With smirking pint-sized comic David Spade looking on from the guest's couch, the band transported the studio audience to some classy dive from the jazz age, Dumont dapper in a pin-stripe suit, Young wearing a top hat (and little else, naturally), while Stefani stepped out in fishnets, heels and the type of hat that wouldn't have been out of place at the Cotton Club. Backstage, in Leno's green room, Young's father, Dumont's mother and both of Stefani's parents happily swilled the free drinks after the high-stepping performance. And yet, despite the obvious backstage bonhomie, the band was coming to grips with the cold fact that *Return Of Saturn* was a flop, at least according to the industry's bean counters and tastemakers, even though it clung to the album chart for almost a year. *Tragic Kingdom* was one hard act to follow.

There was any number of explanations, of course, the most obvious being that the album simply wasn't as tuneful as its predecessor, and the band's maturing had turned off those looking for more of Stefani's answers to Gen X life (even if they were unlikely to find them in the slick pop of Christina Aguilera or Destiny's Child or the God-bothering lite-metal blather of Creed). And after the two-year odyssey flogging *Tragic Kingdom*, the band simply didn't tour this record with the same road-warrior-styled relentless-ness. 'Serious' touring for the album began with dates in Texas in early June, and while the band and crew travelled far and wide, visiting Japan, Malaysia, Thailand, Australia, South Korea and Hawaii, again, *Return Of Saturn* was effectively over when Stefani said goodnight after two dates at KROQ's Acoustic Xmas on December 16 and 17, 2000. They'd only been on the road for six months, a breezy roadtrip in comparison to the long haul of *Tragic Kingdom*.

The band also kept things relatively small scale. Although they played the occasional concrete bunker, they tended to stick with more intimate venues, easily filling such 2500-seaters as Philadelphia's Electric Factory and the Riviera Theater in Chicago, or the 1500 capacity Price Center Ballroom in San Diego and the 1200-seat 9.30 Club in DC. In fact, when they upgraded to larger shows, they had trouble shifting tickets: their June 6, 2000, gig at The Woodlands in Texas, a 12,000 capacity venue, was just over half full, while only 2700 paying punters fronted in Charlotte, North Carolina, even though the room was built for 7000-plus. Worse was to come in Virginia, when only 5800 punters turned up to their show at the 20,000 capacity Virginia Beach Ampitheater, despite a bill that also included retro-rockers Lit and hip-hoppers on the rise the Black Eyed Peas. And the house was barely half full a week later when the same trio played the PNC Bank Arts Center in Holmdel, New Jersey. They faced a similarly half-empty house on July 15 at the legendary Red Rocks Ampitheater in Morrison, Colorado, the site of one of U2's most inspired North American shows in 1983.

Yet, despite their diminishing returns at the box office, there was an upside to the band's 2000 tour. No Doubt may have released their most downbeat album, and were opting for a setlist that included such *Return Of Saturn* navel-gazers as 'Six Feet Under', 'Marry Me' and 'Staring Problem', but the band and crew were losing themselves in some major after-show partying. After most shows, a boombox – sometimes even a full DJ booth, with lights – would be set up backstage and the band would become DJs, spinning their newly discovered dancehall favourites. A cramped backstage space would soon morph into a mass of sweaty, dancing bodies, getting off on the deep Jamaican grooves – in some ways, the band were more enthused about the after-show parties than the gigs themselves. Stefani described the entire tour as a "blast". "Every night we were having these dancehall parties," she said, "and it was just unreal." And the group began to dress a little looser, a little more outlandishly: while Stefani stuck with her flamingo-pink colouring, Dumont would often be spotted proudly sporting a Van Halen visor or a red jumpsuit, Kanal took a fancy to a Karate Kid T-shirt, while the horn section of McNair and Bradley opted for anything, as long as it was in lime green. As for Young, well, he opted to wear as little as possible, as often as possible.

A typical day on the road began with the men of No Doubt, especially the very single Tony Kanal, sampling the hair of the dog around five in the afternoon – the alcohol-wary Stefani remained the most abstemious member of the band, more a spectator than a participant – and then play their show and party well into the next day. Writing from the road on July 30, Dumont summed up the relentlessly good vibes. "This tour has been amazing and is arguably the most fun we've ever had on tour together." (Dumont, who played DJ at most of the band's post-gig bacchanals, admitted that his mind would drift during those Return Of Saturn shows. "During the concert, [I'd] be thinking, 'What am I going to spin tonight?' ") "These guys [partied] so hard," Stefani said afterwards. "They'd have an after-party every night . . . and it was months of it, every single night. The nights we didn't play, they'd go to clubs." As the tour progressed, the idea of bottling some of this bonhomie came to the band; they'd cut their serious record, so maybe it was time to make something a little sexier, a little funkier. And all this backstage madness gave Stefani plenty of lyrical material to draw on; such future tracks as 'Hey Baby' and 'Hella Good' were snapshots of the nights that the band spent "tearing it up," in her own words. In its own drunk and debaucherous way, *Rock Steady* was born.

CHAPTER TEN

Band On The Run

"Jesus Christ!"
    —Gavin Rossdale's response to being tagged No Doubt's "Yoko Ono"

With the brooding *Return Of Saturn* now totally out of their system, No Doubt didn't mess about: within weeks of the final dates of their 2000 tour they began to work on new songs. And this time around, unlike *Saturn*, they were a band with a very specific plan: they were going to cut a party record, one that would make their live shows a joy rather than an endurance test; they were going to embrace life rather than inflict a 90-minute therapy session on their fans. (It's no coincidence that of the band's last three major album tours, *Return Of Saturn* was the only one that wasn't captured on film by the ever-present Sophie Muller.) And this time around No Doubt was totally open to the idea of collaborators, although they didn't know just how many A-listers were keen to work with them.

At a band dinner in September 2000, the idea for this party-hearty record was raised. Rebel Waltz's Jim Guerinot was there. Barely five months had passed since *Return Of Saturn's* release. "Everybody sat down and said, 'What would be the most fun thing to do?'," Guerinot recalled. "They decided to be experimental and just enjoy themselves." And in some ways, the relative failure of *Saturn* lightened the commercial load on the band; they knew that *Tragic Kingdom's* numbers were a fluke, a chance alignment of musical styles and great songwriting – and dollops of sheer dumb luck – that only

197

occurred once in a band's life, if at all. Yet there was still enough momentum, if their records were strong enough, to make the band a steady earner for Interscope.

While *Return Of Saturn* came to life in the rented band house on Woodrow Wilson Drive, this time around the foursome connected at Tom Dumont's place in Hollywood, where he was fast becoming the grandmaster of ProTools. Sessions commenced on January 2, only weeks after the final dates of the Saturn tour. (Something like 80 percent of *Rock Steady's* tracks would be demoed at Dumont's house.) And this time around, Stefani decided to ditch the Sylvia Plath; she was going to try to write some upbeat lyrics, on the fly, rather than indulge in heavy-handed guts spilling. "I usually do this thing where I . . . get all depressed or find different words than inspire me," she said. "It was challenging for me to say, 'I'm gonna write it now, we're gonna record it right now and tomorrow we're gonna write a new song'." Spontaneity was a totally new word in the No Doubt vocabulary. And recording on computer meant that the songs were portable – the band could burn off some Frequent Flyer points making the record, if the mood hit, as would prove to be the case.

They also wanted to experiment with instruments, as Kanal explained. "The instrumentation was whatever made sense at the time," he said. He and Dumont reached an agreement early on that if the song didn't need a bass or guitar part, there was no sense in tacking it on purely to stick with the No Doubt "formula" of bass / guitar / drums / voice. (This led to the heavy use of keyboard on such *Rock Steady* cuts as the juicy single 'Hey Baby', or the saccharine-coated ballad 'Running', where Kanal played a vintage Yamaha organ bought as a gift by his father some 15 years earlier.) "Whatever lends itself to the song" became their new motto, according to Kanal.

In February, the band was in the middle of cutting the track 'Detective', where a trademark Stefani lyric of distrustful lovers is set to a wash of synths, when she announced that London was calling. Bush were off the road and she was going to spend some R&R with Rossdale, thereby further consolidating Rossdale's rep as No Doubt's very own "Yoko". (This was a reference to John Lennon's wife, Yoko One, who, in the eyes of many, single-handedly broke up the Beatles. Rossdale's two-word response – "Jesus Christ!" – pretty much summed up his feelings. Stefani didn't seem to mind; she'd taken to wearing a gold anklet that spelled out his Christian name, something her bandmates couldn't have avoided if they'd tried.) But the Hollywood sessions were proceeding so well that Kanal made a group decision: they'd continue working any way they could. So they decided to play follow the leader; Kanal told Stefani, "Fuck, dude, you can't leave – [so] we're going with you." The band bought some air tickets, located an apartment in Rothwell Street, in Earl's Court, close to Rossdale's splendid London digs, and turned Stefani's UK sojourn into a working holiday, interrupting her lovemaking with requests for lyrics and vocals. Kanal, for one, had no regrets. "I'm so glad we did it," he said, "because 'Detective' came out of those sessions."

The recording of 'Detective' said a lot about this band-on-the-run; the finished version was the result of sessions at four different locales (including the Record Plant in LA) and it was also the band's first collaboration with Nellee Hooper, who'd share a co-production credit for this and four other *Rock Steady* cuts, working out of his London base, Home Recordings. The Bristol-born Hooper was a good fit for No Doubt, especially during this freewheeling, anything-goes phase of their careers. He started out as a DJ and then became part of the Wild Bunch, the collective that eventually morphed into the hugely successful and influential trip-hop outfit Massive Attack. Hooper worked on some era-defining records, making "dance" music that was more for the head than the feet. These albums included Massive Attack's *Protection* (which won him a Best Producer gong at the 1995 Brits), Bjork's *Post* and Madonna's *Bedtime Stories*. He also worked with Ms Smooth Operator, Sade, African / American folkie Tracy Chapman and co-produced Sinead O'Connor's treacly 'Nothing Compares 2 U', a massive hit for the Irish agitator.

In his own way, as part of Soul II Soul, the London-based funk / soul giants of the late 1980s and early '90s, Hooper had replicated the approach of many of the early ska acts that inspired No Doubt to form in the first place: they'd set up a "sound system" and spin records at house and street parties. It was 1950s Jamaica, albeit with a late-20th-century twist (Admittedly, when Hooper first met Soul II Soul mainman Jazzie B in 1985, at a house party, they had a punch-up over some rented gear, although the relationship soon improved.) Along with Jazzie B, Hooper produced the first (and best) two Soul II Soul albums, which included the signature songs 'Back To Life' and 'Keep On Movin' '".

On a number of levels, 'Detective' was a perfect example of where No Doubt was heading with *Rock Steady*. Its trans-Atlantic production job summed up the band's peripatetic lifestyle during 2001, while its sleek soundscape, heavy with digital-age electronics and very light on Dumont's guitar crunch, proved that No Doubt was ready and willing to make another very contemporary-sounding record, a la *Return Of Saturn*. This was one of the few tracks to surface on *Rock Steady* that showed signs of Stefani's old insecurities; in the main, she was in the mood to party.

The band recorded several other tracks with Hooper at sessions later in 2001, including In My Head', 'Hella Good', the album's title track and the sticky-sweet 'Running'. Of these, 'Hella Good' was the standout; it was built around a simple, crisp rhythm from Young, a lurching Kanal bass riff and choppy, minimalist Dumont riffs, with some keyboard squiggles added for colour. It also featured a rare Dumont solo, a shiny-clean lead break that Todd Rundgren would have admired. And 'Hella Good' was deeply and undeniably funky; this was a song created with hips in mind. Stefani wasn't lying when she warned that this track was all about "tearing it up".

'Hella Good' was also a song with a past. Before cutting it in London with Hooper, Kanal and Stefani had written the track with Chad Hugo and Pharrell Williams, aka the Neptunes (and two-thirds of N.E.R.D.), the hottest songwriting / production duo on planet hip-hop. (This dynamic duo had recently worked with hip-hoppers ODB and Mystikal, and were about to strike gold as producers of Britney Spears, 'NSYNC, Nelly and Usher.) Stefani's plan for the track was simple; she wanted to find a way to insert the word "dance" into a pounding chorus. It worked, because this would become their set opener when No Doubt took *Rock Steady* on the road.

Of the other Hooper co-productions, the soppy 'Running' was the weakest, despite the quaintly charming keyboard line played by Kanal on his very old-school Yamaha. 'In My Head' was way more interesting; while the song's lyric placed Stefani back on the couch, trying to decipher the root cause of her paranoia, the song's bare-boned funkiness − it was wrapped around another ridiculously simple Young rhythm and some twitchy keyboards − showed that the work of Dr Dre may have been on their mix tapes during the *Return Of Saturn* after-show parties. Coincidentally, the band did approach Dre about contributing a track to the album, and Stefani went as far as writing some lyrics over the top of a trademark Dre piano loop, but the song was never finished. A jam with hip-hop heavy Timbaland, Missy Elliott's main man, also fell apart. "You work with someone like Timbaland," Stefani explained, "and you're suddenly being lectured. And you're like, 'Dude, I've been doing this for 15 years'."

The final Hooper track, 'Rock Steady', was a few sweet minutes of 21st century dub; this was how The Skatalites might have sounded if they'd formed 50 years later and recorded on ProTools. Stefani dug deeply for one of her best vocals on the album, all gentle charm and sly sexiness, as a burbling Kanal bassline, understated steel drums and wiggly keyboards danced in the background. The song summed up the band's mood at the time, as Stefani explained. "*Rock Steady* is a very happy record, but that's because we were very happy making it." To this she added the band's very clear goals for the song and the album: "We wanted to make simple, sexy songs," she admitted. "We wanted to make a record that we could dance to, that would come on when we were in a club."

Adrian Young, who perfected the craft of playing along to machines during the album, had his own explanation for No Doubt's newfound stability. "We treat each other well within the band," he said. "I think we're pretty good people and I think that comes across. We're not dysfunctional in any way; there aren't any drug habits, there's nothing too crazy or major that seems to come our way." (Young conveniently overlooked the dramatic departure of Eric Stefani, and, admittedly, wasn't around when John Spence killed himself.) Typically, Tom Dumont cut through the crap. "You couldn't play *Return Of Saturn* at a party," he stated. "This [album] is upbeat, like *Tragic Kingdom*. And we love Devo-y bleeps and *Star Wars* noises, so there's lots of that."

The quartet of tunes recorded with Hooper weren't the only songs that the band worked on while in London. Upon the suggestion of Interscope head Jimmy Iovine, Stefani (along with Kanal and Dumont) paid a call on Dave Stewart, the sometimes Eurythmic, and together they wrote a sparse, simple valentine called 'Underneath It All', which some would describe as *Rock Steady's* very own 'Don't Speak'. The song came together in near record time for No Doubt. The lyrical hook – "you're really lovely / underneath it all" – was another act of spontaneity; it had popped into Stefani's head just the day before, when she and Rossdale were in a London park. She quickly jotted it down in her journal. "We were so in love," said Stefani, "and I wrote that line. [It was] like, 'after all the shit we've been through, you're a really good person. I really think I might like you'."

The "shit" Stefani referred to was her brief split with Rossdale, in mid 2000, when he was rumoured to be having a "secret" romance with Andrea Corr and / or All Saints singer Nicole Appleton. "When I was being photographically tracked for my various dalliances, I wasn't with Gwen," Rossdale said in his defence. "So I'm not quite the scoundrel I'm made out to be." The Rossdale / Stefani love match would also briefly come off the rails, in 2004, when a DNA test proved that Rossdale was in fact the father of his teenage god-daughter, Daisy Lowe. Stefani, understandably, was "devastated" by the revelation, but stood by her man.

Dave Stewart, of course, was synth-pop royalty. Born in 1952, the upper-middle-class Englishman had been signed to Elton John's Rocket Records in the '70s, as part of a long-forgotten outfit called Longdancer, but then he met Annie Lennox, the daughter of a bagpipe-playing Scottish shipyard worker. Stewart and Lennox became involved, romantically and creatively; although their relationship didn't last, their music survived, first with the Tourists and then as the creative core of the Eurythmics. Their precisely-crafted hits – 'Sweet Dreams (Are Made Of This)', 'Who's That Girl?', 'Here Comes The Rain Again' – were MTV-era staples and favourites of the very '80s-savvy members of No Doubt.

When we spoke in late 2006, Stewart had nothing but positive memories of the songwriting session that produced 'Underneath It All', although he admitted that the trio seemed a little stunned when they first entered his home. At the time, Stewart lived in a swanky home-cum-studio known as 7 Dials; his high-tech apartment resembled something NASA might have designed, with an added splash of pop culture chic. "It was a very eccentric apartment," he recalled. "I think they were going, "Fucking hell, this is weird." It has these 27-foot tall windows and panoramic views over London, but inside it's this kind of strange, arty, Andy-Warhol's-Factory-on-steroids thing. It was cool."

Stefani and Stewart had been in touch beforehand, and had mapped out a few musical sketches, although 'Underneath It All' wasn't amongst these. "Gwen and I just went away to the kitchen with an acoustic guitar," Stewart recalled, "and came back 15 minutes later with the song. We played it to everybody and we started recording it with Ned Douglas, my programmer / engineer. They walked out with a template that was very similar to the single. Everything, you know, the whole feel of it, the bridge and all the bits were there. It came out really well. They took it to the next step with [Jamaican studio greats] Sly & Robbie." According to Stewart's assistant Douglas, the day was capped with a shot of overproof Jamaican rum – of course. "We started recording," Douglas told me, "Dave's son Django played a sax riff on it and within a couple of hours it was done." (Douglas was pleasantly surprised when some time later he got a call from mixer Mark "Spike Stent, requesting the original programming. "I just assumed that everything would be [re-]done from scratch," he admitted. "The end result was actually not that far from what we had on the day; Django's sax line was still in there and a fair bit of the programming I'd done.")

"There's something with some people, and I think I have it with Gwen," said Stewart, "where it happens very quickly. It's about the emotions of the chords meeting a certain thing with the words and it all goes very quickly, maybe 15 or 20 minutes and you have a strong blueprint of the song, if not a finished version. I never really walk into that kind of situation with expectations; I'm always very open. [I learned that] she's very astute; I think all the band are. I think when Tony came and played the bass I could see what a great bass player and how focused he was." Although Stewart wouldn't go into too much detail, he did tell me that he and Stefani had spoken about the frank lyrics of 'Underneath It All'; Stewart knew Rossdale, so he understood precisely what Stefani was singing about. "She did discuss them, actually," he laughed. "Obviously they're personal lyrics, but when you write a song with someone, you put your cards on the table, so to speak. So I knew what it was about." (A year later, Stefani and Stewart wrote another song, 'Sparkle', still unreleased at the time of writing. Stewart knows of two versions: a spare acoustic take and a Nellee Hooper-produced variation. "I think it's a great song, actually, but I don't know if anyone will hear it," Stewart told me.)

While with the trio, Stewart, who, along with his wife, is a close friend of Stefani and Rossdale, mentioned that he was a huge fan of Jamaican music; he told them that he co-owned a house in the hills overlooking Kingston and spent a lot of time on the island. His friends included Jamaican legends Sly & Robbie, while he'd met Lady Saw, whose scattergun rap would become a key feature of the track he'd written with Stefani. According to Stewart, "Jamaica's a funny little community; there are certain musicians that are obviously the peer group and it goes all the way down to brilliant street musicians; it's just a great place to hang out." As the band continued talking with Stewart, during a "glittery London afternoon", as he remembered it, he got the sense that he'd helped make up their minds about something.

"I think after I'd written that song with them they got into the idea [of Jamaica] after that," Stewart said. Ned Douglas agreed. "Dave has such a love for Jamaica and is so enthusiastic about it that I'm sure that helped inspire them to go." Stewart's house in the hills was another big attractor; he co-owned it with Brian Jobson, who played a huge role in connecting No Doubt with the very best Jamaica had to offer. The members of No Doubt headed there in March 2001, and stayed for two weeks, soon after their sit-down with Stewart. Jobson, and his record-producing brother Wayne, who lived in LA but also sometimes worked on the island – and had spun reggae discs on KROQ, and later Indie 103.1, under the handle 'Native Wayne' – would become go-betweens for No Doubt, whom Wayne dubbed The Doubtless Clan. (Kanal had earlier visited the Jobsons and stayed with them at their base, The Icehouse, in Ocho Rios, Jamaica; it was during this trip that the idea of working on the island was first raised.) "Jamaica's a wonderful place to be and work if you have someone there who knows how it works," said Ned Douglas, "and Brian Jobson is really that person; [he's] someone who can pull all the pieces together." Stewart agreed. "[Jobson] introduced them to this place in Port Antonio, and to Sly & Robbie, probably." The pay-off for the Jobson brothers was an Executive Producer credit on 'Hey Baby', 'Underneath It All' and 'Start The Fire', plus 'New Friend', which didn't make *Rock Steady*'s final cut.

As with many of *Rock Steady*'s tracks, 'Underneath It All' did some miles. Production for this track and 'Hey Baby' came courtesy of aforementioned legends Sly & Robbie, Jamaica's finest local product this side of the island's high-grade marijuana and some stellar cricketers. Drummer Lowell Dunbar (aka Sly, a nod to his hero Sly Stone) and bassman Robert Shakespeare were stone-cold roots music royalty and quite possibly the most prolific studio duo of all time – one estimate has suggested that they've played on and / or produced more than 200,000 tracks (a number that excludes remixes). When Sly & Robbie first met in the 1970s, they found out that their eclectic tastes were very compatible: both were big on the immortal ska records that came out of Clement Dodd's Studio One and Duke Reid's Treasure Isle studio, but they were also mad for Motown, the Philly sound, reggae, even country and western.

Together, they were groundbreakers: in 1976, when they introduced a harder beat to reggae, which they called "rockers", they rendered the then-prevalent "one-drop" style obsolete. In the early 1980s they began playing a "rub a dub" sound, which was just as revolutionary. They were also very progressive with the use of computers and programming in the studio, which surely appealed to the ProTools-crazy members of No Doubt. And the duo's CV was peerless; they'd laid down grooves for Bob Dylan, Joe Cocker, Serge Gainsbourg, Tricky, the Rolling Stones, Sting and literally thousands of others – although, according to Wayne Jobson, they'd never actually heard of No Doubt before working with them (likewise producers Steely & Cleevie and collaborators Lady Saw and Bounty Killer).

Young, Dumont, Stefani and Kanal hooked up with the pair in Jamaica's Geejam and One Pop Studios, hard drives under their arms. "It's easy to move music around with ProTools," Kanal said, "[so] we just brought down the discs." Young was stunned to discover that Sly didn't bother anymore with a regulation drum kit; he simply programmed parts on his drum machine. "That's his thing now," Young explained. (**51**) And despite the heavy partying on their last tour, the foursome wasn't quite prepared for the standard Jamaican breakfast of rum and coke and / or Red Stripe beers, "to get our heads in the right space", according to Kanal. It definitely didn't work for Dumont, who actually passed out while cutting a guitar track. "It's a wonder we got stuff done," said Kanal, shaking his head. "We went out to a lot of local bars in [the district] Drapers," Wayne Jobson recalled, "and they drank a lot of Red Stripe – so it seemed that was the main food." Jobson also turned the band onto a local delicacy, jerk chicken, which they feasted on at Boston Beach, a regular haunt during their stay.

Of the two tracks worked on with the rum-loving pair, 'Hey Baby' was the most noteworthy; it was a sexy dance track, complete with a lyric where Stefani passed judgement on the backstage antics of her bandmates and their many hangers-on. "Misfit, I sit," she sang, "Everybody else surrounded by the girls / With the tank tops and the flirty words." Teamed with a wicked rap from dancehall giant Bounty Killer – who was also unfamiliar with No Doubt before the session – 'Hey Baby' was irresistible; it was both organic and cutting edge, a song for heavy clubbers and pop fans. It was a no-brainer as the lead single from *Rock Steady* and would chart strongly. (In a move that must have impressed the Stefanis, Sly & Robbie, soon after working with No Doubt, produced *The Lone Ranger*, the solo debut from Madness' Suggs. It became a massive UK hit.) As for 'Underneath It All', the highlight was an urgent, insistent rap from Jamaican "bad girl" Lady Saw, another acquaintance of Dave Stewart, who was known universally as "The First Lady of Dancehall".

While in Jamaica, the band also tracked down another dynamic duo, keyboardist Wycliffe "Steely" Johnson and drummer Cleveland "Clevie" Browne, the key production team of the modern dancehall / reggae era. Steely was a player in the Roots Radics, the number one Jamaican band during the early 1980s dancehall revival, while Clevie was a Studio One vet. The pair, who'd first jammed at Lee "Scratch" Perry's famous Black Ark Studios during the late 1970s, were, just like Sly & Robbie, very hip to computer technology. And they were equally prolific, cutting upwards of 10 tracks per week; they'd added their magic touch to hits from Foxy Brown, Cocoa Tea, Johnny P and Dilinger. Also working in Jamaica's Geejam Studios, the pair worked with No Doubt on the *Rock Steady* track 'Start The Fire' and another song entitled 'New Friend', an outtake that ended up on the *Everything In Time* CD of curios.

With their dreads, shades and liquid heart-starters, Sly & Robbie may have resembled your archetypal Jamaican musos, but Steely and Clevie were something else altogether. "They were really nerdy," said a surprised Dumont, "with button-down shirts. [They looked like] college music professors." Dumont found them to be "very particular" about the tracks' drum and bass sound, and for a reason: "They wanted it to hit hard sonically in the cars of Miami, which was something we had never thought about." They got it right, too; "Start The Fire" seamlessly blended a loose-limbed Calypso beat with the type of rhythmic undertow rarely heard this side of the Miami Sound Machine. Once again, with a lot of help from their A-list friends, No

Doubt had bridged the gap between old-school roots music and 21st century dance grooves; while 'Start The Fire' was a song you were bound to hear in some uber-hip club (or booming out of a low-rider in Miami), it was just as likely to become a favourite amongst the poolside, cocktail-sipping set at the Four Seasons in Kingston, Jamaica. It was a song for all seasons.

Wayne Jobson told me that the band won a lot of respect from Jamaican music-makers during their trip, mainly because they bothered to travel to the island and "record at the source, as it were. Most other artists would usually record the music elsewhere and maybe send the tracks to Jamaica for remixes, but No Doubt actually came down and immersed themselves in the vibes and culture and managed to capture the magic." Jobson was impressed by Young's reggae hi-hat playing – "as good as any native" – and his "wicked" golf swing. He admired Dumont's ability to find "the right lick at the right time" and acknowledged that Stefani is "a gifted songwriter". As for Kanal, Jobson, like so many others, had nothing but respect for his juggling skills. "He locks down the rhythm section as wickedly as he masterminds the band's runnings." Rebel Waltz may have overseen the business of No Doubt, but the band was still Kanal's obsession, no matter how big they became.

Their island experience over, No Doubt's wandering minstrels had more miles to cover, but this time they headed to more familiar territory. They hooked up in LA with Ric Ocasek, the gangly, alien-like figure – always in black, rarely seen without shades – best known for his time leading new wave stars the Cars. Ocasek was a Baltimore native, 52 years old when he worked with No Doubt, who'd produced records for Weezer, Hole, Guided by Voices, Bad Religion and numerous others in his post-Cars life. Holed up in LA, Ocasek produced the *Rock Steady* tracks 'Platinum Blonde Life' – another frank Stefani confessional, which dealt with her uncomfortable reaction to the spotlight and was also a heartfelt farewell to her much-loved dog, who'd recently gone to that big kennel in the sky – and 'Don't Let Me Down'. Not surprisingly, Ocasek added a distinctly nervy, new wave-ish character to both tracks, which gave them a totally different flavour to the more groove-heavy cuts that dominated the album.

Another contributor to *Rock Steady* was expat English producer / player William Orbit. His track record was as impressive as anyone else on *Rock Steady*; it included collaborations with erstwhile Spice Girl Melanie C, the all-girl All Saints, alt-folkie Beth Orton, Blur and Seal, although he was best known for his work on Madonna's ethereal *Ray Of Light*, which reinvented the Material Girl as the queen of electronica and in the process scored four

Grammys (including Best Pop Album). He co-produced 'Making Out', a perky Stefani / Kanal / Dumont pop tune that celebrated the simple joys of snogging, Stefani cooing her way through the lyric like some lovestruck teenager.

As freewheeling as *Rock Steady's* globetrotting and high profile collabs was for the band, the album's biggest high – recording with Prince – had actually occurred some time earlier. It was already on tape when the band first decided to make this party album in September 2000. The Prince connection with the band ran deep; as a high schooler, Kanal had used *Purple Rain* as motivational music for swim meets, and his devotion to the over-sexed midget from Minneapolis was so strong that "Tony even thought he was Prince", according to Stefani. She was also a huge fan; Stefani rated him alongside Madness' Suggs – and Rossdale, naturally – as one of the sexiest men in music.

Prince, allegedly, was a fan of the band's way back at the time of their self-titled debut, and had reached out to Stefani via Gavin Rossdale, requesting a collaboration. When the call came, Rossdale looked at Stefani and mouthed "Do it! Do it!" and she swiftly agreed. (It turned out that "Yoko" Rossdale was quite the guru; he'd recommend authors to his wife-to-be, advise her on clothes, hook her up with Prince, and even helped out Dumont's then girlfriend, a schoolteacher, grade her student's papers. According to Dave Stewart, who worked and socialised with both Stefani and Rossdale, "He's really interested in art, literature, everything.") As for Prince, he wasn't backward in coming forward; he turned up at a No Doubt show at the Target Center in Minneapolis on July 1, 1997. He met up with them afterwards and insisted they come back to his Paisley Park palace for a jam. The band, especially Stefani, couldn't quite get their heads around what was happening. "First of all, I do not jam," she said. "I mean, he's not like somebody you meet and walk away going, "Oh, he's a normal person, just like you and me, da, da, da. You walk away going, 'That is the Artist Formerly Known as Prince'." Stefani agreed to sing on his Purpleness' *Rave Un2 the Joy Fantastic* album; in exchange, he worked on No Doubt's 'Waiting Room', with a little help from go-between Rossdale.

'Waiting Room', which was originally planned for *Return Of Saturn*, was first cut by the band and then handed over to Prince to tweak, which explains its distinctively compressed, synths-and-voices-heavy sound. "It's got all these crazy melodies," Stefani gushed. (It actually sounds like a *Sign O' the Times* outtake.) When the track was done, the legendary ladies-man flew the band to his Minneapolis lair, but left Kanal, Young and Dumont waiting outside the studio, as he entertained Stefani one-on-one. "The three of us basically got the couch," said Dumont, "while he ushered Gwen into the studio. Can't say we were surprised." Although not *Rock Steady's* choicest cut – probably the reason it was first put on hold, and then hidden away towards the end of the album – 'Waiting Room' did create a unique and somewhat unsettling situation for Stefani. "It was Prince singing lyrics I had written about Gavin with music I had written with Tony," she said. "It was so weird." It summed up the entire *Rock Steady* experience: the barriers between the band and their heroes (and, in the case of Stefani, her personal life) had been well and truly removed.

On August 2, 2001, Tom Dumont reported that he, Kanal and Young had arrived in London, and expected to be finished recording the record – now officially known as *Rock Steady* – in a few weeks. Although the process had taken up most of the year, and the band had covered thousands of miles, it was actually a far more cohesive production than the interminable grave-yard shifts for *Tragic Kingdom*, or the stop-start train wreck that was *Return Of Saturn*. Some of the band celebrated their good fortune by taking in shows from the Stone Temple Pilots and U2, who No Doubt would soon tour with. While in London, Kanal, Dumont and Young rented a five-bed-room house and set up another No Doubt HQ, although an exploding toi-let almost forced them to search for other digs before they'd unpacked. Still, compared with the dramas of *Return Of Saturn*, an unreliable bog was nothing.

Writing in his on-line diary, Dumont noted how different-sounding *Rock Steady's* songs were; on a track such as 'Hey Baby', for instance, his gui-tar was virtually non-existent. "But I carry great pride in the keyboard work that I did on the song," he wrote. "The great thing is that most of those demo recordings ended up on the actual album tracks. Thanks to studio technology advances, we literally recorded much of this new album in our living room for you to listen to in yours." Mark "Spike" Stent, introduced to Stefani by the ever-resourceful Rossdale, mixed the record in London's famed Olympic Studios. Stent's hitlist included records by Depeche Mode, Bjork, Massive Attack and the Spice Girls' ubiquitous 'Wannabe', while his nickname came about when he was working with Led Zep's John Paul Jones and The Mission in 1987 – the band couldn't remember his name, so they'd refer to him by his hairstyle, hence "Spike".

As the *Rock Steady* mix continued, the men of No Doubt took solace in endless games of ping pong and tennis; the unpredictable London weather meant that they'd become prisoners of the studio, an all-too-familiar sensa-tion. "Mixing can be a long, all-day process," Dumont reported. He also noted that Young was the band's best athlete, hands down. Finally, by the end of September, 2001, mixer Stent had applied what he referred to as "the icing of the cake" and *Rock Steady* was done. No Doubt, however, didn't get much time to relax; within two weeks they were in LA and back in rehearsals for their upcoming U2 dates. In their downtime they were film-ing the 'Hey Baby' video, a vibrant, day-glo number directed by Dave Meyers, that re-created all of the band's recent backstage debauchery with obvious glee. The on-screen cameo from toastmaster Bounty Killer was as irresistible as the song itself, which had more bounce and vitality than a five-year-old who's overdone the sugar.

Rock Steady emerged on December 11, 2001, barely 15 months after the band first kicked around the idea of making the ultimate party record. By No Doubt's terms, it was record-breaking time – in the past, at the 15-month mark they'd probably be hitting Interscope up for more money and re-considering their choice of producer. The album's title and its suggestion of a return to the band's ska roots, however, was a little misleading. Working with Jamaican giants Sly & Robbie and Steely & Clevie had certainly helped add a summery, calypso sway to such tracks as 'Hey Baby' and 'Underneath It All', while the cameos from Lady Saw and Bounty Killer proved that No Doubt knew their dancehall from their dancefloor. Clearly, all those after-show parties spent spinning the various *Biggest Ragga Dancehall Anthems* compilations so loved by the band (which featured Steely & Clevie, Bounty Killer and Lady Saw) had done the trick. And working with Ric Ocasek and Prince – finally – had provided flashbacks to the band's much-loved 1980s. As for the proliferation of *Star Wars*-y bleeps heard throughout *Rock Steady's* soundscape? Well, that was pure indulgence from the George Lucas-obsessed members of the band.

But at the same time, this was an undeniably contemporary record; Stefani's between-album jams with electronic guru Moby (the remix of his 'Southside', with a new Stefani vocal, was a US Top 20 single in 2000) and hip-hop's queen bee Eve (on 2001's Grammy-winning 'Let Me Blow Ya Mind', a huge crossover hit for both singers), had steered No Doubt in the direction of 21st century groove. The significance of these one-offs can't be underestimated, both as sonic signposts for parts of *Rock Steady* and as key influences on the album of sleek, smart, digital-age pop that would herald Stefani's stellar solo career a few years later.

Working with Eve had obviously given Stefani a few style tips, too. Her look for *Rock Steady*, with its emphasis on chunky, oversized bling, and an unmistakable do-not-fuck-with-me attitude, was pure ghetto fabulous, clearly all about Eve. This new look was a million miles away from Stefan's past as a coy, bindi-wearing OC 20-something with an eye for thrift-store threads. The connection with the first lady of hip-hop had come about through Dr Dre. Stefani was so keen to work with him that she phoned her label and insisted, "If Dr Dre ever needs me for anything, call me up." (Dre also recorded for Interscope, which helped.) And Dre did call, suggesting that Stefani and Eve get together on the mic and see what happened. "It was such an awesome experience," Stefani gushed, "this whole kind of cultural collision." The friendship was sealed when Eve sent the ever-girlie Stefani an earring that proclaimed 'Eve' and a gold chain with a paw print. "She's like a homegirl," Eve gushed right back at her. "You'd want to hang out with her." Eve was as good as her word, because she would jam with Stefani on 'Rich Girl' from Stefani's solo album, *Love.Angel.Music.Baby*, a bizarre showtune-meets-pop-song with no less than nine co-writers, including Eve, Stefani and Kanal, with production courtesy of that man Dre.

The Moby hook-up predated her work with Eve; the idea of the two working together was first suggested towards the end of the crazy *Tragic Kingdom* era. "I expected some really self-involved rock star," the elfin Moby admitted, "but she's lovely and down to earth." Moby was nobody's fool, either; he understood exactly why their electro-pop jam became such a hit. "She's the reason our video for 'South Side' got played so much." During the day that the pair spent in the studio, Stefani's attitude impressed Moby as much as the "unique timbre" and "distinctive quality" of her voice. "She worked really hard," he said, sounding as though he expected the exact opposite.

Clearly these two collabs contributed towards the band's decision to write with the Neptunes and use mixer Stent and producers Hooper and Orbit on *Rock Steady*; these guys were all on the cutting-edge of digital-age pop. (As were Dre and Timbaland, even though these sessions were aborted.) *Rock Steady*, clearly, was an album that straddled music's old and new schools. And despite the odd neurotic lapse by Stefani, the lyrical tone of the record was generally positive; she was in love with a hunk who "underneath it all" could just be the right man for her (even if the travelling was a bitch and they were sometimes forced to email each other love letters). Life was as good as it had ever been for Stefani.

'Hey Baby' was a bold first single, a very clear indication that they were ready to party. It was also a positive, life-affirming statement in the aftermath of the 9/11 terrorist strikes on the US. The charts and airwaves were more than just responsive; the song was a major hit throughout the end of 2001 and into the early months of 2002, scoring heavily across charts as diverse as Modern Adult Contemporary and the Adult Top 40 list. And 'Hey Baby' reached the pole position on Billboard's Top 40 Mainstream; the track hung about that key chart for six months. In fact, of the 11 Billboard charts on which it registered, 'Hey Baby' stayed in all, bar one, for at least three months; this song had more legs than Elle MacPherson. It was also a natural fit with much of the chart fodder of the time, too; 2001 was the year of such smooth grooves as Jennifer Lopez's 'I'm Real', Craig David's 'Fill Me In' and Usher's 'U Got It Bad'. It was also a good year for songs that straddled a number of styles, just like 'Hey Baby', including the hip–hop–pop of OutKast's 'Ms Jackson' and the pop-ragga blend of Shaggy's 'Angel', as well as the Stefani collabs 'South Side' and 'Let Me Blow Your Mind' (which, incidentally, would rank 15th and 44th, respectively, in Billboard's list of the Top 100 Songs of 2001). As for rock, at least in commercial terms, it was in poor shape, having been left in the unreliable hands of such bland, corporate unit-shifters as Nickelback, Train and Matchbox Twenty. It was a good time for No Doubt to move on.

'Hey Baby' also gave *Rock Steady* plenty of locomotion at the cash register; with the single still riding high, the band said goodbye to 2001, after yet another *Saturday Night Live* appearance, buoyed by sales fast approaching two million copies. And the LP was embedded in a 76-week run in the Billboard 200. The band was in a euphoric mood; not only was their "comeback" album, of sorts, a hit, but they'd just come off a heady tour with U2, another of their musical heroes. Stefani, who'd now totally embraced hip-hop streetwise patois, referring to her fans as "lambs" (in the best possible way) and signing off her emails as "G-Loc", said it all in a despatch from the road in late November.

"I think we might just be having the time of our lives," she wrote. "Not only did we have the best year ever making our new record, but we are also ending it on tour with a band that has been the soundtrack to our lives. All through our high school and college years, U2 had been there doing their thing. I have always respected and loved them but now with this touring experience it has gone to the next level. These guys are the real deal." It was also a very good year for Adrian Young, who was due to become a father in the early months of 2002, an event that Stefani noticed with a mixture of excitement and envy. Stefani, however, had her own big event in the very near future, because she and Rossdale planned to get hitched in September 2002, during a break in touring for *Rock Steady*. But more on that later.

The critical response to *Rock Steady* was generally favourable. *Spin's* tastemakers could see that it was the next logical step in the reinvention of Gwen Stefani, a slap in the face for those who figured that she was "just some limp-brained So-Cal chickie surfing a moment she'd done nothing to create, destined to be working that sports bra back at the mall in a year". In

the wake of Stefani's very credible jams with Moby and Eve, and the band's
collaborations with such class acts as the Neptunes, Bounty Killer, et al, *Rock
Steady* showed that "suddenly [No Doubt] matter again". And yet the band
gave the impression, at least under *Spin's* critical gaze, that all this hanging
with the cool crowd hardly mattered. "Like all good suburban punks," they
figured, "No Doubt honour their origins and their feelings, without worrying too much about whether they're hip or acceptable." The magazine
also considered, justifiably enough, that Stefani was the star of this show,
calling her a "wonderful dork" and comparing her with such down-home
heroines as Sally Field and Sandra Bullock. As for the "Gavin Report", they
read the forecast this way: "Relationship pretty good but definitely some
clouds on the horizon." It was the review's one real false note; the only
thing on the horizon right now was the pending Stefani / Rossdale nup-
tials.

Rolling Stone also paid due credit to Stefani's honesty and transparency,
the traits that had served her so well so far. "Stefani wears her all-American
vulnerabilities and anxieties in public," they noted, "not because it's some
fashionably alienated pose but because she's vulnerable and anxious. She's a
pure product of the American girl factory: blunt and guileless in detailing
the ways that femininity has screwed her up and screwed her over." (How
Stefani felt about being called "guileless" and "a dork" by America's two
leading music mags is anyone's guess.) Stefani's lyrical bluntness, however,
was something of a distraction; *Rock Steady* was the one No Doubt album
more interested in engaging the listener's hips than their hearts, and yet the
press were once again picking apart Stefani's every utterance as if she was
some late 20th century Joni Mitchell (which she clearly wasn't).

But one question lingered as *Rock Steady* continued its chart-climbing all
around the world, and the band hit the road, first with U2 and then as part
of a woman-power triple-header with Garbage and the Distillers: was
Stefani set to go it alone? *Rolling Stone* didn't think so; they declared in their
review of *Rock Steady* that she "still stands by her band . . . despite all the pre-
dictions that Stefani was a goner for a solo career". Yet Stefani's rising solo
star – and her upcoming bit part as Jean Harlow in the Martin Scorcese-
directed *The Aviator* – suggested otherwise. And the dedication on *Rock
Steady's* inner sleeve read a lot like a fond farewell: "Thank you to our families, our friends and everyone who has supported and inspired us over the
past 15 years," the band wrote. At the time of writing, it remains their final
group recording.

At best these liner notes were deliberately ambiguous, a gesture designed
to leave No Doubt's future in limbo, just in case Stefani's solo career hit a

few bumps. At the same time, the other members of the band, too often undermined by Stefani's high-voltage starpower, quietly pursued their own projects. Dumont, now married to his partner Mieke, would produce an album by singer / strummer Matt Costa; Young, whose son Mason James was born on February 17, 2002, now packed a drummer-for-hire CV that included stints with the Vandals and Bow Wow Wow (and a near-flawless golf swing). Kanal would go on to launch his own label, Kingsbury Studios, work with a reggae singer called Elan and the band Pepper, who were managed by Jon Phillips; he'd also assist with the *50 First Dates* soundtrack, which, in a handy twist of fate, featured re-workings of songs from The Cure, one of Kanal's favourite bands. Kanal would also contribute heavily to Stefani's solo work. So it wasn't as if they were sullenly sitting in their rock star mansions, waiting for a sign in the sky from the Stefani HQ, advising them that she was ready to resume No Doubt operations. After 15 years in each other's pockets, the foursome craved some downtime, a chance to find their own places in the musical world. And even if they'd never get together in a studio again, which was highly unlikely, they'd achieved plenty. In an era when the term "artist development" is an oxymoron, and one failed album means that you're dropped like a steaming turd, No Doubt had managed to forge something that resembled an actual career. (Tony Ferguson has said just this, admitting that No Doubt is one of only three genuine cases of artist development in his time at Interscope.) Sure, they'd only struck pure chart gold once, but *Tragic Kingdom's* follow-ups had generated Platinum-plus sales, while their pulling power as a live act was undeniable.

While their *Return Of Saturn* live, erm, returns were disappointing at times, the *Rock Steady* tour filled one venue after another. Through March and April 2002, they packed rooms in Puerto Rico (the 4,000-capacity Tito Puente Amphitheater, no less); Seattle, where they pulled 5500-plus payers; San Jose (they filled the 7200-capacity Event Center); Denver, Chicago, New York and Philadelphia. They also returned to their happy rocking ground at Universal City's Universal Amphitheater (now known as the Gibson Amphitheater at Universal Citywalk), where over two nights they drew almost 12,000 punters, who deposited upwards of $300,000 through the turnstiles. It was only later in the year, as the headliners on the Garbage / Distillers roadshow, as No Doubt graduated from 4,000–7,000-seaters to concrete bunkers that could hold up to 15,000, that they played to less-than-full houses. Still, their numbers were consistently solid: almost 11,000 fans showed at Worcester, Massachusetts; 10,000-plus in New Jersey; a touch under 14,000 at San Jose and a whopping 40,000 over two nights at the Long Beach Arena, which helped to generate a not-to-be-sneezed-at

$1.3 million. There's no question that the stacked bill helped their returns – neither Garbage nor the Distillers could be called traditional "support" bands – but it appeared as though No Doubt had found their comfortable, profitable niche on the road.

They'd also settled on the perfect setlist, too, the ideal blend of the hits, the favourites and the new stuff, as proved by the excellent live document of the tour, the Sophie Muller-directed *Rock Steady Live*. After opening with the obligatory 'Hella Good' they'd propel themselves into 'Sunday Morning' and 'Ex-Girlfriend', Stefani bounding across the stage like some platinum-blonde aerobics instructor – she even dropped to the stage and executed some painful-looking push-ups during 'Just A Girl'. The men of the band looked great, too; Kanal was going through his bleached-and-sweatband-ed phase; Dumont opted for sharp suits, topped off by a personally monogrammed tie, and a selection of fluorescent-coloured Flying V guitars; while tub-thumper Young wore the fiercest Mohawk this side of Chelsea, 1976. The rest of their set mixed *Rock Steady* cuts 'Underneath it All', 'Platinum Blonde Life', 'Running', et al, with *Saturn's* swinging 'Bathwater' and 'Magic's In The Makeup', plus *Tragic Kingdom's* 'Just A Girl' and a final encore of 'Spiderwebs' and 'Don't Speak'. Sweet pop, sweaty rock, production numbers, crowd favourites, deep groove, lighter-waving ballads – No Doubt's well-rehearsed set now had the works.

Gwen Stefani, though, had more pressing matters to deal with when the band took a pitstop in September, 2002, after one final date in Sydney, Australia (another full house, incidentally). She and Rossdale were engaged nine months earlier, on New Year's Day, 2002, Rossdale sealing the deal with a diamond-encrusted rock that he'd picked up in Amsterdam (which Stefani had re-sized by Beverly Hills jeweller Neil Lane). Now they finally had the time to get married. And, in keeping with their status as rock'n'roll's first couple, the G-rated Kurt and Courtney, they hosted a lavish bash, arranged, in the main, by sometimes-singer and full-time wedding planner, Rossdale, who found himself with loads of spare time now that Bush's career was on a downwards spiral.

Festivities kicked off on September 11, three days before the main event, first with drinks for wedding guests at Rossdale's Primrose Hill townhouse, followed by chow at the nearby Feng Sheng Princess, a swank eatery that was a long-time favourite of the pair. Toasts were made, speeches delivered – one No Doubt member, no doubt aided by a few drinks, admitted that Rossdale was not "the real poser" they expected him to be – and Stefani happily jiggled a niece on her knee, in between mouthfuls of sea bass. Day one ended late at Kabaret, a local club.

The following day was somewhat more serious. Stefani and Rossdale went through their paces during a rehearsal at St Paul's, where the main officiant was Rossdale's childhood religious teacher (he was C of E, which surely created a little Catholic guilt for Stefani, although a Catholic priest also helped out at the ceremony). Across town, at a private club called Home House, staff geared up for the following day's reception for 130 guests (whose numbers included members of both their bands, actor Johnny Lee Miller and a transvestite named Marilyn). A $23,000 blue-and-cream tent was erected, filled with illuminated ficus trees and hundreds of candles, and waiters were advised of their 12-hour shifts; this was a party that would stretch from 6am to 6pm. No Doubt videographer Sophie Muller was in charge of giving the venue's courtyard a makeover, and she adorned trees with roses, silver stars and hydrangeas. The doorway was trimmed with more roses, and topped with two silver Gs, a handy reminder to all the guests as to just who was running this show.

On D-day, September 14, Rossdale awoke and did what any responsible groom would do: he headed for his favourite local, Queens, accompanied by his loyal dog Winston, and his groomsmen. Stefani, every inch the traditionalist, had spent the previous night at Home House, and kept a date with her long-time hairstylist, Danilo (no surname, of course) and designer John Galliano, a friend and fashion adviser to the bride, who also worked with pop princess Kylie Minogue. The white-and-pink silk faille gown that she wore for the wedding was one of his designs (for Christian Dior), and was far more *Vogue* wonderful than ghetto fabulous, in keeping with the formal tone of the event. "She looked beautiful," Galliano told *Us* magazine. On closer inspection, though, the gown had hints of the old Stefani, with its sharp zippers and cargo pockets. "It was very punk rock," said Stefani, "which you couldn't really tell from the pictures." Galliano also designed the bride's wedding ring —a chunky platinum band paved with diamonds and topped with a heart-shaped stone set inside interlocking Gs. (Stefani subsequently namechecked the designer in 'Rich Girl', from her 2004 solo LP, and sported a Galliano creation in the video for 'What You Waiting For?', which was shot at the Beverly Hills Hotel. There was a small problem, though; the huge gown she wore couldn't actually fit in the hotel's front door.)

Over at St Paul's, Stefani arrived 45 minutes late for the scheduled 5pm kick-off, stepping out of a 1970 black-and-cobalt-blue Roller with her father Dennis by her side. Her arrival provided a much-needed break for a team of bagpipers, who'd been blowing non-stop during the nervous silence in the church. 'Bridal Chorus' (Here Comes The Bride) resounded throughout the hallowed hall of St Paul's – both Rossdale and Stefani had resisted using, say, 'Don't Speak' or 'Glycerine' – as she joined her soon-to-be-husband and his six groomsmen, three of them best men. Tears were shed, vows were exchanged – the word "obey" replaced with "protect" – and the party headed back to Home House, where risotto with saffron and bone marrow, and spaghetti with octopus and venison, was served. Four DJs spun funk greats from the 1970s and 1980s, a hefty bouncer checked names at the door, and Macy Gray was, of course, a no-show.

Two weeks later, back in LA, the Stefani / Rossdales threw a second ceremony for their Stateside buddies, including Hollywood's then-golden couple, Brad Pitt and Jennifer Aniston, who'd also attended the London wedding, and MTV mouthpiece Carson Daly. As Stefani explained, simply enough: "We didn't want to impose on anyone, so we decided to do it in both places." This second bash was held at the Tinseltown spread of Jimmy Iovine, the president of Interscope Records, the label that had profited so handsomely from a band that only a few years earlier they'd advised to "focus" or else get back to their day jobs. Oh how things had changed.

Gwen Stefani wasn't a mean woman, and she had little time for irony, but she must have felt a massive wave of satisfaction as the crowd gathered at Iovine's digs. As the leader of the "little band from Orange County" she had endured a friend's horrible death, years of commercial rejection, the unfortunate departure of her brother Eric, the end of her relationship with Tony Kanal, and their very own mid-career crisis – and now she was solid-gold LA royalty, a woman at the very top of the A-list, being hosted and toasted by one of the music industry's heaviest hitters. And all she'd ever really wanted to do was dress like Julie Andrews, make babies and lead a simple kind of life.

POSTSCRIPT

Just A (Solo) Girl

"[Gwen]'s so humble, so grounded, so dorky."

–Linda Perry

As with much of her life in pop, Gwen Stefani was an accidental solo star. Truth be told, her first priority, after the last *Rock Steady* date, played, fittingly, before 13,000 fans at the Pond in Anaheim at the end of November 2002, was to delve deeper into fashion. No empire of any self-respecting 21st century pop star, from Justin Timberlake to Kylie Minogue and P Diddy, was complete without a line of clothes featuring their (trade-marked) signature. It was especially satisfying for Stefani, because it would be fulfilment of a dream that dated back to her Julie Andrews days, when she used to check out the style of Anaheim's Latino teens and dream about catching a little of their streetwise cool.

And throughout her No Doubt career she'd been on the tip of rock'n'roll chic, whether it was copying Dexy's Midnight Runners bib-and-braces look; rocking old-school plaid during 'Trapped In A Box'; flashing a Vivienne Westwood-designed corset in the clip for 'Spiderwebs'; turning a $14 Contempo Casuals knock-off into a pop icon; draping herself in saris or styling up with such designers as Deborah Viereck (who crafted Stefani's punkish look of the mid 1990s) and John Galliano, who described Stefani as "pop princess, rock vixen and Hollywood diva all at the same time". It was no fluke that she won the Rock Style gong at the 2001 VH1 / Vogue

Fashion Awards, because this suburban girl had transformed herself – with a lot of help from her well-connected friends and admirers, some great ideas and wads of cash – from a cartoonish figure into a genuine style leader. "I've always thought about being a fashion designer," Stefani admitted, "but I never did anything about it."

At least that was the case until around the time of *Rock Steady*, when her friend and stylist, Andrea Lieberman, approached Stefani with the idea of her own fashion line, a more formal release of the clothes they'd already been designing together. The LAMB line – a tribute to the pet name of Stefani's dear departed Lhasa Apso, which she'd eulogised in 'Platinum Blonde Life', but also code for 'Love Angel Music Baby', Stefani's four favourite words – was formally launched in spring 2004. Lieberman took on a role similar to that of producer Glen Ballard during *Return Of Saturn*; she was responsible for "streamlining" Stefani, a woman for whom too much was barely enough. Stefani's first commercial venture was hooking up with LeSportsac for a line of bags and accessories, which hit the shelves on September 1, 2003.

The LAMB range was pieced together with the help of Lieberman and designer Annie Younger, whose plan was to create something more substantial than "just another celebrity tracksuit label". What they came up with was a Stefani "retrospective", of sorts, including aspects of every look she'd embraced over the past 10 years, "from my punker pants to the present," according to Stefani. And LAMB's clothes were literally all over the shop: the line included a T-shirt with the story of LAMB written in Stefani's own hand and another with an X-ray of Kanal's broken finger; a Marilyn Monroe-styled halter dress; and destroy-washed jeans trimmed with reggae red-gold-green stitching. In time, it would become the label of choice for such red-carpet queens as Paris Hilton, Carmen Electra and Hilary Duff. And the line wasn't just about clothes; the LAMB logo adorned everything from wristlets to CD and iPod cases, tote bags, wallets, handbags – even woven guitar strap handles. And in a shameless act of cross-promotion, some items were emblazoned with Stefani's lyrics. Stocked in Barney's New York, Saks Fifth Avenue and Henri Bendel, and a few other select stores, the line's price range was reasonable, with some items starting at an affordable $48, and others sporting the more rock-star-like price tag of $325.

Upon LAMB's debut, a forum was set up at www.nodoubt.com, and the feedback was mixed. Some long-time Gwenabees raved – "I love the clothing and if I had the money I would buy pretty much every item" – while others were underwhelmed. "I just got a good look at the clothes made by Gwen," observed one writer, "[and] I can't believe that a woman with her sense of style could design something that ugly." Others weren't totally convinced that Stefani's intentions were as honourable as she insisted they were. "As sad as it may seem, Gwen did not do this line for the fans, she did it for herself," snarled a disgruntled fan.

Nonetheless, LAMB was a hit, so much so that in 2005 Stefani was selected as the celebrity headliner at New York Fashion Week. Estimates had LAMB's 2005 turnover at somewhere around US$40 million, and its expanded range of floral dresses with wisteria prints, skinny-legged jeans, printed cardigans and slip-on sneakers adorned with padlocks and chains was now stocked in more than 200 US stores. While LAMB wasn't quite the same licence to print money as other celeb brands like P Diddy's Sean John or J Lo's Sweetface labels (with annual sales in the US$400 and $200 million ballpark, respectively, according to the *Wall Street Journal*), it was still a handy little earner and more proof, if it were needed, that everything Gwen Stefani touched turned into cash. With future lines, Stefani got on board the ubiquitous *Pirates of the Caribbean* trend for LAMB 2006, and 'Are You Lamb Enough?' became their new slogan. She also looked towards the east for the Harajuku Lovers, a range inspired by the Harajuku Girls, enigmatic Japanese fashionistas who'd play their part on Stefani's upcoming solo albums.

As successful as she was, Stefani, however, had a lot to learn about human rights and sweat-shop life. In order to keep production costs down, LAMB's clothes were mass-produced in China, where labour (and lives) were cheap. When Stefani was asked about conditions in the factories there, and whether she felt any guilt, Stefani quite naively stated that the workers had photos of her hanging on the wall above their machines for inspiration. Now, whether that made their third-world working life more tolerable, however, was unclear – and Chris "Make Trade Fair" Martin wasn't commenting. It went to prove that while you can take the girl out of the valley (or the County, in her case), and turn her into a princess – even a Rock Goddess, according to the January 27, 2005 cover of the *Rolling Stone* – removing the valley from the girl was a whole lot harder.

Apart from some summer dates in 2004, and the occasional one-off (a Superbowl half-time cameo, the 2003 Grammys, a tsunami benefit in March, 2005), No Doubt's self-imposed period of exile continued while Stefani's profile grew. So she started to make other plans – and this time around they actually had something to do with music.

★   ★   ★

In 2002, Gwen Stefani finally attempted to answer the multi-million-dollar question: how much time was left for No Doubt? "I think all of us have things we want to do [and] so many things we haven't done yet," she said. "The boys, Tony and Tom, want to be producing records. Everything post-*Tragic Kingdom* has been such a blessing, we pretty much take it one record at a time. So I don't know if we'll be together forever, because I didn't think we'd be together this long."

Rumours of No Doubt's demise grew even stronger when Stefani started working on what she began calling her "dance record", during another stretch in London in 2002. She stuck to the *Rock Steady* formula, bringing in as many collaborators as Interscope's budget would permit. And, at least in the beginning, she worked with the same people – Nellee Hooper, Dave Stewart – who'd made *Rock Steady* such an all-stars affair. But now Stefani was alone. It wasn't like her first session at 7 Dials with Stewart, where they worked on a song and then played it to the other band members for their approval. Stefani was now her own quality control department, and it caused some problems.

"I have my job in the band – I write the words and I write the melody," she explained. "But then you go and you're writing with some of these people that are so talented. I've had a hard time with my ego, because it gets bruised. Like, 'Oh my God, they're writing some of the melody and they came up something really good, and I didn't come up with it.' So it [was] a whole kind of learning process."

Unsure exactly where she was heading, and with the Stewart co-write, 'Sparkle', on hold, Stefani headed back to LA, where Rossdale was filming a video with avant-gardists the Blue Man Group for their album *The Current*. It was during this time that she checked in on Kanal, hoping for some respite from her solo-album blues. Kanal invited her to his house in Los Feliz, giving Stefani the impression that they'd be going out. Instead he took her into his home studio (aka Kingsbury Studio), where he played some new tracks he'd been working on, written at her request. This was exactly what she was hoping for; Kanal was at the top of her wishlist of solo album collaborators – if nothing else, his contribution would alleviate the guilt she felt from working without the rest of her band. (She later admitted that she felt as though she "cheated" on her bandmates by going solo.)

Stefani was mad for one Kanal song in particular, entitled 'Crash', a "mixture of everything we loved growing up: Prince, Lisa Lisa and Cult Jam and Club Nouveau". She cranked out another song that night with Kanal, a track so good that she declared it was "probably my favourite that I've written so far". Together, ultimately, they'd work on three cuts: 'Luxurious', which Kanal would co-produce with Nellee Hooper; plus 'Crash' and 'Serious', Kanal / Stefani co-writes that were produced by Kanal.

These private jams with her long time bandmate and former lover were just the tonic that Stefani needed; her troubled solo record was back on the rails. Stefani wrote about this in an on-line posting dated March 8, 2004, not long after the release of *The Singles Collection*, another between-studio-albums filler from No Doubt. (The other being the more expansive *Boom Box*, a well-packaged career-to-date wrap up, released in 2003, that compiled the band's 15 singles, both on CD and DVD, a disc of B-sides, remixes and esoterica, and the *Live In The Tragic Kingdom* DVD. *Boom Box* was released simultaneously with *The Singles Collection*, on November 25, 2003.) "It has been really challenging but over the last few weeks I have been able to turn a corner," Stefani wrote. "I have over 16 songs and plan on writing as many as it takes to make it great. It is starting to feel like a record and I can see it coming together. I am hoping to have a single out some time this summer. I have loads of ideas and tricks up my sleeve so watch out. I'm scared for you."

With a working title *What You Waiting For?* – later amended to the ubiquitous *Love.Angel.Music.Baby* – her piecemeal solo record started to take shape in London, Atlanta, New York and LA, throughout 2003 and 2004, with a list of contributors (60 in all, including production crew) that was even lengthier than *Rock Steady*, although nowhere near as imaginative. She was now working with established hitmakers, the platinum club; there'd be no cameos from Bounty Killer or Lady Saw here. Stefani spent studio time with OutKast's Andre 3000; the Neptunes, for a second time; Janet Jackson consorts Jimmy Jam and Terry Lewis; and R&B producer Dallas Austin. Meanwhile, such steady hands as New Order's Bernard Sumner and Peter Hook, plus former Prince sidekicks Wendy Melvoin and Lisa Coleman, played on the album. Stefani even got to complete a track with Dr Dre, the aforementioned 'Rich Girl', where hip-hopper Eve once again shared the mic with Stefani.

Stefani also wrote with Linda Perry, former belter from Four Non Blondes and one of the music biz's leading tunesmiths-for-hire, who'd crafted hits for Pink ('Get This Party Started') and Christina Aguilera ('Beautiful'), amongst many others. Perry told me that she'd always been more a fan of Stefani than No Doubt, and had often floated the idea of writing together. Finally, she cornered the singer at a Grammys after-party, got her in a headlock and told her, "Call me about your solo album." Jimmy Iovine then got the two in a studio together, although Perry sensed right away that Stefani would rather be anywhere but making music. "I said to her, "Can you not want to be here any more?" She told me that she'd rather be at home, in bed with her husband [whom Perry also wrote with, further down the line], eating pizza, watching TV." A lone track, the unreleased 'Fine By You', came out of that uncomfortable first day. "It was cute," according to Perry, "but I didn't run home and tell everyone about it, yet it had the start of something."

However, Stefani's lack of motivation had the reverse effect on Perry; she went home that night and wrote the bulk of 'What You Waiting For?', in part as a taunt to Stefani. "She dragged her feet into the studio," Perry said, "So I had to do something. I put it all down on that one night, and she came back the next day, still uninspired. I told her how she'd really inspired me, and she went, 'I did?' I knew I had something with the track, so I pushed play and put the song through the big speakers and she went, 'Dude, what the *fuck* was that?'."

"The song is really about her," Perry continued. "When she first heard the chorus kick in with "what you waiting for?", she turned to me and said, 'you're challenging me'. I said that I wasn't challenging her, I was inspired by her. I told her I was sitting here wondering what she was waiting for; she had this chance to make her solo record and make it anything she wanted and she was dragging her feet. Everyone was waiting for her 'hot track' and she had her 'million dollar contract'. It's basically addressing her fear: Gwen Stefani from No Doubt was going solo – is she going to succeed? I think it was a scary thing."

All Stefani really needed to do with 'What You Waiting For?' was cut her vocal and the thumping groove-pop track was as good as done. When Jimmy Iovine heard it a few days later, he shouted: "Bingo, first single!" As far as Perry was concerned, the evolution of *L.A.M.B.* started right then, even though Stefani had already worked on songs with Dave Stewart and Tony Kanal. "I really believe that was the beginning of her record, because they now had a song that everybody had to beat."

Perry read her collaborator's initial indifference this way: Stefani had some other serious business to attend to; she had to film her Jean Harlow cameo in *The Aviator* and was also about to launch her fashion label. But Perry also felt that Stefani was uncomfortable with her new-found sense of autonomy; rather than have Kanal, Young and Dumont to lean on for words of encouragement or a deciding vote on some band business, she was now totally alone. "I think she was afraid of being without the boys; all these decisions were hers, it's not like being in the band where they vote on things, this was all in her hands," Perry said. She also felt that Stefani was uncertain about working with a woman, especially a straight-fucking-shooter like Perry. In her 15-plus years of music-making, Stefani had never collaborated with a female, apart from her jam with Eve on 'Let Me Blow Ya Mind'.

Together, Perry and Stefani co-wrote eight songs, although if Perry had her way, she would have had more than three tracks on *L.A.M.B.* Perry became an unstoppable force of musical ideas in their latter sessions; she hit such a purple patch that at one stage Stefani pulled her aside and said, "Dude, slow down. I've got so many lyrics to write, I'm overwhelmed." Stefani impressed Perry, who has witnessed her share of prima-donna antics during her super-successful career. "She's so humble, so grounded, so dorky". There was only one occasion when Stefani lost her composure. Perry, who in the main is a writer of music, not words, had improvised some lyrics – "poetry, really" – and showed them to Stefani, who burst into tears. "I explained that these were the words that came into my mind when I was listening to the song – and she got really offended and started crying," Perry recalled. "She said that she wanted to write this song about her friend. I think she cried because she was overwhelmed, rather than actually about what I'd done. I was just trying to help her out, throw some lyrics at her and see if she got inspired. I realised that I shouldn't have done that."

But overall, it was one of Perry's best co-writing experiences. "A lot of people [I work with] don't have any ideas and they don't have any input to give," she explained. "[But] Gwen was very clear about what she wanted; she had certain subjects that she wanted to sing about. Some people I've worked with before Gwen couldn't have come up with an idea to save their life. Now I tell people that they have to write something, I can't just sit there holding their hand.

"I don't care about credit; I could care less," added Perry. "What I have a problem with is learning that there are plenty people out there with more talent than someone I'm working with. You have a wonderful opportunity here, I tell them; if I were you I'd get off your ass and put in more than explaining what your hairstyle is and what kind of car you drive. In the end I stopped working with these people."

Rock Steady may have suffered from a lack of cohesion, but *Love.Angel.Music.Baby* was a thoroughly modern mess, in part because the signature sound of Stefani's guests weighed down most tracks. (Perry sensed that, too. As she told me: "That's the unfortunate thing with so many records today – when you've got seven producers and a dozen songwriters, or whatever, there's no real unity.") For instance, the song to which Hook and Sumner contributed, 'The Real Thing' – another Stefani / Perry co-write – was a dead-ringer for New Order, with Hook's thudding bass prominent in the mix; Stefani's jam with Andre 3000, 'Long Way To Go' was dominated by the Prince-like antics of the man from OutKast; while the Neptunes-produced 'Hollaback Girl' came on like some tub-thumping anthem for a high-school marching band. (Stefani would wear a drum majorette outfit while playing the song on her 2005 solo tour.) Stefani's heliumated vocals were as distinctive as ever, but the album had no real soul or character. Instead, it was the quintessential high-tech, big-budget, digital-age dance-pop record, with an '80s sonic undercurrent – some critics, justifiably enough, accused Stefani of becoming "just another vacuous pop diva". As for her lyrics, Stefani didn't devote much time to the subject that had been her obsession since the days of 'Don't Speak': herself. And the album suffered because of that. There were one key exception: 'Danger Zone' dealt with her reaction to Rossdale's recent discovery of his long-lost daughter, Daisy, whose mother was Pearl Low from the cult 1990s band Powder. But these revelatory moments weren't common. Most of *L.A.M.B.*'s lyrics were well-written fluff, set dressing for the album's slick grooves and all-star cameos.

"There are some weird twists to the themes," Stefani explained, "but it's not heartfelt, deep, painful subject matter. That's why I don't call it a solo record," she added. "A solo record to me is like a heart-pouring [and] that's not what this record is." As with the bulk of *Rock Steady*, Stefani was content to make an album that was custom-built for dancefloors. (This would explain the exclusion of 'Sparkle', her second co-write with Dave Stewart, which he described as a "very personal" song. Depth was not the theme of *L.A.M.B.*) And if you were hoping for just a hint of ska, you were in the wrong place, my friend.

Nonetheless, there were standouts: the peculiar 'Rich Girl', which included an updated take of *Fiddler on the Roof*'s 'If I Were A Rich Man', was a strange commingling of showtune and sleek dance cut, while the urgent 'Crash' was one of her finest co-writes with Kanal. And then there was 'Harajuku Girls', Stefani's tributes to her new 'besties' (i.e. best friends), the bizarrely-dressed crews of young women usually found hanging about Harajuku in Japan – although they could be spotted all over Japan"s larger cities – whose various out-there styles were known as Gothic Lolita, Cyber Fashion, Sex Kitten, Wamono (an east-meets-west fusion) and Decora, a brightly-coloured, day-glo style that had endless appeal for budding fashionista Stefani, who even named her publishing company Harajuku Lover Music. (Interestingly, the Japanese didn"t use the term "Harajuku Girls".)

Even with its many flaws, *Love.Angel.Music.Baby*, which dropped on November 23, 2004, was a massive hit, selling in far more substantial numbers than either *Return Of Saturn* or *Rock Steady*. (Seven million world-wide.) It generated a stunning six charting singles: "What You Waiting For?", "Rich Girl", "Hollaback Girl", "Cool", "Luxurious" and "Crash".

Stefani toured heavily in the later months of 2005, covering 16 US cities. By the time the Stefani roadshow reached the West Coast on Christmas Eve, 2005 – and there wasn't a single No Doubt song on the live setlist, by the way – the album had sold almost four million copies in North America alone. It was no overstatement on the part of the *Los Angeles Times* when they crowned Stefani "the biggest female rock star of the last decade". If magazine covers, red carpets and column inches counted for anything – and they appeared to be the barometer of a star's worth in these strange, Paris Hilton-obsessed times – then Stefani was an even bigger name than Madonna. And Stefani was now spawning her own imitators; *The Duchess*, the 2006 solo LP from Black Eyed Pea Fergie, was virtually a carbon copy of *Love.Angel.Music.Baby*.

The final dates of Stefani's first solo tour, however, were a struggle. Stefani was pregnant, finally; the story of her impending joyous occasion had broken when *US Weekly* magazine called Rossdale's father in the UK, who innocently (and proudly) confirmed the rumour. Stefani responded by loosening the waistband on her drum majorette outfit and imploring audiences to let her baby know that she wasn't alone by making loads of noise. Five months later, on May 25, 2006, shortly before 1pm, Kingston James McGregor Rossdale was delivered via Caesarean section at LA's Cedars-Sinai Medical Center, his Christian name a handy reminder of where the No Doubt ska-pop trip had started all those years ago: in deepest Jamaica. Dave Stewart, a regular visitor to the stately homes of the Stefani / Rossdales, confirmed what everyone suspected, given that the child's parents were blessed with movie-star good looks. "It's beautiful; it's a very sweet baby," he said.

★   ★   ★

Now that Stefani had finally fulfilled her life-long dream of becoming a parent, it seemed inevitable that she'd take a break: what else was there for her to achieve? She was fabulously rich, incredibly famous, happily married – and a parent, to boot. Here was the ideal chance to slow down, keep one eye on the LAMB cash cow, and the other on the newborn. Yet a little over six months after her son's birth, Stefani returned to the airwaves and charts with *The Sweet Escape*, her second solo set, which was a simultaneous release with *Harajuku Lovers Live*, another Sophie Muller-directed live DVD, shot during a hometown show in Anaheim from Stefani's 2005 solo tour.

Again, Gwen called in the A-list; contributors to her second album included Kanal, who produced three tracks, including 'Fluorescent', where Fishbone's Angelo Moore played sax; Dave Stewart; Depeche Mode's

Martin Gore; Nellee Hooper, who produced two tracks, one featuring Keane's Tim Rice-Oxley on piano; Sean Garrett; Swizz Beats; Senegalese star Akon (who'd support Stefani on her 2007 US tour); and the Neptunes. The latter worked on five cuts, including the lead single 'Wind It Up' – where Stefani managed to channel both Julie 'Lonely Goatherd' Andrews and Missy Elliott – and 'Orange County Girl', Stefani's life story spelled out in a few poptastic minutes.

The reality, however, was that much of the album was assembled from leftover tracks from *L.A.M.B.*, including 'Wonderful Life', one of the eight songs she co-wrote with Linda Perry back in 2004. 'Wind It Up', meanwhile, was a rejigged version of a track she'd recorded with the Neptunes in 2005.

"This album is surprisingly different than the last one," Stefani said in an official press release. "I started recording it last year before Kingston was born and it's definitely evolved over the last year. The dance sound is very 'now'. It's modern, not so retro," she said.

Everything about *The Sweet Escape*, from the highly stylised cover image of an airbrushed, Photoshop-ped Stefani, every inch the queen of pop, draped in a platinum blonde wig and staring icily into the middle distance, to the album's glacial-cool dance-pop, succeeded in putting even more distance between the singer and her No Doubt past. Was this really the same woman who sobbed 'Don't Speak' and spilled her guts over the course of five No Doubt albums? While the rest of No Doubt quietly went about their business – Kanal writing, producing and working on his new label; Dumont also producing; Young golfing, drumming and parenting – Stefani showed no signs of slowing down. She took *The Sweet Escape* on the road in April 2007.

Many No Doubt / Stefani long-time observers, including Sublime manager Jon Phillips, remain amazed by her mega-stardom and the longevity of the band. "I just remember them as kids, seriously," he told me. "And then in the blink of an eye she's grown up, she's got fashion lines and she's got *Vogue* covers. It was only a matter of a few years ago when I saw Gwen at a club and she had braces. This was after she became a star, but she had like these little braces to straighten her teeth up or something.

"They're good people. They didn't forget about anybody; they're still really approachable," Phillips continued. "Obviously that much success is going to change you, but they're not like evil, you know? Adrian's mellow; he likes to do his golf thing, plays naked. They're nice folks. They never got caught up in the drug scene, they've made a lot of money and get to enjoy life on their own terms."

Even though her solo star was rising even higher, there was, apparently, a little life left in No Doubt. According to their management, the band, while not actually recording together, are "just starting to work on some new ideas – long term, though. Next chapter is still a way off". But given that Stefani spent much of 2007 pushing *The Sweet Escape*, it seems unlikely that anything will emerge from the band until at least 2008, if at all.

Linda Perry, who likens Gwen to Madonna, feels that Stefani's solo records provide her with the opportunity to indulge in styles and sounds that may not quite fit No Doubt, but that doesn't necessarily signal the end of the band. "She never said that she was leaving No Doubt [while we worked together]; there was no talk of her being simply Gwen Stefani from now on. There'll be another No Doubt record, for sure," Perry said. "But Gwen's a star, and as great a band as they are, there's limitations. I think No Doubt have gone as far as they could into other types of music and Gwen had all these other areas she wanted to go. I don't think No Doubt could have made the records she wanted to make."

Dave Stewart remains convinced that the band has the ability to continue making – and selling – albums, despite Gwen's unstoppable solo success. The band's secret, according to Stewart, is an uncanny ability to adapt and survive in an ever-changing pop culture environment. They're chameleons. And it doesn't matter that all of the band members, at the time of writing, are staring 40 right between the eyes.

"They live it, you know?" Stewart said in November 2006. "They're like pop culture engineers. It's an art form in itself and it has to be the whole thing for it to work. Morrissey's the whole thing; Beck's the whole thing in a different way. Nirvana were an example, too, in their ripped jumpers and sleeves. An artist creates their world and their world has to survive in the changing trends of popular culture. No Doubt does that. I can see why the band are very successful."

In short, remain seated please, as the ticket collector at Disneyland instructs, this ride isn't over yet.

No Doubt Discography

No Doubt Albums

No Doubt
March 17, 1992 / Interscope
BND / Let's Get Back / Ache / Get On The Ball / Move On / Sad For Me /
Doormat / Big City Train / Trapped In A Box / Sometimes / Sinking /
A Little Something Refreshing / Paulina / Brand New Day.

The Beacon Street Collection
March 1995 / Sea Creature Records
Open The Gate / Blue In The Face / Total Hate 95 / Stricken /
Greener Pastures / By The Way / Snakes / That's Just Me / Squeal / Doghouse.

Tragic Kingdom
October 10, 1995 / Trauma/Interscope
Spiderwebs / Excuse Me Mr / Just A Girl / Happy Now? / Different People /
Hey You / The Climb / Sixteen / Sunday Morning / Don't Speak /
You Can Do It / World Go 'Round / End It On This / Tragic Kingdom.

Return Of Saturn
April 11, 2000 / Trauma/Interscope
Ex-Girlfriend / Simple Kind Of Life / Bathwater / Six Feet Under /
Magic's In The Makeup / Artificial Sweetener / Marry Me / New / Too Late /
Comforting Lie / Suspension Without Suspense / Staring Problem /
Home Now / Dark Blue (Bonus track: Big Distraction)

Rock Steady
December 11, 2001 / Interscope
Intro / Hella Good / Hey Baby / Making Out / Underneath It All /
Detective / Don't Let Me Down / Start The Fire / Running /
In My Head / Platinum Blonde Life / Waiting Room / Rock Steady.

228

Compilations

The Singles 1992–2003
November 25, 2003 / Interscope
Just A Girl / It's My Life / Hey Baby / Bathwater / Sunday Morning / Hella
Good / New / Underneath It All / Excuse Me Mr / Running / Spiderwebs /
Simple Kind Of Life / Don't Speak / Ex-Girlfriend / Trapped In A Box.

Boom Box
November 25, 2003 / Interscope
Disc 1: Just A Girl / It's My Life / Hey Baby / Bathwater / Sunday Morning /
Hella Good / New / Underneath It All / Excuse Me Mr / Running /
Spiderwebs / Simple Kind Of Life / Don't Speak / Ex-Girlfriend /
Trapped In A Box.
Disc 2: The Videos 1992-2003 (same track listing as disc 1)
Disc 3: Big Distraction / Leftovers / Under Construction / Beauty Contest /
Full Circle / Cellophane Boy / Everything in Time (Los Angeles) /
You're So Foxy / Panic / New / Everything in Time (London) / Sailin' On /
Oi to the World / I Throw My Toys Around / New & Approved [New Remix]
/ A Real Love Survives / A Rock Steady Vibe.
Disc 4: *Live In The Tragic Kingdom* DVD (see DVD section for track listing)

Everything In Time
October 12, 2004 / Interscope
Big Distraction / Leftovers / Under Construction / Beauty Contest /
Full Circle / Cellophane Boy / Everything in Time (Los Angeles) /
You're So Foxy / Panic / New / Everything in Time (London) / Sailin' On /
Oi to the World / I Throw My Toys Around / New & Approved [New Remix] /
A Real Love Survives / A Rock Steady Vibe.

DVDs

Live In the Tragic Kingdom
Interscope 1997 (reissued 2006)
Tragic Kingdom / Excuse Me Mr / Different People / Happy Now? / DJs /
End It On This / Just A Girl / The Climb / Total Hate / Hey You /
The Imperial March / Move On / Don't Speak / Sunday Morning /
Spiderwebs / Ob-La-Di, Ob-La-Da.

Rock Steady Live
Interscope 2003
Intro / Hella Good / Sunday Morning / Ex-Girlfriend / Underneath It All /
Platinum Blonde Life / Bathwater / Don't Let Me Down / Magic's In The

Makeup / Running / In My Head / New / Simple Kind Of Life / Just A Girl / Hey Baby / Rock Steady / Spiderwebs / Don't Speak.

The Videos 1992-2003
Interscope 2004
Just A Girl / It's My Life / Hey Baby / Bathwater / Sunday Morning / Hella Good / New / Underneath It All / Excuse Me Mr / Running / Spiderwebs / Simple Kind Of Life / Don't Speak / Ex-Girlfriend / Trapped In A Box.

No Doubt Solo

Gwen Stefani

Love.Angel.Music.Baby.
November 23, 2004 / Interscope
What You Waiting For? / Rich Girl / Hollaback Girl / Cool / Bubble Pop Electric / Luxurious / Harajuku Girls / Crash / The Real Thing / Serious / Danger Zone / Long Way To Go. (Bonus track: The Real Thing)

The Sweet Escape
December 2, 2006 / Interscope
Wind It Up / The Sweet Escape / Orange County Girl / Early Winter / Now That You Got It / 4 In The Morning / Yummy / Flourescent / Breakin' Up / Don't Get It Twisted / U Started It / Wonderful Life.
Harajuku Lovers Live (DVD)
December 2, 2006 / Interscope
Harajuku Girls / What You Waiting For? / The Real Thing / Crash / Luxurious / Rich Girl / Danger Zone / Long Way To Go / Wind It Up / Orange County Girl / Cool / Serious / Bubble Pop Electric / Hollaback Girl

Also appears on:
Sublime 'Saw Red' (1997)
Gameface *Good* (1997)
The Brian Setzer Orchestra 'You're The Boss' (1998)
Bush *Science of Things* (1999)
Eve 'Let Me Blow Ya Mind' (2001)
Moby 'South Side' (2000)

Tony Kanal

Kelis *Wanderland* (2001)
Unwritten Law *Elva* (2002)
Toots & The Maytals *True Love* (2004)

Gwen Stefani *Love.Angel.Music.Baby* (2004)
Various Artists: *50 First Dates* soundtrack (2004)
Gwen Stefani *The Great Escape* (2006)
Pepper *No Shame* (2006)
Elan *Together As One* (2006)

Adrian Young

The Vandals *Hitler Bad, Vandals Good* (1998)
Kelis *Wanderland* (2001)
Fishbone *Essential Fishbone* (2003) [Liner notes]
Toots & The Maytals *True Love* (2004)
Gwen Stefani *Love.Angel.Music.Baby* (2004)
Unwritten Law *Here's To The Mourning* (2005)
Matt Costa *Songs We Sing* (2006)
The Bangkok Five *Who's Gonna Take Us Alive?* (2006)

Tom Dumont

Kelis *Wanderland* (2001)
Black Sabbath *Black Box* (2004) [Liner notes]
Shifty *Happy Love Sick* (2004)
Toots & The Maytals *True Love* (2004)
Various Artists *Look At All The Love We Found: A Tribute To Sublime* (2005)
Matt Costa *Songs We Sing* (2006)

Eric Stefani (includes artwork)

Shplang *Self Made Monk* (1997)
My Superhero *Solid State 14* (1998)
Rancid *Life Won't Wait* (1998)
Rancid 'Brad Logan' (1998)
Various Artists *Chef Aid: The South Park Album* (1998)
Donkey Show *Just Can't Get Enough of The Donkey Show* (2000)
Bush *Golden State* (2001)

This is a selective list; for full details and more information go to www.allmusic.com; for a list of soundtracks, etc, go to: www.nodoubt.com/music/soundtracks.asp

No Doubt Acknowledgements

Many thanks to former No Doubt band members Eric Carpenter, Alex Henderson and Alan Meade and all at Rebel Waltz, NxD HQ; Dito Godwin, co-producer of the *No Doubt* album; Gerald Lokstadt, Doug Fatone and Paul Oberman; Dave Stewart; Jerry Miller of the Untouchables; Aaron Barrett of Reel Big Fish (special thanks to Jenny Jensen); The Skeletones' Paul Hampton and Rick Bonin; Mike Miller, Shawn Nourse, Kim Segovia, Sean Jones, Robert Dagnall, Scot Thiesmeyer, Mario Artavia II, Andrew Medlin, Brian Elledge and various other OC friends and Anaheim High classmates of the band; Howard Paar (owner of The ON Klub, LA's first ska venue); Ken Phebus (from Fender's Ballroom in Long Beach); Sam Lanni; Rick Gershon; John Pantle (who booked various No Doubt shows); Daniel Arsenault (*Tragic Kingdom* sleeve photographer); *Los Angeles Times* writers, both past and present, Ken Boehm, Steve Hochman and Don Snowden; Rob 'Bucket' Hingley of Moon Ska Records and the Toasters; Jon Phillips from Sublime HQ and Mike 'Mongo' Stevens; Tony Keys at www.rocksbackpages.com; Ned Douglas and Tina Adamian from Weapons of Mass Distraction; William Petersen at Rebel Management; the lovely Linda Perry; Wayne and Brian Jobson; Amy at www.nodoubtlive.com; Rhianne Smith for digging deep; Paul Tollett at Goldenvoice; Eric Keyes; Gordon Murray and Bob Allen at Billboard; Emily Koch at the Anaheim Pond (sorry, make that the Arrowhead Pond of Anaheim); Billy Poveda at Oil Factory; Paris Thongsiri and all at the Tragic Kingdom fanzine.

Special thanks to Albino Brown of the Ska Parade and SP Radio One live radio/online programs for his sage advice and candid observations, especially during the early stages of this book. Ditto Tazy Phillipyz. I highly recommend checking out www.skaparade.com (SPradio1@aol.com) for everything ska.

Also a heavyweight thank you to Chris Charlesworth, Andrea Rotondo and Melissa Whitelaw at Omnibus Press for their support and advice; and to Diana and Lili for being way more than understanding.